THE AMERICAN LAW INSTITUTE

THE WTO CASE LAW OF 2009

LEGAL AND ECONOMIC ANALYSIS

This book is the seventh report of the American Law Institute (ALI) project on World Trade Organization Law. The project undertakes yearly analysis of the case law from the adjudicating bodies of the WTO. These studies cover a wide range of WTO law: this volume focuses on the year 2009. Each case is jointly evaluated by well-known experts in trade law and international economics. The contributors critically review the jurisprudence of WTO adjudicating bodies and evaluate whether the ruling 'makes sense' from an economic as well as a legal point of view, and, if not, whether the problem lies in the interpretation of the law or in the law itself. The studies do not cover all issues discussed in a case, but they seek to discuss both the procedural and the substantive issues that form the 'core' of the dispute.

HENRIK HORN, Professor of International Economics, is Senior Research Fellow at the Research Institute of Industrial Economics (IFN), Stockholm. He is a member of the Editorial Board of the *World Trade Review* and is a member of the Centre for Economic Policy Research. He has previously worked for the Economic Policy Research and Analysis Division of the World Trade Organization, and has been a judge on the Swedish Market Court (supreme court for competition law).

PETROS C. MAVROIDIS is Edwin B. Parker Professor at Columbia Law School, Professor at the University of Neuchatel, and a member of the Centre for Economic Policy Research. He was previously Chair of Competition Law, EUI, Florence, and a member of the Legal Affairs Division of the World Trade Organization.

THE AMERICAN LAW INSTITUTE

THE WTO CASE LAW OF 2009

LEGAL AND ECONOMIC ANALYSIS

Edited By

HENRIK HORN

AND

PETROS C. MAVROIDIS

CAMBRIDGE
UNIVERSITY PRESS

CAMBRIDGE
UNIVERSITY PRESS

University Printing House, Cambridge CB2 8BS, United Kingdom

One Liberty Plaza, 20th Floor, New York, NY 10006, USA

477 Williamstown Road, Port Melbourne, VIC 3207, Australia

314-321, 3rd Floor, Plot 3, Splendor Forum, Jasola District Centre, New Delhi - 110025, India

79 Anson Road, #06-04/06, Singapore 079906

Cambridge University Press is part of the University of Cambridge.

It furthers the University's mission by disseminating knowledge in the pursuit of education, learning and research at the highest international levels of excellence.

www.cambridge.org
Information on this title: www.cambridge.org/9781107681781

A catalogue record for this publication is available from the British Library

ISBN 978-1-107-68178-1 Paperback

CONTENTS

Foreword

This is the seventh volume analyzing legal decisions of the World Trade Organization for publication by The American Law Institute (ALI) and the Cambridge University Press. The WTO decisions, most of them from the Appellate Body, demonstrate a gradual process of creating trade law doctrine that applies one of the world's most important treaties to significant economic disputes. We believe that the contributions made by economists and lawyers in describing and criticizing the WTO's outcomes and the reasoning that supports them are a step toward the establishment of a body of international law that is now, and will increasingly be, essential to a world economy based on huge cross-border trade. Our books have now analyzed all the important WTO decisions issued in the first decade of the twenty-first century.

The ALI is also at work on books that propose governing principles for trade law. In 2008, we published *The Genesis of the GATT*, by Professors Douglas A. Irwin, Petros C. Mavroidis, and Alan O. Sykes. In the next year, we expect to publish a comprehensive analysis of the principle of nondiscrimination in international trade, with particular attention to the economics of trade agreements. The volume will discuss nondiscrimination with regard to both border instruments (GATT Article I) and domestic instruments (GATT Article III (national treatment)).

We appreciate the intellectual and administrative leadership of Professors Henrik Horn and Petros Mavroidis, the creative scholarship of the authors of these essays, the valuable comments and criticisms from expert professors and engaged professionals, and the financial support we have received from The Jan Wallander and Tom Hedelius Foundation and from the Milton and Miriam Handler Foundation.

LANCE LIEBMAN
Director
The American Law Institute

Introduction

HENRIK HORN AND PETROS C. MAVROIDIS

This volume contains five reports on the World Trade Organization (WTO) case law of 2009, written in the context of the American Law Institute (ALI) project *Legal and Economic Principles of World Trade Law*, which aims to provide systematic analysis of WTO law based on both economics and law. Each report in the volume is written jointly by an economist and a lawyer, and each discusses a separate WTO dispute. The authors are free to choose the particular aspects of the dispute they wish to discuss. The aim is to determine for each dispute whether the Appellate Body's (or occasionally the Panel's) decision seems desirable from both an economic and a legal point of view, and, if not, whether the problem lies in the interpretation of the law or the law itself.

Earlier versions of the papers included in this volume were presented at a meeting in Geneva in June 2010, and we are very grateful for the comments at the meeting provided by Robert L. Howse and Frieder Roessler. We would also like to thank all of the other meeting participants for providing many helpful comments, and the WTO for providing a venue for the meeting.

Our sincere thanks also go to The American Law Institute, particularly to Director Lance Liebman, President Roberta Cooper Ramo, former President Michael Traynor, Deputy Director Stephanie Middleton, and former Deputy Director Elena Cappella, all of whom have been instrumental in bringing this project about. We would further like to express our gratitude to Nina Amster, Judy Cole, Todd David Feldman, Sandrine Forgeron, and Marianne Walker of the ALI's staff for providing very efficient administrative and editorial help. Finally, we are extremely grateful for financial support from the Milton and Miriam Handler Foundation, The Jan Wallander and Tom Hedelius Research Foundation, Stockholm, and the WTO Secretariat (especially Alejandro Jara and Patrick Low) for helping us with the organization of the meeting at the WTO headquarters.

Turning to the content of the volume, the year of 2009 saw relatively few disputes being adjudicated and then coming to an end. As always, anti-dumping was a common theme among those that did, and the zeroing issue was raised again in these disputes. In their paper, **Hoekman** and **Wauters** review the WTO Appellate Body (AB) Reports on *United States–Zeroing* (*Article 21.5 DSU – EC*), and *United States–Zeroing* (*Article 21.5 DSU – Japan*). The AB found that the United States had not brought its anti-dumping measures into compliance with the WTO Anti-Dumping Agreement as it continued to use zeroing in annual reviews of anti-dumping orders. The authors argue that this conclusion – based on a complicated discussion of what constitutes a 'measure taken to comply' – could have been reached through a much simpler and more direct argument. Continued noncompliance by the United States generates costs to traders targeting the United States and the trading system more generally. They further argue that, from a broader WTO compliance perspective, consideration should be given to stronger multilateral surveillance of anti-dumping practice by all WTO members and to more analysis and effective communication by economists regarding the costs of zeroing and anti-dumping practices more generally.

The zeroing methodology is also discussed in the contribution by **Prusa** and **Vermulst** in their comment on *United States – Continued Existence and Application of Zeroing Methodology*. They note that this is the eighth AB Report in which some aspect of zeroing was adjudicated. As in the prior cases, the AB again found the US practice inconsistent with several aspects of the WTO Anti-Dumping Agreement. The authors point out that the novelty in this dispute was the EC attempt to broaden the concept of what constitutes an appealable measure. The EC challenged whether a WTO decision regarding zeroing could apply to subsequent proceedings that might modify duty levels, and it asked the AB to decide whether the United States' continued use of zeroing in the context of a given case was consistent with WTO obligations. The AB stated that in its attempt to bring an effective resolution to the zeroing issue, the EC was entitled to frame its challenge in such a way as to bring the ongoing use of the zeroing methodology in these cases under the scrutiny of WTO dispute settlement. The AB then cautiously applied the new perspective to US zeroing practice.

Other disputes raised more novel issues. For instance, the Panel Report on *China–Intellectual Property Rights* was the first Report focusing on China's policies with respect to enforcement of intellectual property rights. The Report, discussed by **Saggi** and **Trachtman**, addressed three main issues: first, the relationship between China's censorship laws and its obligations to protect copyright under the WTO Agreement on Trade Related Intellectual Property Rights (TRIPS); second, China's obligations under TRIPS to ensure that its customs authorities are empowered to dispose properly of confiscated goods that infringe intellectual property rights; and, third, whether China's volume and value-of-goods thresholds for application of criminal procedures and penalties with respect to trademark counterfeiting or copyright piracy comply with TRIPS requirements for application of criminal procedures and penalties. In the authors' view, international trade agreements are generally intended to cause states to internalize policy externalities. The policy externalities that arise from domestic decisions regarding intellectual property protection may deprive foreign intellectual property owners of the monopoly profits that they would otherwise derive from intellectual property protection. In connection with intellectual property protection, even a state that lacks 'traditional' market power on world markets may be able to impose terms-of-trade externalities on other states by reducing its protection of intellectual property below the global optimum. For this reason, and because of the international public-goods aspects of intellectual property, states have incentives to undersupply intellectual property protection. At least in part, TRIPS seems to be an attempt to reduce these policy externalities. All contracts, and all international treaties, are incomplete. This case involves, in the authors' view, some good examples of treaty incompleteness. Incompleteness can arise from circumstances of uncertainty regarding the possible tradeoffs, and the optimal balance, between different goals, including state autonomy in censorship on the one hand and internalizing policy externalities in intellectual property protection on the other. The authors analyze the possibility that it might be efficient to allow states broad discretion over censorship. Alternatively, in connection with the requirement for criminal penalties, incompleteness can arise from uncertainty regarding the particular industry structure that might be involved, and what would constitute production of 'commercial scale' for that industry. The authors also question the rationale for the limitation on the use of nonviolation complaints in connection with the TRIPS, since nonviolation complaints may be used to reduce the possibility that states will use discretion, such as that granted with respect to censorship, in a manner that is inconsistent with the rationale for that discretion – so as to defect from the general commitment to provide copyright or other intellectual property rights.

Another highly interesting dispute was *China–Publications and Audiovisual Products*, where a series of Chinese restrictions on the importation and distribution of certain 'cultural' or 'content' goods and services were found to violate GATT, GATS, and China's Accession Protocol. The AB Report in this dispute is analyzed by **Conconi** and **Pauwelyn**. The authors review the definition of what is a 'good' (is a 'film' a good or a service?) and the extent to which GATT Article XX exceptions can justify violations under WTO instruments other than the GATT itself. In the case at hand, the issue was whether this GATT provision could serve as an exception justifying deviations from obligations assumed under the Chinese Protocol of Accession. This was the first time that WTO adjudicating bodies had to address this particular issue. The authors argue that trade volumes are unlikely to rise significantly as a result of this ruling, as it does not affect China's right to keep out foreign films and publications if China finds them objectionable. However, foreign producers of audiovisuals can now gain potentially large economic rents by being able to export and distribute their products into the Chinese market. Finally, the authors discuss the issue of the protection of cultural goods and review the recent literature on trade and culture that has put forward economic arguments to justify, under some conditions, the protection of cultural goods. The authors include in their comment an extensive discussion of the AB findings regarding violations of China's Protocol of Accession, an issue that is gaining pace in WTO dispute-settlement practice.

Grossman and **Sykes** discuss the Report on *United States – Subsidies on Upland Cotton (Recourse to Arbitration by the United States under Article 22.6 of the*

DSU and Article 4.11 and Article 7.10 of the SCM Agreement). In the authors' view, the case raises a range of interesting issues regarding the rationale for retaliation in the WTO system and the proper approach to its calibration. The authors entertain the following questions in this context: Should the approach to retaliation differ in cases involving prohibited or actionable subsidies? When should cross-retaliation be allowed? Should retaliation be based only on the harm to the complaining nation, or to other nations as well? And, most importantly, what economic content can be given to the standard of countermeasures 'equivalent to the level of nullification or impairment'? Grossman and Sykes point to a number of puzzling features of the DSU. For instance, the fact that the DSU allows WTO members to maintain illegal measures for an extended period of time without suffering any formal sanction suggests that the system is designed neither to 'ensure compliance', nor to ensure 'efficient compliance' (and its corollary 'efficient breach'). Furthermore, they see no economic rationale in using the amount of the subsidy as a basis for determining the amount of retaliation; nor do they see any valid economic reason why the approach to retaliation should differ in subsidies cases generally, or in prohibited-subsidies cases in particular. But Grossman and Sykes identify certain restrictive assumptions under which it makes economic sense to allow the retaliator to reduce the value of its imports by an amount equal to the value of its lost exports due to the violation. At the same time, the authors note that the use of prohibitive tariffs for purposes of retaliation is puzzling, as these tariffs cannot in general restore lost welfare for the complainant – nonprohibitive tariffs that enhance the terms of trade seem to make more sense. Their analysis suggests that the same information required to compute the nonprohibitive tariffs that will produce an equal trade-volume effect could instead be used to compute the tariffs that would offset the terms-of-trade loss due to the violation. Such an approach seemingly holds more promise as a way to approximate the level of retaliation that would restore the welfare of the complainant.

US Compliance with WTO Rulings on Zeroing in Anti-Dumping

United States–Zeroing (EC); United States–Zeroing (Japan)
Article 21.5 DSU Implementation Reports

BERNARD HOEKMAN
World Bank and CEPR
JASPER WAUTERS

Abstract: This paper reviews the WTO Appellate Body Reports on *United States–Zeroing* (*EC*) (Article 21.5 DSU – EC) (WT/DS294/AB/RW, 14 May 2009) and *United States–Zeroing* (*Japan*) (Article 21.5 DSU – Japan) (WT/DS322/AB/RW, 18 August 2009). The Appellate Body found that the United States had not brought its anti-dumping measures into compliance with the WTO Anti-Dumping Agreement as it continued to use zeroing in annual reviews of anti-dumping orders. We argue that this conclusion – based on a complicated discussion of what constitutes a 'measure taken to comply' – could have been reached through a much simpler and direct argument. Continued noncompliance by the United States generates costs to traders targeting the United States and the trading system more generally. We argue that from a broader WTO compliance perspective consideration should be given to stronger multilateral surveillance of anti-dumping practice by all WTO members and to more analysis and effective communication by economists regarding the costs of zeroing and anti-dumping practices more generally.

Introduction

This paper reviews the WTO Appellate Body (AB) Reports on *United States–Zeroing* (*EC*) (Article 21.5 DSU – EC) (WT/DS294/AB/RW, 14 May 2009)[1] and *United States–Zeroing* (*Japan*) (Article 21.5 DSU – Japan) (WT/DS322/AB/RW,

The paper is a contribution to The American Law Institute project on the case law of the WTO, led by Henrik Horn and Petros Mavroidis. We thank Marco Bronckers, Chad Bown, and Tom Prusa for helpful discussions and Henrik Horn, Rob Howse, Petros Mavroidis, and participants in the June 7, 2010 American Law Institute conference in Geneva for comments on the first draft. The views expressed are personal and should not be attributed to our employers.

1 Appellate Body Report, *United States – Laws, Regulations and Methodology for Calculating Dumping Margins ('Zeroing') – Recourse to Article 21.5 of the DSU by the European Communities*, WT/DS294/AB/RW and Corr.1, adopted 11 June 2009.

18 August 2009).[2] These disputes concerned the manner in which the United States implemented – or failed to implement – the WTO rulings relating to the prohibition of zeroing in anti-dumping investigations and reviews. The main legal issue dealt with in these compliance cases was what prospective implementation means in the context of a retrospective system of administering anti-dumping measures.

As the United States is the only country with such a system, the Reports are very specific to the US situation and are limited to the question of implementation in the context of anti-dumping measures. The Reports are nonetheless of interest in that they provide further insight into the approach taken by the AB in assessing compliance with WTO rulings. In the two Reports, the AB found that the United States was not in compliance, in that any action taken after the expiry of the 'reasonable period of time' (RPT) for implementation of previous AB Reports, whether a legal determination of the amount of duties due or the simple collection of duties, must be consistent with the WTO Anti-Dumping (AD) Agreement.

In what follows, we first summarize the disputes (Section 1), the Panel Reports (Section 2), and the appeals and the AB Reports (Section 3). In Section 4, we discuss the reasoning in the AB Reports. We argue that the Appellate Body conclusion could have been reached in a much more direct way rather than after a lengthy and unnecessarily complicated discussion of what constitutes a 'measure taken to comply'. Given extensive prior analysis of the technical aspects of zeroing, in Section 5 we focus on the available evidence on the economic impact of (continued) US zeroing. As the practice potentially affects all exporters to the United States, we argue that the chilling effect of continued use of zeroing may be nontrivial. Moreover, continued use of zeroing can be expected to lead to both WTO-legal retaliation in the future by affected WTO members and, potentially more important, emulation by other countries. As anti-dumping is increasingly used by developing countries, we argue that from a broader WTO compliance perspective consideration should be given to strengthening multilateral surveillance of anti-dumping practice around the world to make the effects of zeroing and other methodologies on anti-dumping margins more transparent. Section 6 concludes.

1. The dispute

This dispute concerns the manner in which the United States implemented a number of rulings by the WTO in respect of the use of zeroing in anti-dumping investigations and reviews. In the context of the dispute known as *US–Zeroing (EC)*, the European Union (the 'EU') challenged the use of zeroing both as such, and as applied by the United States in the specific context of a large number of original investigations and reviews relating to different products from the EU. The

2 Appellate Body Report, *United States – Measures Relating to Zeroing and Sunset Reviews –Recourse to Article 21.5 of the DSU by Japan*, WT/DS322/AB/RW, adopted 31 August 2009.

dispute known as *US–Zeroing (Japan)* concerned a similar challenge by Japan of the use of zeroing as such, and as applied by the United States in the context of a number of original investigations and reviews relating to a number of steel-related products such as ball bearings from Japan.

The question of zeroing has been at the heart of many Panel and Appellate Body Reports. It essentially relates to the way in which dumping margins are calculated in the context of anti-dumping measures. In order to determine whether a product has been dumped, the export price of the product will be compared to its normal value, which is the comparable price for which the like product is sold in the ordinary course of trade on its domestic market. This comparison will normally involve a large amount of transactions. When 'zeroing', an investigating authority will not allow transactions in which the export price was actually equal to or higher than the normal value (no dumping) to offset the transactions in which the export price was below the normal value (dumping). In other words, if there are 100 transactions, 50 of which are dumped because the export price is 10 % lower than the normal value and 50 of which are not dumped because the export price is 20 % higher than the normal value, dumping will be found to exist, even though, on average, the margin of dumping was below zero. The margin of dumping will be determined on the basis of the first 50 transactions, as a 'zero' margin will be assigned to the latter 50 transactions, even though their margin was actually negative (–20 %). As negative margins cannot be used to offset positive margins, a finding of dumping is more likely and the amount of the margin of dumping will be inflated.

The Panel in its Report on *US–Zeroing (EC)* found that the United States had acted inconsistently with Article 2.4.2 AD Agreement as regards the 15 original investigations at issue. The Panel considered that this was so because 'USDOC [US Department of Commerce] did not include in the numerator used to calculate weighted average dumping margins any amounts by which average export prices in individual averaging groups exceeded the average normal value for such groups'.[3] The Panel also found that, in the context of original investigations, the zeroing methodology as such, and thus independent of any specific application, was inconsistent with Article 2.4.2 AD Agreement.[4] However, the Panel considered that zeroing was permissible in the context of administrative reviews. The AB reversed the Panel on this and held that by using zeroing in the administrative reviews, the USDOC had violated Article 9.3 AD Agreement and Article VI:2 GATT.

3 Panel Report, *United States – Laws, Regulations and Methodology for Calculating Dumping Margins ('Zeroing')*, WT/DS294/R, adopted 9 May 2006, as modified by Appellate Body Report, WT/DS294/AB/R, DSR 2006:II, 521 (*US–Zeroing (EC)*), para. 7.32. Furthermore, having adjudicated the claims of the EC under Article 2.4.2 AD Agreement, the Panel considered it unnecessary to rule on its claims under Article 2.4 AD Agreement.

4 Panel Report, *US-Zeroing (EC)*, para. 7.106.

Similar issues arose in the *US–Zeroing (Japan)* case, where the Panel found that the use of zeroing in the context of weighted-average-to-weighted-average comparisons ('model zeroing') by the USDOC in the context of original investigations is 'as such' inconsistent with Article 2.4.2 AD Agreement because the dumping margin so calculated does not take into account all comparisons between the normal value and the export price. The Panel also held that by applying model zeroing in the anti-dumping investigation of imports of certain cut-to-length carbon-quality steel products from Japan, the United States had infringed Article 2.4.2 AD Agreement. This aspect of the Panel's findings was uncontroversial.

In respect of zeroing in the context of transaction-to-transaction comparisons ('simple zeroing'), the Panel considered that this could be permissible and was overturned on appeal. The AB found that zeroing while using the transaction-to-transaction comparison method in original investigations is inconsistent with Article 2.4.2 AD Agreement:

> In the light of our analysis of Article 2.4.2 of the Anti-Dumping Agreement, we conclude that, in establishing 'margins of dumping' under the T–T comparison methodology, an investigating authority must aggregate the results of all the transaction-specific comparisons and cannot disregard the results of comparisons in which export prices are above normal value.[5]

Therefore, it held that the USDOC violated Article 2.4.2 AD Agreement by using zeroing in the transaction-to-transaction comparison method in original investigations.[6]

The AB reversed the Panel's findings in respect of the permissibility of zeroing in the context of reviews, ruling that zeroing is not permitted in the context of any type of review. In particular, the AB found that the United States had violated Articles 9.3 and 9.5 AD Agreement and Article VI:2 GATT by maintaining simple zeroing in *administrative reviews* (also known as 'periodic reviews') and *new-shipper reviews*.[7] The AB also held that zeroing in administrative and new-shipper reviews is inconsistent with the fair-comparison requirement of Article 2.4 AD Agreement. As a result, it held that the United States had acted in contravention of its WTO obligations by applying simple zeroing in the 11 administrative reviews in

5 Appellate Body Report, *United States – Measures Relating to Zeroing and Sunset Reviews*, WT/DS322/AB/R, adopted 23 January 2007, DSR 2007:I, 3 (*US–Zeroing (Japan)*), para. 137.

6 The Appellate Body also found that this method of dumping-margin calculation is not unbiased or even-handed and accordingly zeroing in transaction-to-transaction comparisons violates the fair-comparison requirement. Consequentially, the Appellate Body reversed the Panel's decision in this regard and held that the United States infringed Article 2.4 AD Agreement by maintaining simple zeroing in original investigations.

7 The Appellate Body considered that dumping and dumping margins can only exist at the level of a product and that this equally prohibits zeroing in administrative reviews as the dumping margin acts as a ceiling for the total amount of anti-dumping duties that can be collected in any type of duty-assessment system.

question. Finally, the AB reversed the Panel in respect of the use of zeroing in *sunset reviews*, concluding that the presence of the terms 'review' and 'determine' in Article 11.3 AD Agreement require a reasoned conclusion based on positive evidence and a sufficient factual basis. If, in sunset reviews, the authorities relied on historical dumping margins, these margins should be in conformity with Article 2.4 AD Agreement. Hence, the AB held that by relying in sunset reviews on the dumping margins calculated in the administrative reviews using zeroing, the United States had infringed Article 11.3 AD Agreement.

The RPT for the United States to implement the recommendations and rulings of the Dispute Settlement Body (DSB) in the case of *US–Zeroing* (*EC*) was set, by agreement of the parties, at 11 months, expiring on 9 April 2007.[8] On 13 September 2007, the EU requested the establishment of a Panel pursuant to Article 21.5 of the Dispute Settlement Understanding (DSU),[9] which applies 'when there is disagreement as to the existence of consistency with a covered agreement of measures taken to comply with the recommendations and rulings' of the DSB. In the context of the *US–Zeroing* (*Japan*) dispute, the RPT for the United States to bring its measures into conformity expired on 24 December 2007.[10] On 7 April 2008, Japan requested the establishment of a Panel[11] pursuant to Article 21.5 of the DSU.

Complainant arguments and the US defense

The United States was required to implement the rulings of the DSB in the disputes on *US–Zeroing* (*EC*) and *US–Zeroing* (*Japan*) relating to the zeroing methodology 'as such' both in the context of original investigations (*US–Zeroing* (*EC*)) and in the context of administrative reviews and new-shipper reviews (*US–Zeroing* (*Japan*)). It was also required to correct the use of zeroing 'as applied' in a number of original investigations, as well as administrative reviews and sunset reviews. We briefly discuss the arguments of the parties in respect of each case.

US–Zeroing (*EC*)

The EU's challenge related first of all to the measures expressly identified by the United States as 'measures taken to comply' with the DSB rulings. The EU thus challenged the Section 129 determinations adopted by the United States to implement the recommendations and rulings of the DSB. The EU argued that one such determination was vitiated by a calculation error. Of a number of other determinations, the EU argued that they were inconsistent with the United States's

8 WT/DS294/19.
9 WT/DS294/25.
10 WT/DS322/20.
11 WT/DS322/27.

obligations under the AD Agreement since no new injury analysis was performed, even though the recalculation of the dumping margins without zeroing led to the exclusion of a number of exporters previously found to be dumping. The EU also challenged the US determination of the all-others rate based on margins that were below de minimis or based on facts available. These sets of claims could be qualified as 'ordinary' implementation issues as they relate to the measures taken to comply with a DSB ruling and examine their consistency under the relevant Agreement. These claims are unrelated to the question of zeroing as it is undisputed that, in these redeterminations, the United States indeed no longer used 'zeroing'.

In addition, the EU challenged a number of reviews that were undertaken by the United States as part of the normal ongoing life of the anti-dumping orders originally challenged by the EU. The EU thus claimed violations in respect of subsequent administrative reviews, changed-circumstances reviews, and sunset reviews adopted in relation to the 15 original investigations and the 16 administrative reviews at issue in the original proceedings, as well as liquidation and assessment instructions and final liquidation of duties resulting from those subsequent reviews. The EU argued that all of these subsequent reviews undertaken in the context of AD orders of which the original determination or the administrative review were found to be WTO-inconsistent, were sufficiently related to the challenged measures to be considered as 'measures taken to comply'. Since the United States continued to use zeroing in these subsequent reviews, the EU argued that the United States continued to violate the AD Agreement. Similarly, the EU argued that any liquidation instructions based on a determination vitiated by zeroing that were made after the expiry of the RPT were WTO-inconsistent actions. Finally, the EU argued that the United States, by omission, had failed to implement the DSB's rulings. In particular, the EU noted that there was a gap between the end of the RPT for implementation and the adoption of some of the Section 129 determinations through which the United States sought to implement the WTO rulings.

The United States considered it had fully implemented the DSB rulings by amending, through several so-called 'Section 129 determinations', the challenged original determinations[12] and reviews[13] and by making an effective end to the use of

12 On 9 April 2007, the USDOC issued Section 129 determinations in which it recalculated, without zeroing, the margins of dumping for 11 of the original investigations at issue in the original proceedings. The results of those Section 129 determinations became effective two weeks later, on 23 April 2007. The Section 129 determination in the remaining case was issued on 20 August 2007, effective 31 August 2007.

13 With respect to the 16 administrative reviews at issue in the original proceedings, the United States considered that the cash-deposit rates calculated in those proceedings – with the exception of one exporter – were no longer in effect because they had been superseded by subsequent administrative reviews. Consequently, 'no further action was taken by the United States in order to implement the DSB recommendations and rulings in respect of these administrative review[s]'.

model zeroing in original investigations.[14] According to the United States, only these Section 129 determinations are 'measures taken to comply' in respect of which the Panel has a mandate under article 21.5 of the DSU. The United States acknowledged that the USDOC issued, in the ordinary course, administrative-review determinations with respect to anti-dumping duty orders relating to the original investigations at issue in the original proceedings. The USDOC continued to apply zeroing when calculating margins of dumping in those administrative reviews.[15] It also acknowledged that sunset reviews were conducted with respect to some of the measures at issue in the original proceedings. Twelve sunset-review determinations of these measures resulted in the continuation of the relevant AD duty order.[16] According to the United States, these subsequent reviews should not be considered as 'measures taken to comply' with the DSB rulings.

US–Zeroing (Japan)

Japan considered that the United States had failed to comply with the recommendations and rulings of the DSB. It argued that the United States had done nothing to implement the DSB rulings in respect of the 'as such' claims relating to the zeroing methodology in the context of transaction-to-transaction comparisons in original investigations, and under any comparison methodology in periodic and new-shipper reviews. It further alleged that the United States had not amended the importer-specific assessment rates in the context of five periodic reviews that were found to be WTO-inconsistent in the original proceedings. In addition, Japan considered that the United States committed the same zeroing violation in the case of four subsequent periodic reviews, one of which was only adopted in the course of the Panel's proceedings, which Japan considered to be 'measures taken to comply'. Japan also argued that the United States failed to bring into compliance the sunset-review determination of 4 November 1999, which was found to be vitiated by the use of zeroing. Finally, Japan argued that by continuing with certain liquidation actions relating to reviews that were completed before the end of the RPT, but where such actions were taken after the expiry of the RPT, the United States acted in violation of Articles II:1(a) and II:1(b) of the GATT 1994.

The United States argued it had brought its measures into compliance. It asserted that the zeroing procedures challenged 'as such' by Japan in the original proceeding no longer exist, as on 27 December 2006 USDOC published a final

14 On 27 December 2006, the United States announced that it would terminate the use of 'model zeroing' in original investigations in which the margins of dumping are determined on the basis of weighted-average-to-weighted-average comparisons of export prices and normal value. This modification became effective on 22 February 2007.

15 See Panel Report, *United States – Laws, Regulations and Methodology for Calculating Dumping Margins ('Zeroing') – Recourse to Article 21.5 of the DSU by the European Communities*, WT/DS294/RW, adopted 11 June 2009, as modified by Appellate Body Report WT/DS294/AB/RW (Panel Report, *US–Zeroing (EC) Article 21.5 DSU*) para. 3.1(c).

16 Panel Report, *US–Zeroing (EC)* (Article 21.5 DSU), para. 3.1(e).

notice announcing that it would no longer apply zeroing in weighted-average-to-weighted-average comparisons in original investigations.[17] It also held that it complied regarding certain of the challenged administrative reviews by withdrawing the WTO-inconsistent cash-deposit rates with prospective effect, replacing them with new cash-deposit rates determined in subsequent administrative reviews. The United States denied it was required to take any compliance action in respect of the importer-specific assessment rates determined in several administrative reviews. In addition, it asserted that a number of reviews challenged by Japan that were not challenged in the original proceedings should not be considered as 'measures taken to comply' within the meaning of Article 21.5 of the DSU, and therefore fell outside the scope of these proceedings. It also argued that a review which was not terminated at the time Japan requested the establishment of the implementation Panel was not within the Panel's terms of reference. Finally, the United States asserted that it was not required to take any action to comply with the DSB's recommendations and rulings regarding the 4 November 1999 sunset review, because the relevant likelihood of dumping determination continues to be based on a number of dumping rates not called into question by the findings of the Appellate Body.[18]

2. The Panel Report

We next briefly discuss the main elements of the Panel's ruling in both cases.

US–Zeroing (EC)

In its Report on *US–Zeroing (EC)*, the Panel upheld some, but not all of the EU's claims. As to what actions are to be considered as 'measures taken to comply', the Panel noted that 'a nexus-based analysis, as articulated in *Australia–Leather II* (Article 21.5 – US), *Australia–Salmon* (Article 21.5 – Canada), and *US–Softwood Lumber* (Article 21.5 – Canada) is useful in examining which measures challenged by a complainant properly fall within the scope of an Article 21.5 proceeding'. It thus found that if the 'contested measures are closely connected with the measures at issue in the original dispute or with the steps taken by the Member to implement the DSB's recommendations and ruling', they are measures taken to comply.[19]

The Panel examined the links, 'in terms of their *nature* and of their *effects*', that exist in general between the subsequent reviews challenged by the European Communities and the measures at issue in the original dispute and the

17 'Antidumping Proceedings: Calculation of the Weighted Average Dumping Margin During an Antidumping Investigation', Final Modification, 71 Fed. Reg. 77722, 77723 (USDOC, 27 December 2006).

18 Panel Report, *United States – Measures Relating to Zeroing and Sunset Reviews – Recourse to Article 21.5 of the DSU by Japan*, WT/DS322/RW, adopted 31 August 2009, upheld by Appellate Body Report WT/DS322/AB/RW, paras. 3.2–3.5.

19 Panel Report, *US–Zeroing* (*EC*) (Article 21.5 DSU), paras. 8.97–8.98.

recommendations and rulings of the DSB. It found that 'successive determinations of different types are made in the context of a single trade remedy proceeding, involving the imposition and assessment of anti-dumping duties on imports of a particular subject product, from the same country. They all concern the imposition and collection of anti-dumping duties under a particular anti-dumping order. In this sense, these determinations form part of a continuum of events and measures that are all inextricably linked.'[20] It then considered the links, 'in terms of the *timing* of the determinations at issue' and found that 'only those subsequent reviews that were decided after such [DSB] adoption could be taken into consideration as part of a compliance panel's examination of the implementation of DSB recommendations and rulings'.[21] In other words, the Panel was of the view that only 'measures adopted following the adoption of the DSB's recommendations may have a close link with the DSB's recommendations and rulings and with the steps, if any, taken by the implementing Member to achieve compliance with the recommendations and rulings, and therefore warrant inclusion in the scope of an Article 21.5 proceeding'.[22] This is so, according to the Panel, because 'the application of a nexus-based test should primarily aim at bringing within the scope of the compliance dispute measures that potentially circumvent implementation or undermine measures officially taken to comply'. Therefore, 'none of the subsequent reviews challenged by the European Communities that were decided before the adoption of the DSB's recommendations and rulings fall within our terms of reference'.[23]

Having established the measures that fell within its terms of reference, the Panel examined the relevant claims of the EU in respect of such measures. It agreed with the EU that the United States had violated its WTO obligations by making determinations of the final amount of duty assessment after the end of the RPT in certain administrative reviews, and by continuing to apply cash-deposit rates to certain imports established in an administrative review that was found to be WTO-inconsistent. Liquidation of anti-dumping duties calculated with zeroing pursuant to final duty-assessment determinations made *before* the end of the RPT was deemed not to be WTO-inconsistent. In essence, the Panel was of the view that any final determination in a related periodic review made after the end of the RPT must comply with the WTO prohibition on zeroing, even when it relates to imports that entered the country before the end of the RPT. However, according to the Panel, when the final determination using zeroing is made before the end of the RPT and thus at a point in time that the United States's violation was not subject to a sanction, it is irrelevant that the execution of that determination through liquidation instructions takes place after the end of the RPT. According to the Panel,

20 Ibid., para. 8.103.
21 Ibid., para. 8.100; para. 8.115.
22 Ibid., para. 8.116.
23 Ibid., para. 8.119.

'the relevant date for implementation of DSB recommendations and rulings concerning anti-dumping duties by a Member operating a retrospective duty assessment system is the date of the final determination of liability'.[24]

The Panel further found that the United States had violated Article 3 of the AD Agreement by maintaining the AD duty orders, in certain cases, without having made a new determination of injury and of the volume of dumped imports even though the redeterminations without zeroing led to the exclusion of a number of exporters that were no longer considered to have been dumped. However, the Panel found that the United States did not act inconsistently with Article 9.4 of the AD Agreement in the establishment of 'all others' rates in the Section 129 determinations in the relevant cases since it was of the view that Article 9.4 does not impose any obligations on authorities when all margins are either de minimis, zero, or based on facts available. The Panel did not make findings for technical reasons on a number of other claims.

US–Zeroing (Japan)

The Panel upheld almost all of the arguments of Japan. It found that the United States had failed to comply with the DSB's recommendations and rulings regarding the importer-specific assessment rates determined in a number of administrative reviews in respect of imports that were liquidated after the expiry of the RPT. It concluded that the United States was thus in continued violation of its obligations under Articles 2.4 and 9.3 of the AD Agreement and Article VI:2 of the GATT 1994. It also found that the United States acted inconsistently with Articles 2.4 and 9.3 of the AD Agreement and Article VI:2 of the GATT 1994 by applying zeroing in the context of those administrative reviews that were not challenged in the original dispute but which could be considered as measures taken to comply with the DSB rulings and recommendations because of their close nexus with the determinations challenged in the original proceedings.

In addition, the Panel held that the United States failed to comply with the recommendations and rulings of the DSB regarding the maintenance of zeroing procedures challenged 'as such' in the original proceedings. It found that the United States had not implemented the recommendations and rulings in the context of transaction-to-transaction comparisons in original investigations and under any comparison methodology in periodic and new-shipper reviews. It thus found that the United States remained in violation of Articles 2.4, 2.4.2, 9.3, and 9.5 of the AD Agreement and Article VI:2 of the GATT 1994. It also found that the United States was in violation of Articles II:1(a) and II:1(b) of the GATT 1994 with respect to certain liquidation actions taken after the expiry of the RPT, even

24 Ibid., para. 8.174. The Panel made no findings with respect to the EU claim that the United States violated the DSU by failing to take any measure to comply in respect of certain determinations found to be WTO inconsistent until well after the end of the RPT but before the start of the implementation proceedings.

when they were based on reviews terminated prior to the end of the RPT. The Panel thus adopted a different approach from that of the Panel on *US–Zeroing (EC)*.[25] Finally, the Panel found that the United States had not complied with the DSB recommendations and rulings with respect to the 1999 sunset review.[26]

3. The appeal and the Appellate Body Reports

We next outline the major arguments raised on appeal and summarize the findings of the AB in respect of the most relevant matters in both cases.

US–Zeroing (EC)

A number of issues were raised on appeal.[27] Most importantly, the EU argued the Panel erred in finding that subsequent reviews that predated the adoption of the recommendations and rulings of the DSB did not fall within its terms of reference, because they did not have a sufficiently 'close nexus' with the original measures at issue and the recommendations and rulings of the DSB. The EU also considered that the Panel erred by not extending the US compliance obligations to actions consequent to the assessment of duties, including the collection or liquidation of duties occurring after the end of the RPT when they related to administrative-review determinations completed before that date.

In addition, the EU challenged a number of other aspects of the Panel's findings, such as the Panel's refusal to make a finding in respect of measures taken to comply after the end of the RPT but before the request for establishment of an implementation Panel was submitted by the EU. The EU also challenged the Panel's refusal to examine an alleged calculation error in a measure taken to comply for reason of the fact that this error could have been challenged in the original dispute as it had also been present in the original measure. It also contested the Panel's findings in respect of the lack of disciplines in respect of the 'all others' rates when all margins are determined based on zeroing or are de minimis.

The United States challenged a number of the Panel's findings, most importantly the 'close nexus' test developed by the Panel that formed the basis for the inclusion of a significant number of reviews that had not been challenged in the original dispute since they postdated the original request for establishment.

The Appellate Body Report

The Appellate Body sided with the EU on an important number of claims overturning the Panel's findings. Our discussion in what follows focuses mainly on the

25 The Panel expressly recognized this difference in approach. Panel Report, *US–Zeroing (Japan)* (Article 21.5 DSU), para. 7.208 and footnote 220.

26 Ibid., para. 8.1.

27 On 13 February 2009, the EU notified the DSB of its intention to appeal certain issues of law and legal interpretations developed in the Panel Report and filed a Notice of Appeal (WT/DS294/28). On 25 February 2009, the United States notified the DSB of its intention to appeal certain issues of law and legal interpretations developed in the Panel Report and filed a Notice of Other Appeal (WT/DS294/29).

scope of the term 'measures taken to comply' in the specific context of US anti-dumping proceedings. We also briefly discuss the manner in which the AB dealt with a number of other issues on appeal, i.e. sunset reviews, the implementation gap between the end of the RPT and actual compliance, the challenge of aspects of a measure that were part of the original measure and were not challenged at the time of the original dispute, and the limits imposed by the AD Agreement in respect of the 'all others' rate under Article 9.4 AD Agreement.

1. 'Measures taken to comply' and 'subsequent reviews'

The EU argued that the Panel erred, inter alia, in finding that the subsequent reviews that *predated* the adoption of the recommendations and rulings of the DSB did not fall within its terms of reference because they did not have a sufficiently close nexus with the original measures at issue and the recommendations and rulings of the DSB.

The AB first clarified that it considered 'that successive administrative, changed circumstances, and sunset review determinations issued in connection with the measures at issue in the original proceedings constitute separate and distinct measures, which therefore cannot be properly characterized as mere "amendments" to those measures',[28] thus rejecting the EU's argument that any subsequent reviews were, in any case, mere amendments of the challenged measures and for that reason alone properly before the Panel.[29] The AB recalled that it had previously 'expressed the view that a panel's mandate under Article 21.5 of the DSU is not necessarily limited to measures that the implementing Member maintains are taken "in the direction of" or "for the purpose of achieving" compliance with the recommendations and rulings of the DSB.'[30] It reiterated its view that 'measures with a "particularly close relationship" with the declared measure "taken to comply", and to the recommendations and rulings of the DSB, may also fall within the purview of a compliance panel',[31] and that 'a panel's determination of whether such a "close relationship" exists will depend upon the particular factual and legal background, and may call for an examination of the timing, nature, and effects of the various measures before the panel'.[32]

28 Appellate Body Report, *US–Zeroing (EC)* (Article 21.5 DSU), para. 192.

29 The Appellate Body recalled that, in a previous case, it had already found that subsequent reviews are 'connected stages under the same anti-dumping duty order', and that it had also made clear before that subsequent reviews involve 'successive determinations' and thus do not constitute 'mere "amendments" to the immediately preceding measure, because they constitute *distinct* determinations'. Appellate Body Report, *US–Zeroing (EC)* (Article 21.5 DSU), para. 192.

30 Appellate Body Report, *US–Zeroing (EC)* (Article 21.5 DSU), para. 202.

31 Ibid., para. 204.

32 Ibid., para. 204.

The AB then explained why it *agreed* with the nexus test as developed by the Panel but *disagreed* as to the impact of the factor time when applying this test:

> At the outset, we agree with the Panel that measures taken to comply with recommendations and rulings of the DSB ordinarily post-date the adoption of the recommendations and rulings. As the Appellate Body noted in *US – Softwood Lumber IV (Article 21.5 – Canada)*, '[a]s a whole, Article 21 deals with events *subsequent* to the DSB's adoption of recommendations and rulings in a particular dispute'.
>
> However, the Panel's finding that 'a measure taken before the adoption of the DSB's recommendations and rulings could rarely, if ever, be found to be a measure taken "to comply" with such recommendations and rulings' seems premised on the notion that a panel's mandate under Article 21.5 is limited to those measures taken 'in the direction of' or 'for the purposes of achieving' compliance with the recommendations and rulings of the DSB. As we have noted earlier, in the Appellate Body's interpretation, '[t]he fact that Article 21.5 mandates a panel to assess "existence" and "consistency" tends to weigh against an interpretation of Article 21.5 that would confine the scope of a panel's jurisdiction to measures that *move in the direction of*, or *have the objective of achieving*, compliance.' For this reason, measures with a 'particularly close relationship' with the declared measures 'taken to comply', and to the recommendations and rulings of the DSB, may also fall within the scope of a panel proceeding under Article 21.5 of the DSU, even though such measures are not, strictly speaking, measures taken with the purpose of achieving compliance with those recommendations and rulings.
>
> In this respect, we agree with the European Communities and the United States that the *timing* of a measure cannot be determinative of whether it bears a sufficiently close nexus with a Member's implementation of the recommendations and rulings of the DSB so as to fall within the scope of an Article 21.5 proceeding. Since compliance with the recommendations and rulings of DSB can be achieved *before* the recommendations and rulings of the DSB are adopted, a compliance panel may have to review events pre-dating the adoption of those recommendations and rulings in order to resolve a disagreement as to the 'existence' or 'consistency with a covered agreement' of such measures. Indeed, the United States argued before the Panel that it did not have to take further action to implement the recommendations and rulings of the DSB in respect of the administrative reviews at issue in the original proceedings, because they were superseded by subsequent administrative reviews that pre-dated the adoption of the DSB's recommendations and rulings. We also note the United States' argument that, where a measure is withdrawn prior to the DSB's recommendations and rulings, a Member may not need to take any further measures to comply with those recommendations and rulings after they are adopted. We do not see why a compliance panel should be unable to take such prior withdrawal into account. (footnotes omitted)[33]

33 Ibid., paras. 222–224.

In sum, the AB reversed the Panel's finding that reviews that predated the adoption of the Panel and AB Reports by the DSB could not be considered as 'measures taken to comply':

> In our view, the Panel's formalistic reliance on the date of issuance of the subsequent reviews in ascertaining whether these reviews had a close nexus with the recommendations and rulings of the DSB was in error. The relevant inquiry was not whether the subsequent reviews were taken with the intention to comply with the recommendations and rulings of the DSB; rather, in our view, the relevant inquiry was whether the subsequent reviews, despite the fact that they were issued before the adoption of the recommendations and rulings of the DSB, still bore a sufficiently close nexus, in terms of *nature*, *effects*, and *timing*, with those recommendations and rulings, and with the declared measures 'taken to comply', so as to fall within the scope of Article 21.5 proceedings.[34]

Applying the nexus test to the reviews challenged, the AB concluded that 'the use of zeroing in the excluded subsequent reviews provides the necessary link, in terms of *nature* or subject matter, between such measures, the declared measures "taken to comply", and the recommendations and rulings of the DSB'.[35] In terms of effects, the AB found that 'to the extent that these administrative reviews generated assessment rates and cash deposit rates calculated with zeroing that replaced those found to be WTO-inconsistent in the original proceedings with the effects of assessment rates and cash deposit rates that continued to reflect the zeroing methodology, this would provide a sufficient link, in terms of *effects*, between those administrative reviews and the recommendations and rulings of the DSB, insofar as the requirement to cease using the zeroing methodology is concerned'.[36]

However, the AB added that the situation was different in respect of those administrative reviews that related to determinations for which section 129 redeterminations without zeroing had been made:

> With respect to the 15 original investigations subject to the recommendations and rulings of the DSB, the United States issued Section 129 determinations in which it recalculated margins of dumping without zeroing that served as the basis for the going-forward cash deposit rates for the relevant anti-dumping duty orders. This recalculation without zeroing replaced the effects of the cash deposits calculated with zeroing in previous administrative reviews with the effects of cash deposits calculated *without* zeroing. Consequently, to the extent that the effects of the administrative and sunset reviews excluded from the Panel's terms of reference were replaced with those of a subsequent Section 129 determination in which zeroing was not applied, those subsequent reviews would generally not have the necessary link, in terms of *effects*, with the declared

34 Ibid., para. 226.
35 Ibid., para. 230.
36 Ibid., para. 231.

> measures 'taken to comply', and with the recommendations and rulings of the DSB, so as to fall within the Panel's terms of reference.[37]

Finally, the AB confirmed its view on the lack of significance of the factor 'time'. It concluded that 'the fact that the likelihood-of-dumping determinations in the sunset reviews listed above pre-date the adoption of the recommendations and rulings of the DSB is not sufficient to sever the pervasive links that we have found to exist, in terms of *nature* and *effects*, between such sunset reviews, the recommendations and rulings of the DSB, and the declared measures "taken to comply"'.[38]

The AB logically rejected the US cross-appeal on the Panel's nexus test, stressing the risk involved in adopting the US approach to implementation, arguing that:

> the use of zeroing in subsequent determinations could undermine implementation in respect of original investigations. Although the Appellate Body noted in *US – Softwood Lumber IV (Article 21.5 – Canada)* that there are some limits on the scope of compliance proceedings, 'these limits should not allow circumvention by Members by allowing them to comply through one measure, while, at the same time, negating compliance through another.'[39]
> The use of zeroing to calculate assessment rates in administrative reviews issued after the end of the reasonable period of time is an indication that these reviews could undermine the compliance allegedly achieved by the United States. Indeed, the Section 129 determinations do not apply to entries prior to the end of the reasonable period of time and thus do not relate to compliance with respect to administrative reviews issued after the end of the reasonable period covering imports occurring before that date.[40]

The AB also rejected the US allegation that zeroing in a weighted-average-to-weighted-average context is not the same as zeroing in the context of a transaction-to-transaction comparison and that, for that reason, there is 'no nexus' between the challenged measures and some of the reviews in which a different methodology was used. The argument concerning the risk of undermining the objective of effective compliance led one member of the AB to issue a separate opinion in which this member pointed to the lack of risk of circumvention in respect of two reviews in which no going-forward cash-deposit rates were set.[41]

37 Ibid., para. 232.

38 Ibid., para. 234.

39 Appellate Body Report, *US – Softwood Lumber IV* (Article 21.5 – Canada), para. 71; Appellate Body Report, *US–Zeroing (EC)* (Article 21.5 DSU), para. 250.

40 Appellate Body Report, *US–Zeroing (EC)* (Article 21.5 DSU), para. 252.

41 Ibid., paras. 267–268. According to this member, 'to the extent that the Section 129 determinations led to the revocation of the underlying anti-dumping duty orders, the 2004–2005 administrative reviews in Cases 1 and 6 had no bearing on the cash deposit rates that they would have otherwise "updated" or "superseded" in those Cases. Rather, the results of the 2004–2005 administrative reviews merely had a retrospective effect, which was the establishment of final anti-dumping duty liability for importers on entries taking place long before the end of the reasonable period of time.'

This member thus warned against the overly broad reading of the term 'measures taken to comply'.[42]

Turning to the Panel's findings in respect of the timing of measures taken to comply, the AB agreed with the Panel in rejecting the US argument that the date of importation was the relevant date and that measures taken after the end of the RPT, even if they related to imports that entered prior to the end of the RPT should be 'zeroing-free'. However, the Panel also considered that a failure to comply could not be found with respect to actions occurring after the expiry of the RPT, such as assessment instructions by the USDOC to Customs, liquidation instructions by Customs to local port authorities, or actions to collect or liquidate duties, to the extent that these actions resulted from administrative reviews concluded *before* the end of the RPT. The AB rejected this approach and considered that any action taken after the end of the RPT, whether the determination of the amount of duties due or the actual liquidation of the entries after the end of the RPT should be consistent with the WTO Agreement:

> Given the scope of the recommendations and rulings of the DSB, in order to achieve compliance, the United States had to cease using zeroing in the assessment of duties with respect to Cases 16 through 31 by the end of the reasonable period of time. Having said that, we consider that these compliance obligations are not limited to the cessation of zeroing in the calculation of assessment rates; rather, by implication, these obligations also extend to connected and consequent measures that are simply 'mechanically' derived from the results of an assessment review and applied in the ordinary course of the imposition of anti-dumping duties.[43]

The AB rejected the allegation that this approach would imply a retroactive implementation, which goes against the prospective nature of WTO implementation.

> We observe, first, that an administrative review determination issued after the end of the reasonable period of time in which duty liability has been assessed for entries that occurred before that date also has an impact on entries taking place after the end of the reasonable period of time, because this determination sets going-forward cash deposit rates that apply to future entries. Under the United States' approach, prospective implementation would imply that cash deposit rates on entries after the end of the reasonable period of time do not reflect zeroing. Moreover, because compliance with the recommendations and rulings of the DSB implies cessation of zeroing in the assessment of final duty liability, and in the measures that, in the ordinary course of the imposition of anti-dumping duties, derive mechanically from the assessment of duties, whether the implementation is prospective or retroactive should not be determined by reference to the date when liability arises, but rather by reference to the time when

42 Ibid., para. 262.
43 Ibid., para. 306.

> final dumping duty liabilities are assessed or when measures that result mechanically from the assessment of duties occur. We consider that the obligation to cease using zeroing in the assessment of anti-dumping duty liability at the latest as of the end of the reasonable period of time 'is eminently prospective in nature'.[44]

The AB thus reversed the Panel's interpretation that the United States's obligation to implement the recommendations and rulings of the DSB does not extend to the actual collection and liquidation of duties, and to the issuance of assessment or liquidation instructions, when these actions result from administrative-review determinations made before the end of the RPT.[45]

Somewhat mysteriously, the AB added at the very end of this long discussion about compliance that it was not expressing 'any opinion on the question of whether actions to liquidate duties that are based on administrative review determinations issued before the end of the reasonable period of time, and that have been delayed as a result of judicial proceedings, fall within the scope of the implementation obligations of the United States, as we do not need to do so in the context of our analysis of this issue in this case'.[46] The AB then applied this reasoning to the facts of the different cases/reviews before it to consistently conclude that any action taken after the end of the RPT based on zeroing, even actions that derive mechanically from prior review determinations and actions not setting forth any forward cash deposit, are WTO-inconsistent.

2. Sunset reviews

As regards the various sunset reviews that were challenged, the AB referred to its prior report on *US–Continued Zeroing* to find that it is premature to challenge a sunset review when only USDOC has made a likelihood-of-dumping determination 'considering that such preliminary results could be modified by the final results'[47] or when such reviews were still pending before the USITC (US International Trade Commission) and it had not yet made its likelihood-of-injury determination. It further held that if sunset reviews, even when based on zeroing, led to the revocation of the measure, the Panel was right not to have considered such reviews:

> As we have noted above, these are compliance proceedings and the issue before the Panel was whether the United States had failed to comply; that is, the Panel was called on to establish whether the USDOC's determinations in these sunset reviews had any impact on compliance by the United States. We consider that the USDOC's affirmative final likelihood-of-dumping determinations in these sunset reviews did not ultimately undermine compliance by the United States with the

44 Ibid., para. 309.
45 Ibid., para. 311.
46 Ibid., para. 314.
47 Ibid., para. 374.

> recommendations and rulings of the DSB, considering that the anti-dumping duty orders were revoked at the end of the sunset reviews with an effective date of 7 March 2007. We consider this to be the case even assuming that the European Communities had demonstrated that these likelihood-of-dumping determinations relied on margins of dumping calculated using zeroing.[48]

What was important to the AB was the fact that 'the sunset reviews resulted in revocation orders and that these revocation orders became effective on a date prior to the end of the reasonable period of time'.[49]

3. Failure to comply – time gap

The AB upheld the Panel's refusal to make findings in respect of the US failure to take certain action by the end of the RPT when implementing measures were subsequently taken and adopted before the establishment of the implementation Panel. The AB agreed that any findings in respect of such noncompliance which was remedied prior to the establishment of a 21.5 DSU Panel would not be pertinent:

> In this case, the Panel acted in a manner consistent with the objective of securing a positive and effective solution to the dispute, and did not exceed the bounds of its discretion when, in its analysis of whether the United States had complied with the recommendations and rulings of the DSB, it took into account implementation actions taken subsequent to the expiry of the reasonable period of time but before the Article 21.5 Panel was established.
>
> When an Article 21.5 panel makes a finding that a WTO Member has not complied with the recommendations and rulings of the DSB in the original proceedings, the implication of that finding is that the WTO Member remains subject to obligations flowing from the recommendations and rulings issued by the DSB in the original proceedings. However, if the compliance panel finds that compliance has been achieved at the time of its establishment, but not at the end of the reasonable period of time, the responding WTO Member will not need to take additional remedial action.[50]

4. Prior nonchallenged aspects of the original measures

The AB found that the fact that part of the original measure was previously not challenged or not found to be WTO-inconsistent because no final ruling was

48 Ibid., para. 380.

49 Ibid., para. 380. In respect of another sunset review in which both the USDOC and the USITC had made their final determinations but the actual continuation of the duty was only made effective through a continuation order after establishment of the compliance Panel, the AB considered that this sunset review should have been reviewed by the Panel since this continuation order did not change the essence of the measure in question and that this order risked undermining compliance by the United States. The AB concluded that this sunset review was inconsistent with the US obligations under the AD Agreement.

50 Ibid., paras. 411–412.

made in this respect does not mean that it cannot be challenged in 21.5 DSU proceedings:

> We disagree with the notion that a Member may be entitled to assume in Article 21.5 proceedings that an aspect of a measure that was not challenged in the original proceedings is consistent with that Member's obligations under the covered agreements ... If certain claims against aspects of a measure were not decided on the merits in the original proceedings, they are not covered by the recommendations and rulings of the DSB and, therefore, a Member should not be entitled to assume that those aspects of the measure are consistent with the covered agreements.[51]

According to the AB, allowing a complaining Member to make a case that it did not establish in the original proceedings would not provide it with an unfair 'second chance', nor would it compromise the finality of the DSB's recommendations and rulings. The AB was of the view that 'While claims in Article 21.5 proceedings cannot be used to re-open issues that were decided on substance in the original proceedings, the unconditional acceptance of the recommendations and rulings of the DSB by the parties to a dispute does not preclude raising new claims against measures taken to comply that incorporate unchanged aspects of original measures that could have been made, but were not made, in the original proceedings.'[52] It thus reversed the Panel's contrary finding. The AB did qualify its position, putting it in the context of a 'new' implementation measure that incorporates unchanged aspects of the original measure that are not separable from the implementation measure.

5. 'All others' rate

On the question of the 'all others' rate in situations where all margins are determined on the basis of facts available or are below de minimis, the AB reversed the Panel's finding that in such cases Article 9.4 of the AD Agreement does not impose any limits on the discretionary powers of the investigating authority. However, the AB offered no solution to the obvious problem posed by the text of Article 9.4:

> In this regard, we do not agree with the Panel's statement that, in situations where all margins of dumping are either zero, *de minimis*, or based on facts available, Article 9.4 'simply imposes no prohibition, as no *ceiling* can be calculated.'[53] In our view, the fact that all margins of dumping for the investigated exporters fall within one of the categories that Article 9.4 directs investigating authorities to disregard, for purposes of that paragraph, does not imply that the investigating authorities' discretion to apply duties on non-investigated exporters is unbounded. The lacuna that the Appellate Body recognized to exist in Article 9.4 is one of a specific *method*. Thus, the absence of guidance in Article 9.4

51 Ibid., para. 424.
52 Ibid., paras. 426–427.
53 Panel Report, *US–Zeroing* (*EC*) (Article 21.5 DSU), para. 8.283 (original emphasis).

> on what particular methodology to follow does not imply an absence of any obligation with respect to the 'all others' rate applicable to non-investigated exporters where all margins of dumping for the investigated exporters are either zero, *de minimis*, or based on facts available. In any event, the participants have not suggested specific alternative methodologies to calculate the maximum allowable 'all others' rate in situations where all margins of dumping calculated for the investigated exporters fall into the three categories to be disregarded, and we do not need to resolve this issue to dispose of this appeal.[54]

Interesting is also the AB's position that the possibility of determining margins on the basis of facts available under Article 6.8 'applies exclusively to those "interested parties" from which information *was* required, rather than to those parties from which information was not requested. Thus, the disciplines in relation to the application of "facts available" under Article 6.8 and Annex II do not apply to non-investigated exporters that eventually will be subject to the "all others" rate.'[55]

US–Zeroing (Japan)

On 20 May 2009, the United States filed a Notice of Appeal,[56] challenging several aspects of the Panel Report. First, the United States argued that a review which was not yet terminated at the time of Japan's request for establishment of a Panel was not within the Panel's terms of reference. The United States considered that the general terms 'any subsequent closely connected measures' was not sufficiently specific in the sense of Article 6.2 DSU. In addition, the United States argued that this review was a 'future measure' that had not yet come into existence at the time of Japan's Panel request, and therefore could not be considered to be part of the Panel's terms of reference.

Second, in respect of the determination of the relevant moment in time for determining compliance, the United States considered that the Panel's basic error consisted of using the date of collection of duties as the determining factor for assessing whether the United States had brought itself into compliance. According to the United States, it is rather the date of importation that prevails. This implies that reviews relating to imports that entered the United States prior to the expiration of the RPT and that apply zeroing are not inconsistent with the US obligations, even when this leads to the collection of duties after the RPT. In addition, the United States submits that, even if the date of liquidation was relevant for assessing compliance, liquidation actions that take place after the RPT as a result of domestic litigation cannot provide a basis for a finding of noncompliance. Relying on the AB Report in *US–Zeroing (EC)* (EC – Article 21.5), the United States further maintains that the liquidation actions that have been delayed as a result of

54 Appellate Body Report, *US–Zeroing (EC)* (Article 21.5 DSU), para. 453.
55 Ibid., para. 459.
56 WT/DS322/32.

domestic litigation cannot be said to 'derive mechanically' from the challenged periodic reviews, and therefore cannot be deemed to be WTO-inconsistent.[57] In addition, the United States challenges the finding concerning Reviews 4, 5, and 6, on the grounds that these reviews did not have effects after the expiration of the RPT because assessment of duties calculated in these reviews was enjoined prior to the conclusion of the RPT and continues to be enjoined.

Appellate Body Report
The AB rejected the US arguments on both issues.

1. Inclusion of reviews not terminated at the time of the request for establishment

The AB rejected the US appeal considering that in the context of this dispute the challenged review was sufficiently clearly identified in the request that expressly referred to the previous eight reviews in respect of the same anti-dumping order. It also 'agree[d] with the Panel's conclusion that "a finding that the phrase 'subsequent closely connected measures' satisfies the terms of Article 6.2 would not violate any due process objective of the DSU"'.[58] Regarding the formalistic US argument that the DSU does not allow for the inclusion of such 'future measures' within a Panel's terms of reference,[59] the AB reasoned as follows:

> We observed earlier that the requirements of Article 6.2 must be read in the light of the specific function of Article 21.5 proceedings and that the 'specific measures at issue' to be identified in these proceedings are measures that have a bearing on compliance with the recommendations and rulings of the DSB. A measure that is initiated before there has been recourse to an Article 21.5 panel, and which is completed during those Article 21.5 panel proceedings, may have a bearing on whether there is compliance with the DSB's recommendations and rulings. Thus, if such a measure incorporates the same conduct that was found to be WTO-inconsistent in the original proceedings, it would show non-compliance with the DSB's recommendations and rulings. To exclude such a measure from an Article 21.5 panel's terms of reference because the measure was not completed at the time of the panel request but, rather, was completed during the Article 21.5 proceedings, would mean that the disagreement 'as to the existence or consistency with a covered agreement of measures taken to comply' would not be fully resolved by that Article 21.5 panel. New Article 21.5 proceedings would therefore be required to resolve the disagreement and establish whether there is compliance. Thus, an *a priori* exclusion of measures completed during Article 21.5 proceedings could frustrate the function of compliance proceedings. It would also be inconsistent with the objectives of the DSU to provide for the 'prompt settlement of situations in which a Member considers that any benefits accruing to it directly or indirectly under the covered agreements are being impaired', as

57 Appellate Body Report, *US–Zeroing (Japan)* (Article 21.5 DSU), para. 148.
58 Ibid., para. 119.
59 Ibid., para. 120.

> reflected in Article 3.3, and to 'secure a positive solution to a dispute', as contemplated in Article 3.7.[60] (footnotes omitted)

The AB agreed with the Panel that it was proper to include this review as it was 'necessary for the Panel to assess whether compliance had been achieved, and thereby resolve the "disagreement as to the existence or consistency with a covered agreement of measures taken to comply with the recommendations and rulings"'.[61] It considered that 'Review 9 had been initiated at the time the matter was referred to the Panel and was due to be completed during the Article 21.5 proceedings. Under these circumstances, we consider that the Panel was correct in finding that Review 9 was within its terms of reference, as doing so enabled it to fulfil its mandate to resolve the "disagreement" between the parties and determine, in a prompt manner, whether the United States had achieved compliance with the DSB's recommendations and rulings.'[62]

2. Relevant moment of time for assessing compliance

The AB also rejected the US arguments on appeal in respect of the Panel's finding that the date of collection of duties is the determining factor for assessing whether the United States had brought itself into compliance. The AB first examined the scope and timing of the compliance obligations under Article 21.5 DSU and concluded that 'Article 21.3 requires that the obligation to implement fully the DSB's recommendations and rulings be fulfilled by the end of the reasonable period of time at the latest and, consequently, the WTO-inconsistent conduct must cease at the latest by that time'.[63] The AB then examined the first issue raised by the United States's appeal, i.e. whether the obligation to comply applies also in respect of imports that entered the territory of the implementing WTO Member prior to the expiration of the RPT, when matters concerning those imports have not been fully settled by the end of the RPT. It referred to its ruling in the *US–Zeroing (EC)* case and confirmed that the relevant date is not the date of importation as argued by the US:

> Irrespective of the date on which the imports entered the territory of the implementing Member, the WTO-inconsistencies must cease by the end of the reasonable period of time. There will not be full compliance where the implementing Member fails to take action to rectify the WTO-inconsistent aspects of a measure that remains in force after the end of the reasonable period of time. Likewise, actions taken by the implementing Member after the end of the reasonable period of time must be WTO-consistent, even if those actions are in respect of imports that entered the Member's territory before the end of the reasonable period of time. Therefore, we agree with the Panel's statement that,

60 Ibid., para. 122.
61 Ibid., para. 125.
62 Ibid., para. 124.
63 Ibid., para. 158.

> '[i]f a measure found to be WTO-inconsistent is to be applied after the expiry of the reasonable period of time, that measure must have been brought "into conformity", irrespective of the date of entry of the imports covered by that measure'.[64] (footnotes omitted)

Applying this test to the facts of the case it agreed with the Panel that the United States had failed to bring itself into compliance:

> The measures at issue in the present case are periodic reviews of anti-dumping duty orders. The Panel explained that, in the United States' anti-dumping system, periodic reviews involve the determination of 'importer-specific assessment rates for previous entries imported during the review period' and 'exporter-specific cash deposit rates that will apply prospectively to future import entries'. Where the importer-specific assessment rates or cash deposits rates determined by the implementing Member are found to be WTO-inconsistent, that Member is under an obligation to rectify the inconsistencies. In order to comply fully with this obligation, the inconsistencies must be rectified by the end of the reasonable period of time. Where the periodic reviews cover imports that entered the implementing Member's territory prior to the expiration of the reasonable period of time, the WTO-inconsistencies may not persist after the reasonable period of time has expired. Thus, for example, importer-specific assessment rates that were found to be WTO-inconsistent may not remain in effect after the expiration of the reasonable period of time. In other words, the WTO-inconsistent conduct must cease completely, even if it is related to imports that entered the implementing Member's territory before the reasonable period of time expired. Otherwise, full compliance with the DSB's recommendations and rulings cannot be said to have occurred.[65] (footnotes omitted)

An important part of the US argument was that this approach disadvantages WTO Members with retrospective anti-dumping systems, i.e. the United States. The AB rejected this argument considering that it 'is difficult to reconcile with the text of Article 9.3.2 of the *Anti-Dumping Agreement*, which requires that WTO Members with prospective anti-dumping systems provide a mechanism allowing importers to request refunds of any duty paid in excess of the margin of dumping'.[66] The AB explained its view as follows:

> Therefore, where actions or omissions relating to a refund procedure are challenged both domestically and in WTO dispute settlement, delays in the completion of a refund procedure until after the end of the reasonable period of time cannot be excluded. Should such a refund procedure not be completed before the end of the reasonable period of time, a WTO Member with a prospective anti-dumping system would have compliance obligations in respect of that refund procedure concerning past imports. Such a Member would thus find itself in a situation similar to that of an implementing Member applying a retrospective

64 Ibid., para. 160.
65 Ibid., para. 161.
66 Ibid., para. 166.

> anti-dumping system. This confirms that, under both retrospective and prospective anti-dumping systems, entries made prior to the expiration of the reasonable period of time also may be affected by compliance obligations. As a consequence, we disagree with the United States that disregarding the date of entry of the merchandise for purposes of determining compliance would result in retrospective anti-dumping systems being treated less favourably than prospective anti-dumping systems.[67]

The AB also recalled that the obligation of Article 9 relates to the imposition and collection of duties which must comply with the obligations of the AD Agreement, including the prohibition on zeroing. Therefore, according to the AB, 'Where a WTO Member has been found to have violated the *Anti-Dumping Agreement* and the GATT 1994 by using zeroing in a periodic review, it fails to comply with the DSB's recommendations and rulings if it collects, subsequent to the expiration of the reasonable period of time, anti-dumping duties based on rates that were determined in the periodic review using zeroing. If it did so, the obligation in Article 9.3 that "[t]he amount of the anti-dumping duty shall not exceed the margin of dumping as established under Article 2" would not be respected.'[68]

The second aspect of the US appeal on this matter concerned the impact on compliance of domestic-court proceedings by which reviews are suspended until after the expiration of the RPT. As phrased by the AB 'the question is whether actions or omissions that occur after the expiration of the reasonable period of time due to domestic judicial proceedings are excluded from the implementing Member's compliance obligations'.[69]

The United States had argued that the compliance obligation had to be read in the light of the obligation in Article 13 of the AD Agreement of allowing for

67 Ibid., para. 166.

68 Ibid., para. 168. This is similar to what would occur if zeroing were allowed in periodic reviews, while being disallowed in the original anti-dumping determination. As the Appellate Body explained in *US–Stainless Steel (Mexico)*: 'a reading of Article 9.3 of the *Anti-Dumping Agreement* that permits simple zeroing in periodic reviews would allow WTO Members to circumvent the prohibition of zeroing in original investigations that applies under the first sentence of Article 2.4.2 of the *Anti-Dumping Agreement*. This is because, in the first periodic review after an original investigation, the duty assessment rate for each importer will take effect from the date of the original imposition of anti-dumping duties. Consequently, zeroing would be introduced although it is not permissible in original investigations' (Appellate Body Report, *US – Final Anti-Dumping Measures on Stainless Steel from Mexico*, WT/DS344/AB/R, adopted 8 May 2008, para. 109).

69 Appellate Body Report, *US–Zeroing (Japan)* (Article 21.5 DSU), paras. 170–171. It is important to understand that in the US system, liquidation instructions are given following the conclusion of the periodic review. However, where litigation is initiated before the USDOC has issued the liquidation instructions and a US court enjoins liquidation, the USDOC will issue instructions to Customs ordering it not to liquidate the entries during the pendency of domestic litigation. If litigation is initiated after the issuance of liquidation instructions but before actual liquidation, the court may issue an injunction, and the USDOC will send instructions to Customs notifying it of the injunction and will require Customs to suspend liquidation of the entries until the conclusion of domestic litigation. Upon the conclusion of domestic litigation and the consequent lifting of any applicable injunctions, the USDOC will send instructions to Customs ordering liquidation of the entries in accordance with the court's decision and Customs will collect duties accordingly.

independent review by domestic tribunals of anti-dumping determinations. The AB rejected this argument in no unclear terms:

> The fact that WTO Members are required to maintain independent review procedures for administrative anti-dumping actions does not exonerate them from the requirement to comply with the DSB's recommendations and rulings within the reasonable period of time. We see no conflict between the obligation to maintain independent review procedures under Article 13 and the obligation to comply with the DSB's recommendations and rulings. Accordingly, we do not consider that Article 13 provides support for the proposition that a WTO Member is excused from complying with the DSB's recommendations and rulings by the end of the reasonable period of time, where a periodic review has been challenged in that Member's domestic courts and this has resulted in the collection of duties being delayed.[70]

It also considered very relevant the requirement of prompt compliance of Article 21.3 DSU:

> the very text of Article 21.3 indicates that the 'reasonable period of time' is an exception to immediate compliance, thus implying that further delays would not be justified, whatever the circumstances. In *US – Zeroing (EC) (Article 21.5 – EC)*, the Appellate Body stated that the 'implementing Member would be able to extend the reasonable period of time and delay compliance depending on when it chooses to undertake final duty assessment' if the approach based on the date of entry, as advocated by the United States, was followed. The Appellate Body also cautioned there that '[s]uch a result would deprive of meaning the notion of "reasonable period of time" in which a Member shall comply, as provided for in Article 21.3 of the DSU, and be contrary to the implementation mechanism of the DSU.' *The same rationale is applicable in respect of delays in implementation due to domestic judicial proceedings. Such delays in implementation cannot exonerate a Member from its compliance obligations and are not consistent with the overall objectives of 'prompt' and 'immediate' compliance in Articles 21.1 and 21.3.* (emphasis added; footnotes omitted)[71]

The AB rejected the US argument that 'the timing of liquidation is controlled by the independent judiciary and *not* the administering authority' and that therefore it could not be blamed for not respecting the RPT. The AB recalled that a WTO Member 'bears responsibility for acts of all its departments of government, including its judiciary', and concluded that 'the United States cannot seek to avoid the obligation to comply with the DSB's recommendations and rulings within the reasonable period of time, by relying on the timing of liquidation being "controlled by the independent judiciary"'.[72] Finally, the AB was not persuaded by the

70 Ibid., para. 175.
71 Ibid., para. 178.
72 Ibid., para. 182.

US argument that the initiation by private parties of domestic judicial proceedings is relevant for determining the scope of US compliance obligations.

4. Legal analysis

The two 'zeroing' Reports discussed above do not concern the question of the legitimacy of zeroing. Rather, the issues before the AB in these cases related to the way in which adverse rulings in respect of US anti-dumping measures have to be implemented. Thus, the implementation-related issues of these Reports are mainly of interest to trade-remedy lawyers, especially those dealing with US anti-dumping measures. They do not raise any systemic legal issues of major importance to the implementation of WTO rulings, although as discussed in the next section, they do raise some more general issues regarding determination of compliance with WTO rules and rulings from an economic perspective.

Periodic reviews as 'measures taken to comply'

The main issue in this case related to the manner in which the United States was supposed to have implemented adverse rulings relating to zeroing in anti-dumping investigations. The implementation issues that arose are specific to the United States, which is the only country that uses a retrospective anti-dumping system rather than a prospective anti-dumping system. To put it simply, in a retrospective system, the original investigation into dumping, injury, and the causal link will allow for the imposition of anti-dumping measures and will set the amount of cash deposits for imports entering the country following imposition of the measure. The actual amount of duties to be paid, however, will normally only be determined in the course of a periodic (yearly) review of the measure. At the time of the review, it will be examined whether, in the course of the past review period, imports were actually entering the country at dumped prices and what the level of the dumping margin was. Based on the level of the margin of dumping – which may well be higher than the margin of dumping determined at the time of the original investigation – a definitive determination of the amount of duties that are due will be made and on that basis the duties will be collected ('liquidated'). At the same time, a cash-deposit requirement will be imposed for future imports entering the country, the level of which is set on the basis of the margin of dumping that was determined at the time of the review. And that story repeats itself until the end of the normal five-year life cycle of the anti-dumping order when a sunset review may be conducted to examine whether there is a likelihood of continuation or recurrence of dumping causing injury if the duty were removed.

The EU and Japan challenged a number of original determinations and a number of periodic reviews in which dumping was determined by the US authorities using the WTO-inconsistent zeroing methodology. Following the original dispute in which the EU and Japan prevailed, the United States revisited the dumping calculations of the original investigations to determine whether, even without zeroing, dumping existed. If so, the measure continued to exist. The United States considered that it was not required to do anything in case subsequent periodic reviews had superseded the reviews that had originally been challenged. And it thus continued to zero in the course of these subsequent reviews. Obviously, this type of implementation was considered to be completely meaningless to the EU and Japan since, at the end of the day, their exporters were still required to pay duties based on margins of dumping determined through the use of zeroing.

The EU and Japan argued that these subsequent reviews in which the United States continued to zero were 'measures taken to comply' with the DSB ruling and could thus be examined by the implementation Panel in the context of an Article 21.5 DSU implementation dispute. As explained above, the Panel and AB agreed, applying the 'close nexus' test: the subsequent reviews conducted in the context of the same AD orders that had been the subject of the original dispute were sufficiently closely linked in terms of the nature, effect, and timing with the previously challenged measures that they could be seen as 'measures taken to comply'. The AB considered that this was true even for reviews that had been initiated well before the adoption of the Reports they were supposed to be 'complying with'.

We do not disagree with the outcome of this dispute and consider that ultimately the AB got it right. However, we do find that there is something bizarre about the AB's reasoning – how can a measure be a 'measure taken to comply' with a Report when that Report has not even been adopted or even issued? It is simply counter-intuitive to treat reviews initiated and completed even before adoption of the Panel and AB Reports as measures 'taken to comply' with these Reports.

The AB explained that any measure adopted in the course of the dispute but before adoption of a Report could well impact on the country's compliance with its WTO obligations and should therefore be treated as a 'measure taken to comply' if a sufficiently close link existed between the originally challenged measure and the alleged measure taken to comply. However, we wonder whether there was actually any need to develop the rather complicated reasoning that the AB adopted in this case in respect of these reviews arguing that they were 'measures taken to comply'. In our view, the problem could have been dealt with in a simple and straightforward manner, avoiding problematic statements such as the one referred to before about measures complying with Reports even before the Report was released let alone adopted.

What was the original problem? That anti-dumping duties were imposed based on a WTO-inconsistent method for determining dumping; that cash deposits were required and duties were collected on the basis of dumping margins calculated using this same methodology. We recall that GATT Article II allows for the imposition of duties and charges only up to the level of the bound tariff and that 'other charges' may only be imposed if they are included in the Schedule of Concessions. GATT Article II.2 allows, by way of exception, for the imposition of anti-dumping measures, as long as they are imposed in a GATT-consistent manner. Similarly, GATT Article VI and the WTO AD Agreement allow for the imposition of anti-dumping measures on imports of certain countries only, thus deviating from the general MFN rule of GATT Article I, and set forth certain disciplines in terms of the determination of the margin of dumping. The United States lost the original dispute because the 'zeroing' method for calculating the margin of dumping that was used in a number of anti-dumping cases was considered to be WTO-inconsistent. The United States was to correct this error and was given a reasonable period of time to do so. Upon expiry of this period of time, the question is whether the United States has complied with the ruling of the DSB that its method of determining margins of dumping and thus of imposing anti-dumping duties based on zeroing is WTO-inconsistent. It seems normal to examine the situation at the end of the RPT to determine whether duties are still in place, whether cash deposits are still required, and whether duties are still being collected in respect of the originally challenged AD orders and this based on the WTO-inconsistent method of zeroing. If that is the case – and the United States did not deny that this was indeed the case – then it seems pretty clear that the United States has failed to comply with the DSB ruling. What can be so complicated about this conclusion that would warrant a lengthy discussion about the meaning of the term 'measures taken to comply'?

The basic question is whether there exists compliance. The imposition of charges (cash deposits) and the collection of additional import duties (anti-dumping duties) based on zeroed margins clearly demonstrate, not that the measures taken to comply were WTO-inconsistent, but that no measures were taken to comply. The existence of such GATT/WTO-inconsistent cash deposits and duties is inconsistent with the AD Agreement, GATT Article VI, and thus ultimately also with GATT Article II. Interestingly, this is also what the AB appears to ultimately find: that any action taken after the expiry of the RPT that concerns the same subject matter and is not consistent with the WTO obligations of a Member demonstrates a failure to comply with the DSB ruling dealing with that subject matter.

In our view, the AB inappropriately was led down a pseudo-technical path distinguishing between original determinations, periodic reviews, new periodic reviews, sunset reviews, prospective systems, retrospective systems, cash deposits, duty collection, duty liquidation, etc. If this had not been an anti-dumping dispute but a simple tariff violation, it is very doubtful that the AB would have complicated matters as much as it did in this case. In addition, its acceptance of these technical nonarguments required it to effectively disregard one of the three tests it had itself developed for determining whether there existed a sufficient nexus between the measure challenged and the 'measure taken to comply': the timing of the measure. Clearly, the sensible rationale for including the 'timing' of any measure as part of the analysis of whether a new measure was a measure taken to comply and thus part of the implementation Panel's terms of reference was whether it was taken following release and/or adoption of the Report. The AB in these zeroing cases rejected the idea that timing is a determinative factor but failed to explain what role, if any, this factor should play if it actually does not matter whether the measure was adopted even before the release of the Report to the parties. It seems that the three-pronged 'nexus' test that was developed by the AB in the context of Article 21.5 implementation disputes has effectively been reduced to a two-pronged test in these zeroing cases.

Timing of compliance – any action following the expiry of the RPT is captured

A second important clarification offered by the AB in these cases concerned the importance of the end of the RPT. We are of the view that the AB was right that the relevant moment in time for determining compliance is the end of the RPT and that any action taken after the end of the RPT that is inconsistent with a country's WTO obligations demonstrates a failure to comply. For many WTO Members, this solution is obvious and there is no reason why the same conclusion would not apply to the United States as well.

This being said, we agree with the United States that this puts it at a disadvantage in comparison with Members that use the prospective system of duty collection. Under a prospective system, imports entering the country prior to the end of the RPT will be subject to the payment of duties in a final manner and such duties will effectively escape the WTO disciplines since they were collected prior to the end of the RPT. In a retrospective system, such duties are collected only in a provisional manner. If a subsequent review that determines the final duty liability is conducted after the end of the RPT, it will be subject to the WTO disciplines and the duties may not be collected in full. In sum, it is clear that the AB's approach implies that the United States will have to accept the consequences of its retrospective system, which disadvantages the United States in this particular case. However, in many other ways, this retrospective system has important 'advantages' from the point of view of protecting the domestic industry. There are good reasons why domestic industry associations argue so strongly in favour of maintaining this administratively burdensome system, the usefulness of which is currently under discussion in the United States.

In this respect, it is not clear that the AB's approach does *not* disadvantage the retrospective system. The AB argues that in a prospective system (used everywhere else in the world), interested parties may also request refunds after the end of the RPT. However, such refund requests are rather uncommon. Moreover, we wonder whether an importer could request the refund of excess duties paid in the course of the RPT. After all, throughout the RPT a Member would be allowed to continue to act in a manner inconsistent with its WTO obligations without there being any remedy. On what basis would such a refund be requested? The Panel's position on this question seems more appropriate: that every system has its advantages and disadvantages and that each Member must accept the consequences, whether good or bad, of the system it adopts. This was essentially also the view adopted in the context of the *US–FSC* (Foreign Sales Corporations) dispute where, to put it somewhat simplistically, the United States suffered the negative consequences of the international tax regime that it had adopted.

A related matter of some importance concerns the impact that delays caused by domestic-court proceedings have on compliance. We consider that the AB was right to say that it does not matter why liquidation was delayed since any action taken after the expiry of the RPT has to be WTO-consistent. But why then did the AB not immediately say so when this first came before it in the Article 21.5 *US–Zeroing* (*EC*) case? After all, it is merely the logical consequence of its general approach to focus on the date of the expiry of the RPT and on the actions adopted since that time, rather than on the legal basis for the action in isolation (the determination of the margin of dumping).

In the Article 21.5 *US–Zeroing* (*EC*) case, the AB stated that it did 'not express any opinion on the question of whether actions to liquidate duties that are based on administrative review determinations issued before the end of the reasonable period of time, and that have been delayed as a result of judicial proceedings, fall within the scope of the implementation obligations of the United States, as we do not need to do so in the context of our analysis of this issue in this case'.[73] This was surprising since its entire reasoning, which focused on the fact that any action taken after the expiry of the RPT has to be WTO-consistent, clearly suggested that it had in fact expressed itself on this issue.

This is a typical example of the AB throwing in a statement to say that it is not expressing a view on a certain matter when it actually has already done so, thereby creating the impression that it may adopt a different approach with respect to this question. Why else would you add a paragraph saying that your views should not be read to imply that this or that is also inconsistent? The signal that is being given is clearly that a different conclusion may need to be drawn in such circumstances. But then, six months later when the issue is again before the AB in the Article 21.5 *US–Zeroing* (*Japan*) case, the AB does actually follow its own logic and does consider that such actions are also WTO-inconsistent irrespective of whether the delay was caused by court proceedings. Why did the AB not say that before and why did it suggest that a different outcome may actually be warranted if 'security and predictability' are the main guiding principles of the dispute-settlement system?[74]

This is not the first time the AB has done so. Its entire zeroing jurisprudence is the consequence of such failure to express itself clearly in respect of this issue from the first time the issue was raised before it. The AB stated that it did not express a view on whether zeroing was inconsistent with the fair-comparison requirement of Article 2.4 in, for example, *US–Zeroing* (*EC*) and stated that it was not expressing a view on whether zeroing in transaction-to-transaction comparisons is also prohibited in *US–Softwood Lumber V*, to later find that zeroing is unfair and that

73 Appellate Body Report, *US–Zeroing* (*EC*) (Article 21.5 DSU), para. 314.
74 Article 3.2 DSU.

zeroing violates the fair-comparison requirement. This false restraint by the AB is not consistent with its important role in securing the predictability of the system.

The 'all others' rate – how to deal with a loophole?

Another missed opportunity in clarifying the rules has been the AB's reasoning on the 'all others' problem in this case. Article 9.4 of the AD Agreement provides that the 'all others' rate that applies to nonsampled exporters should not exceed the average margin of dumping, while excluding margins that are zero or de minimis or based on facts available. But what to do if all margins are either zero or de minimis or are based on facts available? That was the problem the Panel was confronted with. It reached the conclusion that in such a case there is no obligation to respect under Article 9.4. The Panel found that Article 9.4 merely 'establish[es] a methodology for the calculation of a "ceiling" which the "all others" rate may not exceed', but does not 'specify a method for or imposes disciplines on the calculation of the "all others" rate itself.'[75] According to the Panel, in cases where all the margins of dumping for the investigated exporters are zero, *de minimis*, or based on facts available, 'there are simply no margins of dumping from which the investigating authority ... may calculate the maximum allowable 'all others' rate and therefore, in such circumstances, 'Article 9.4 simply imposes no prohibition, as no *ceiling* can be calculated.'[76]

The AB disagrees:

> The lacuna that the Appellate Body recognized to exist in Article 9.4 is one of a specific *method*. Thus, the absence of guidance in Article 9.4 on what particular methodology to follow does not imply an absence of any obligation with respect to the 'all others' rate applicable to non-investigated exporters where all margins of dumping for the investigated exporters are either zero, *de minimis*, or based on facts available. In any event, the participants have not suggested specific alternative methodologies to calculate the maximum allowable 'all others' rate in situations where all margins of dumping calculated for the investigated exporters fall into the three categories to be disregarded, and we do not need to resolve this issue to dispose of this appeal.[77]

Thus, the AB considers that Article 9.4 imposes an obligation, but it refuses to clarify what this obligation is and what an authority is to do in such circumstances. It hides behind the fact that no alternative methodologies have been suggested by the parties. In our view, it would have been very useful and even necessary given the objective of providing 'security and predictability to the multilateral trading system' had the AB clarified its view of what, if any, obligation Article 9.4 imposes in such circumstances. Unfortunately, the AB said A without saying B.

75 Panel Report, *US–Zeroing (EC)* (Article 21.5 DSU), para. 8.281.
76 Ibid., para. 8.283 (original emphasis).
77 Appellate Body Report, *US–Zeroing (EC)* (Article 21.5 DSU), para. 453.

5. Economic perspectives and policy considerations

Anti-dumping-related disputes – both zeroing and others – accounted for a significant share of the WTO dispute-settlement caseload – some 30 % on average during 2001–2008, compared to 15 % in the 1995–2000 period (Bown and McCulloch, 2010). This is a reflection of the frequency with which AD measures are imposed by WTO members. The instrument is increasingly employed by 'non-traditional' users – emerging market and other developing countries – as well as the EU, United States, and other OECD [Organisation for Economic Co-operation and Development] members. The frequent recourse to the DSU is also a reflection of the detailed rules of the game that are contained in the AD Agreement, which are the result of efforts by targeted exporting countries over the past 20+ years to discipline specific practices that at some point in time were employed by the major users – the EU and United States in particular – to protect domestic industries.

Previous studies of zeroing disputes that have been undertaken for the ALI (American Law Institute) project on the case law of the WTO have analyzed many of the economic dimensions of the practice of zeroing in some depth, clarifying how zeroing inflates margins and documenting how the different varieties of zeroing methodologies employed by the Department of Commerce operate (Bown and Sykes, 2008; Prusa and Vermulst, 2009). We have little to add in terms of analysis of the economics of zeroing and we will not seek to do so in this paper.

From an economic perspective, a first-order question is how much zeroing matters. It is well known that investigating authorities can be and often are 'creative' in pursuing AD investigations in ways that increase the likelihood of finding positive dumping margins and that inflate average calculated margins. From this perspective, it is somewhat puzzling why the specific question of zeroing is the focus of such intense dispute-settlement activity. One reason is that the United States is currently the only jurisdiction to use zeroing. Another is that the United States is a major user of anti-dumping. Anti-dumping affects only a small share of global trade – much less than 1 % – but the United States accounts for about 10 % of global AD actions and is a major market for many exporters.

Although several developing countries, most notably India, have become more frequent AD users (India accounted for 15 % of global investigations in 2009, up from less than 4 % in 1995),[78] their increased 'market share' has come at the 'expense' of a small number of traditional users such as the EU and South Africa. These two WTO members accounted for some 30 % of all AD investigations in the mid 1990s, as compared to 9 % in 2009. The US share of total investigations in contrast has been quite stable at 10 %, although the US share of AD measures imposed has declined relative to the second half of the 1990s when it was on the order of 15 % of the global total. In recent years, the US share of AD measures in force has averaged around 10 % of the global total. On average, 4.6 %

78 Unless noted otherwise, data reported in this paragraph are from the WTO website.

of all US imports by value were subject to temporary trade barriers in the 1997–2007 period, with AD accounting for over 80 % of the products affected (Bown, 2010).

Thus, US anti-dumping is a significant market-access concern. How much zeroing matters in this regard depends on the extent to which it increases dumping margins. Empirical analysis of this question is very scarce. Nye (2009) estimates that zeroing accounts for only 2.5 percentage points of an average 47 % anti-dumping duty imposed by the United States in a sample of cases, suggesting that zeroing is of marginal relevance from an economic perspective. Bown and Prusa (2010) come to a very different conclusion, arguing that if the United States was to cease using zeroing, a significant number of AD measures would be removed altogether. They determine that up to *half* of all US AD measures that have been contested in WTO cases would have to be removed (because there would not be a positive AD margin anymore) and that the duties in the other cases would fall significantly.[79] While many of the duties that would be removed are relatively low – mostly in single digits – the uncertainty created by zeroing for exporters that confront substantial variation in export prices can have a significant chilling effect on trade. It is not just the dumping margin that matters but the probability of being subject to an anti-dumping investigation and the associated direct costs and chilling effects/uncertainty generated by the reactions of importers/ buyers.

The Bown and Prusa analysis helps to explain the amount of time and resources that have had to be devoted by the DSB to the issue of zeroing and the continuing expansion of the zeroing caseload. It matters for the affected exporters. As of the time of writing, zeroing cases have accounted for 20 % of all AB cases, and about half of all Art. 21.5 DSU compliance cases. The recurring cases on zeroing are a problem, both for the system and for affected exporters. For the trading system, the recurring zeroing cases are a problem because repeated cases against a member that is not willing to comply can only reduce the perceived value of the institution. The importance of this dimension may increase the longer the Doha Round goes nowhere – as it raises the relative profile of the DSU as the part of the WTO that does work. For exporters, the lack of compliance by the United States implies continuing uncertainty regarding the conditions of market access in a large economy, while for the WTO system the repeated zeroing cases imply a misallocation of scarce resources given that the legal issues have been settled.[80] Noteworthy in

79 This estimate is most likely an upper bound regarding the effects of zeroing on margins (presumably there is a selection effect).

80 However, it also needs to be pointed out that the process has had positive results. The first zeroing case (against the EC) was brought in 1998, and the EC eventually brought its AD regime into compliance in this respect, after having gone through an Art. 21.5 Panel (Janow and Staiger, 2003; Grossman and Sykes, 2006). In the case of the United States, zeroing is no longer applied by the United States in investigations. Of course, the problem is that the stock of past AD orders in the United States is large so that

this regard is that five new dispute-settlement cases were brought to the WTO following the two Art. 21.5 cases that are the subject of this paper: by Brazil, Thailand, Mexico, Korea, and Vietnam – the last two in May 2010. Vietnam's case is the first this country has brought to the WTO, and is particularly noteworthy because it is treated as a nonmarket economy by the United States for AD purposes – so that there are many other ways the Department of Commerce can determine high dumping margins.

Needed: more effective surveillance and analysis

The role of the compliance Panels that are the subject of this paper was to determine whether the United States took action (implemented new measures) to become compliant with the AD Agreement. They concluded that the United States had not done so. As of the time of writing, both the EU and Japan had launched Art. 22.6 DSU proceedings, seeking authorization to retaliate against the United States for the losses incurred as a result of noncompliance by the United States. Paralleling the limited economic analysis of the effects of zeroing discussed above, the parties have wildly different estimates of the economic impacts of US zeroing, with the EU claiming upwards of $300 million per year and the United States arguing it is closer to one-hundredth of that figure. Much will depend on the answer to the question posed above – i.e. the extent to which the use of zeroing in each case inflated the calculated dumping margin. The availability of information on this matter (more accurately, the lack thereof) will affect the feasibility of generating an accurate estimate of the amount of compensation-cum-retaliation that is appropriate.

This information problem also applies at the compliance Panel stage. A fundamental problem affecting the efficacy of the DSU is that the process of determining if compliance has occurred is left to Panels that are required to limit their remit to the issues raised in the original Panel. What may be missing – and is in the case of zeroing – is information on what is being implemented by the country found to have violated the WTO. For example, it is not clear whether the United States has in fact stopped using zeroing in original investigations. In at least one recent case, it has reportedly reverted to the practice.[81] It is generally held that the United States continues to use zeroing in reviews, but it is not necessarily true that it does so in all reviews, and we do not know for all these reviews how much the dumping margin is affected by the practice.

the effect of ceasing to use zeroing in original investigations is limited due to the retroactive nature of the way duties are collected in the United States.

81 See Robert L. LaFrankie and Alicia Winston, 'US Government Expands the Use of Zeroing in Antidumping Investigations', 13 May 2010, commenting on *Polyethylene Retail Carrier Bags from Taiwan: Final Determination of Sales at Less than Fair Value*, 75 Fed. Reg. 14569 (26 March 2010). Available at http://www.mondaq.com/unitedstates/article.asp?articleid=100460 (last visited 27 September 2010).

Zeroing affects not only EU and Japanese exporters. The first zeroing cases were brought by India and Brazil (against the EU), and, as noted above, more recently Thailand, Mexico, Korea, and Vietnam have now brought cases against the United States. It is rather inefficient if continued noncompliance by the United States results in recurring cases that are all dealing with an issue that has already been litigated. Rather than force individual exporting countries to initiate their own disputes, imposing unnecessary costs on the system and the countries concerned, it would be much better that if the United States has no intention of complying, the focus be put on compensating affected trading partners. Given that the US methodology is (can be) applied to all exporters, it would be more efficient to address this matter in a cooperative manner, rather than through a recurring series of cases that impose an excess burden on the DSB and on affected exporting countries and their exporters.[82]

Of course, the best way to resolve the matter would be for the United States to bring its measures into compliance. At the time of writing, the United States is reportedly still working towards this – which can be inferred from the decision in early September 2010 by the EU to request that the Art. 22.6 arbitration be suspended for a one-year period to provide the United States more time to reform its AD regime.[83] In the absence of full compliance, one way to facilitate either an agreement with exporters on compensation or to reduce the costs to the WTO system of continued litigation is to make available information on a country-by-country basis how much dumping margins have been affected by zeroing. That information can then be used to provide the affected countries with compensation, or be the basis for retaliatory action by the affected countries. At some point, if enough countries retaliate the United States may be induced to change its policy. However, as noted by Bown and Prusa (2010) the amounts involved – even though subject to great uncertainty at this point because of the lack of data – may not be large enough to have much of an impact on US exporters and thus to change the political-economy equilibrium in the United States on zeroing. But a system of transparent compensation-cum-retaliation based on the actual effects of zeroing would be better than another possible reaction to continued noncompliance by the United States: emulation by trading partners.

There are some parallels between the zeroing saga and the use of quantitative restrictions in the 1970s and 1980s that resulted in the Mutifibre Arrangement (MFA). Quantitative restrictions on textiles and clothing – which clearly violated the GATT but were accommodated by the system – emerged gradually but became widespread over time. A similar phenomenon could arise with zeroing, except in reverse, with developing countries adopting the practice. This would be very

82 It could be argued that allowing (forcing) a series of disputes to be brought by exporters, each of which ultimately result in retaliation – if a country thinks this is productive – also opens the United States up to accusations that it is not demonstrating good faith.

83 See http://www.foxbusiness.com/markets/2010/09/08/eu-suspend-tariff-dispute-sanctions/, September 8, 2010 (last visited 28 September 2010).

unfortunate.[84] The textiles episode generated a GATT Textile Surveillance Body to monitor the implementation of the MFA and a Textiles Monitoring Body that was responsible for surveillance of all measures taken under the Uruguay Agreement on Textiles and Clothing (ATC) to liberalize trade in textiles and clothing. Agreement to establish a multilateral surveillance mechanism that documents the continued use by the United States of zeroing could increase the transparency of US policy in this area and help in quantifying the likely effects of zeroing on dumping margins. Such information would facilitate the work of both compliance and arbitration Panels, and help to inform the policymaking process in the United States.

The need for greater transparency goes beyond zeroing. AD has become by far the most frequently used contingent trade-policy instrument by WTO members and there is only limited multilateral surveillance of what countries are doing and what the effects are. The conventional wisdom is that the aggregate effects of AD are small. Egger and Nelson (2010) estimate that between 1960 and 2000 anti-dumping actions reduced imports in the countries applying these measures by 1.6 percentage points. It has long been pointed out by economists that such aggregate estimates ignore both the incidence of actions – the targeted exporters may be severely affected even if on average most are not – and the chilling effects of the uncertainty of market-access conditions created by the threat of AD.[85] A recent empirical analysis that explicitly considers the counterfactual – how much trade would be expected to be observed without the threat of AD – by incorporating information on the date when a country adopts AD legislation concludes that use of AD measures reduced imports by some 6–7% in active users, such as Brazil and India (Vandenbussche and Zanardi, 2010). However, the results also show that the reduction in imports resulting from AD actions in major users (which constitute a relatively small number of countries, albeit ones that are large) only partially offsets the increase in trade that resulted from overall liberalization of trade policy during the sample period in the countries considered. The estimated offsets ranged between one-sixth and one-half.

These results provide support for the notion that AD can be a useful (political) safety valve that allows countries to implement and sustain more general trade liberalization. As noted by Egger and Nelson (2010) this is an argument that has a long pedigree in the economic literature, dating back to Viner (1923). Finger and Nogués (2006) provide case-study evidence how AD and similar measures were used in Latin America as a proliberalization, safety-valve device. However, the trend in the prevalence of AD is clearly upward, with the 2009–2010 period seeing an additional boost in response to calls by firms for assistance to cope with the global economic crisis (Bown, 2010). The spread of AD may generate incentives for 'retaliation' – tit-for-tat responses by targeted countries – and this may serve to

84 This is true even if it eventually results in a multilateral solution as occurred in the case of the MFA: the costs of widespread use of zeroing are likely to be high for the most efficient producers.

85 These issues are recognized and discussed by Egger and Nelson (2010).

constrain the growth of AD. There is some evidence that retaliation threats are one reason for the use of AD by major exporters, and that it may help restrain the use of AD by importing countries (Blonigen and Bown, 2003; Feinberg and Reynolds, 2006).

Whatever the dynamics may turn out to be, one conclusion we draw from the continuing zeroing saga is that greater transparency would be beneficial. What the WTO does in terms of surveillance is very narrow – essentially it is limited to a biannual compilation of AD investigations initiated and measures imposed without detail on trade volumes affected and no information on the methodologies used to determine dumping margins. The Temporary Trade Barriers database created by Chad Bown offers greater detail in terms of information on products affected and the amount of trade involved,[86] but there is no effort currently to collect and report information on how margins were calculated. This is a major task that in practice will require the cooperation of the investigating authorities. As far as zeroing is concerned, if the United States were to decide to continue to zero in reviews and to go down the renegotiation/compensation route, such an exercise would need to be done just once, assuming that continued zeroing is limited to the existing stock of AD orders – i.e. to the reviews. Whatever the eventual outcome of this extended litigation and the decision of the United States regarding the use of zeroing, greater surveillance and information will be beneficial to the system.

6. Concluding remarks

To some extent the repeated recourse to the DSU on zeroing reflects ambiguities in the text of the AD Agreement, which in turn reflects serious, fundamental disagreement on this matter that could not be addressed in the Uruguay Round negotiations, and subsequent strong opposition by the United States towards efforts by the Appellate Body to 'write law' by interpreting an agreement that was somewhat ambiguous with respect to zeroing. While US noncompliance is the trigger for continuing litigation, this has been facilitated by the approach taken by the AB towards zeroing. Bown and Sykes (2008) argue that the strategy of the AB towards zeroing has been to decide each case narrowly as opposed to ruling on the legality of zeroing in general, i.e. independent of the case-specific context. This generated a series of cases that contest specific instances of zeroing methodologies along different segments of the AD 'supply chain' – original investigations, administrative reviews, sunset reviews, etc. The narrow and limited approach of the AB has been one determinant of the continuing stream of zeroing-related cases.

86 The anti-dumping data is available at http://econ.worldbank.org/ttbd/gad/ (last visited 29 September 2010).

In the two Art 21.5 cases at hand, the AB has clearly stated that zeroing 'as such' is not permitted in either original investigations or reviews. The convoluted legal reasoning used by the AB to arrive at what is an obvious conclusion from a practical perspective – in that the United States continues to zero in reviews and does not contest this – is rather striking, but it has now been made clear that zeroing is disallowed, whether in investigations or in the administrative or sunset reviews that are used in the US retrospective system to determine applicable AD duties.

Continued noncompliance by the United States regarding zeroing in reviews creates a systemic risk as well as a continuing economic burden on affected exporters that confront higher AD duties than they otherwise would. Indeed, the limited extant research suggests that, absent zeroing, a substantial number of exporters would not be subject to AD measures at all. This is an area where greater transparency is important as it currently is virtually impossible to determine what the impact of zeroing is. If zeroing continues to be applied in reviews by the United States, affected exporting countries are confronted with the decision whether to launch disputes. A number of countries have already started down the road of invoking the DSU, and more may follow. This is arguably a waste of WTO resources. Continued noncompliance may also lead countries to start to zero themselves.

The best outcome of course would be that the United States reforms its regime to bring it into conformity with the AD Agreement. At the time of writing this, the prospects of this happening have increased, reflected in the request of the EU to suspend arbitration under Art. 22.6 to determine the magnitude of permitted retaliation so as to give the United States more time to reform its regime. In the absence of such an outcome, it would be desirable for the United States to provide information on the impacts that zeroing has on AD duty levels and either agree to compensate all affected exporters for the associated mark-ups (i.e., based on an analysis that 'but for' the zeroing the duty would have been X instead of Y) or to facilitate (lower the costs for the WTO/DSB) the calculation of what is the appropriate level of retaliation that affected countries are permitted to apply if they choose to do so.

More generally, given the steady expansion in the number of countries using AD, there is a need for greater transparency on process and methodologies, so as to enhance the understanding of what is driving dumping margins. This is needed independent of whether one believes that AD is a useful tool that helps governments undertake across-the-board liberalization or is a potential slippery slope. More detailed reporting by WTO Members on dumping-margin calculations in investigations to the WTO can be designed to address confidentiality concerns. For example, detailed data reported to the Secretariat could be kept confidential, but could be used to calculate and publish estimates of the impact certain types of methods have on average margins across a set of cases in a certain time period.

References

Blonigen, Bruce A. and Chad P. Bown (2003), 'Antidumping and Retaliation Threats', *Journal of International Economics*, **60**(2): 249–273.

Bown, Chad P. (2010), 'Taking Stock of Antidumping, Safeguards, and Countervailing Duties, 1990–2009', mimeo.

Bown, Chad P. and Rachel McCulloch (2010), 'Developing Countries, Dispute Settlement, and the Advisory Centre on WTO Law', World Bank Policy Research Working Paper No. 5168.

Bown, Chad P. and Thomas J. Prusa (2010), 'US Antidumping: Much Ado about Zeroing', World Bank Policy Research Working Paper No. 5352.

Bown, Chad P. and Alan O. Sykes (2008), 'The Zeroing Issue: A Critical Analysis of Softwood V', *World Trade Review*, 7(1): 121–142.

Egger, Peter and Douglas Nelson (2010), 'How Bad is Antidumping?: Evidence from Panel Data', *The Review of Economics and Statistics*, forthcoming.

Feinberg, Robert M. and Kara Marie Reynolds (2006), 'The Spread of Antidumping Regimes and the Role of Retaliation in Filings', *Southern Economic Journal*, **72**(4): 877–890.

Finger, J. Michael and Julio J. Nogués (eds.) (2006), *Safeguards and Antidumping in Latin American Trade Liberalization: Fighting Fire with Fire*, Washington, DC: World Bank.

Grossman, Gene M. and Alan O. Sykes (2006), 'European Communities – Anti-Dumping Duties on Imports of Cotton-Type Bed Linen from India: Recourse to Article 21.5 of the DSU by India', *World Trade Review*, 5(1): 133–148.

Janow, Merit E. and Robert W. Staiger (2003), '*EC–Bed Linen European Communities* – Anti-Dumping Duties on Imports of Cotton-Type Bed Linen from India', in Henrik Horn and Petros C. Mavroidis (eds.), *The WTO Case Law of 2001*, Cambridge: Cambridge University Press, pp. 115–139.

Nye, William W. (2009), 'The Implications of "Zeroing" for Enforcement of US Antidumping Laws', *Journal of Economic Policy Reform*, **12**(4): 263–271.

Prusa, Thomas J. and Edwin Vermulst (2009), 'A One–Two Punch on Zeroing: *US–Zeroing (EC) and US–Zeroing (Japan)*', *World Trade Review*, **8**(1): 187–241.

Vandenbussche, Hylke and Maurizio Zanardi (2010), 'The Chilling Trade Effects of Antidumping Proliferation', *European Economic Review*, **54**(6): 760–777.

Viner, Jacob (1923), *Dumping: A Problem in International Trade*, Chicago: University of Chicago Press (reprinted in 1991 by Augustus M. Kelley, Fairfield, NJ).

United States – Continued Existence and Application of Zeroing Methodology: the end of Zeroing?

THOMAS J. PRUSA
Rutgers University and NBER
EDWIN VERMULST
Vermulst, Verhaeghe, Graafsma & Bronckers

Abstract: This is the eighth Appellate Body Report in which some aspect of zeroing was adjudicated. As in the prior cases, the AB again found the US practice inconsistent with several aspects of the Anti-Dumping Agreement. The novelty in this dispute was the EC attempt to broaden the concept of what constitutes an appealable measure. The EC challenged whether a WTO decision regarding zeroing could apply to subsequent proceedings that might modify duty levels and asked the AB to decide whether the United States' continued use of zeroing in the context of a given case was consistent with WTO obligations. The AB stated that in its attempt to bring an effective resolution to the zeroing issue, the EC is entitled to frame the subject of its challenge in such a way as to bring the ongoing use of the zeroing methodology in these cases, under the scrutiny of WTO dispute settlement. The AB then cautiously applied the new perspective to US zeroing practice.

1. Introduction

United States – Continued Existence and Application of Zeroing Methodology[1] is yet another dispute related to the US practice of zeroing in anti-dumping proceedings. As is well known to anyone familiar with WTO Appellate Body disputes, zeroing is the single most litigated subject in the history of the WTO. Indeed, this is the eighth Appellate Body (AB) Report in which some aspect of zeroing was adjudicated.[2]

The views expressed in this paper are those of the authors and all omissions and errors are also of the authors.

1 *United States – Continued Existence and Application of Zeroing Methodology* (WT/DS350/AB/R, 4 February 2009) [hereinafter: *US–Continued Zeroing* (*EC*)].

2 Previous cases in which the AB ruled concerning zeroing: (1) *European Communities – Anti-Dumping Duties on Imports of Cotton-Type Bed Linen from India*, WT/DS141/AB/R of 1 March 2001 [*EC–Bed Linen*]; (2) *United States – Sunset Review of Anti-Dumping Duties on Corrosion-Resistant*

On 2 October 2006, the EC requested consultations with regard to zeroing in certain specified anti-dumping (AD) measures. As has been the case for every dispute involving zeroing, consultations proved fruitless and on 10 May 2007 the EC requested the establishment of a Panel. The Panel issued its Report in 1 October 2008. As in several prior disputes, the Panel Report reflected some ambiguity regarding the WTO consistency of zeroing.[3] Both parties appealed certain aspects of the Panel decisions. The AB issued its report on 2 February 2009. And, as it had done in every prior case involving zeroing, the AB's rulings were unambiguous – it upheld all Panel findings that zeroing was inconsistent with the WTO Anti-Dumping Agreement (ADA) and generally overturned the Panel's findings that ruled against the EC's claims against zeroing.

In many respects, this case seems very similar to previous complaints about the US practice of zeroing. The dispute concerns EC claims related to the use of zeroing in anti-dumping proceedings carried out by the US Department of Commerce. In this case, the EC challenged 'the specific instances of application of what it describes as the "zeroing methodology" in 4 anti-dumping investigations, 37 periodic reviews and 11 sunset reviews'.[4] With respect to these specific 52 claims, we have little to add to the already voluminous literature critiquing the AB's approach toward zeroing.[5] We agree with the legal-justification logic behind the AB's decisions – given that this case largely follows the script developed in prior

Carbon Steel Flat Products from Japan, WT/DS244/AB/R of 9 January 2004; (3) *United States – Final Dumping Determination on Softwood Lumber from Canada*, WT/DS264/AB/R of 11 August 2004 [*US–Softwood Lumber V*]; (4) *United States – Laws, Regulations and Methodology for Calculating Dumping Margins (Zeroing)*, WT/DS294/AB/R of 18 April 2006 [*US–Zeroing (EC)*]; (5) *United States – Final Dumping Determination on Softwood Lumber from Canada*, WT/DS264/AB/RW of 15 August 2006 [*US–Softwood Lumber V (compliance)*]; (6) *United States – Measures Relating to Zeroing and Sunset Reviews*, WT/DS322/AB/R of 9 January 2007 [*US–Zeroing (Japan)*]; (7) *United States – Final Anti-dumping Measures on Stainless Steel from Mexico*, WT/DS344/AB/R of 30 April 2008 [*US–Stainless Steel (Mexico)*]. In addition to these AB reports, zeroing was discussed by Panels in: (1) *EC – Anti-Dumping Duties on Malleable Cast Iron Tube or Pipe Fittings from Brazil*, WT/DS219/R of 7 March 2003; (2) *United States – Anti-Dumping Measure on Shrimp from Ecuador*, WT/DS335/R of 30 January 2007; and (3) *United States – Measures Relating to Shrimp from Thailand*, WT/DS343/R of 29 February 2008.

3 In *US–Stainless Steel (Mexico)* and *US–Zeroing (Japan)*, the Panels ruled that zeroing in original investigations was inconsistent, but zeroing in review proceedings was consistent. In both cases, the AB overturned the Panel with respect to zeroing in review proceedings.

4 *US–Continued Zeroing (EC)*, Panel, para. 2.1.

5 See, e.g., Merit E. Janow and Robert W. Staiger (2003), 'EC – Bed Linen European Communities – Anti-Dumping Duties on Imports of Cotton-Type Bed Linen from India', in Henrik Horn and Petros C. Mavroidis (eds.), *The WTO Case Law of 2001*, Cambridge: Cambridge University Press; Gene M. Grossman and Alan O. Sykes (2006), 'European Communities – Anti-Dumping Duties on Imports of Cotton-Type Bed Linen from India: Recourse to Article 21.5 of the DSU by India', in Henrik Horn and Petros C. Mavroidis (eds.), *The WTO Case Law of 2003*, Cambridge: Cambridge University Press; Chad P. Bown and Alan O. Sykes (2008), 'The Zeroing Issue: A Critical Analysis of *Softwood V*', *World Trade Review*, 7(1): 121–142; Thomas J. Prusa and Edwin Vermulst (2009), 'A One–Two Punch on Zeroing: *US–Zeroing (EC)* and *US–Zeroing (Japan)*', *World Trade Review*, 8(1): 187–241; Meredith Crowley and Robert Howse (2010), '*US–Stainless Steel (Mexico)*', *World Trade Review*, 9(1): 117–150.

cases, this should not be surprising. Further, as we have argued in the past, we also believe that standard economic statistical inference methods demand that all transactions be included in a 'fair' comparison.[6]

What gives this case gravitas is a new type of zeroing challenge – in this case the EC asked the AB to comment on what constitutes an appealable measure and whether a WTO decision regarding zeroing could apply to *subsequent* proceedings that might modify duty levels. Given the United States' refusal to stop zeroing despite numerous WTO decisions, it is easy to assume that the word 'continued' in the case title is used in the same way Hollywood uses numerals to denote sequels to blockbuster movies – in one year the challenge might involve zeroing with respect to steel bars, and the next-year challenge might involve zeroing with respect to pasta. Given the breadth of the EC products under US AD orders, we know of no Hollywood movie franchise that has the potential to match the number of potential EC zeroing disputes!

In this case, however, the term 'continued' is used in a different sense. In this case, the EC asked the AB to decide whether the United States' continued use of zeroing in the context of a given case was consistent with WTO obligations.

A bit of perspective is needed to understand the nature of the EC's claim. First, the United States has a retrospective duty-assessment system. In the retrospective system used by the United States, the dumping margin calculated in the initial investigation only establishes the deposit rate. The actual dumping margin is established during annual administrative reviews, although they often occur less frequently in practice. Second, the United States has responded to previous AB determinations by no longer zeroing in original investigations. The United States still contends, however, that the WTO ADA allows zeroing during administrative reviews. Given that the actual collected margins are determined during the administrative-review phase, the United States still practices zeroing when it really matters. Third, even if the AB finds zeroing as practiced in a review for a specific product and supplier is inconsistent, the United States' current policy is that the AB decision applies only to that particular measure. If the US Department of Commerce does a new administrative review, then the onus is back on the EC (or any other affected member country) to file another dispute with regards to that new review. The current US practice creates a 'cat and mouse' game with its trading partner. The measure currently in effect is almost always different from the one that is being challenged at the WTO.

The EC submission included claims requesting the AB to find that the US ongoing or continued zeroing is inconsistent with the ADA. For all intents and purposes, the meat of this dispute is this continued-zeroing claim.

6 Prusa and Vermulst (2009), 'A One–Two Punch on Zeroing: *US–Zeroing (EC)* and *US–Zeroing (Japan)*'.

2. What measures can be challenged?

Beyond the specific instances of zeroing enumerated in the aforementioned 52 claims, the EC also challenged the continued application by the United States of anti-dumping duties resulting from the anti-dumping orders enumerated in 18 cases, as calculated or maintained in place at a level in excess of the margin of dumping that in the EC's view would have resulted from the correct application of the relevant provisions of the Anti-Dumping Agreement.[7] These 18 alternative claims are quite different from the zeroing claims made in previous disputes. The Panel's discussion and analysis of these claims clearly suggests a struggle to properly fit these claims into WTO dispute rules. Without any prior jurisprudence, the Panel floundered as it sought to put this new and broadened sense of 'measure' into proper legal context.

In an Annex to the request for establishment of the Panel (REP), the EC numbered the 18 orders from I to XVIII and the administrative determinations from 1 to 52. In Table 1, we provide an excerpt from the Annex to the EC's REP in an attempt to clarify the relationship between the two concepts. In this example, the EC challenged the continued application of zeroing in 'Case XIII' *Certain Pasta from Italy* in general, as well as various types of zeroing applied in four periodic reviews and one expiry review conducted in the framework of this case.

The motivation for the EC's request for the WTO AB to decide on zeroing in the context of a case rather than just for each separate dumping calculation is understandable. If member countries can only challenge each application of zeroing in a specific determination, there is the prospect of a never-ending cycle of ineffective complaints (the cat-and-mouse game alluded to above). By the time the EC (or any other member country) prevails at the WTO on a zeroing complaint, the challenged determination almost surely has been replaced by a new administrative-review determination, which in effect makes the sanctioned zeroing measure moot. In turn, this means the new measure would need to be challenged again. The combination of the US system of annual retrospective reviews, its continued use of zeroing in administrative reviews, and the two+ year duration of a WTO dispute mean the WTO AB rulings are largely meaningless.

In our view, the question of what is a measure is the single most compelling aspect of this dispute.

3. Commentary

A significant part of this dispute and the accompanying AB report concerns what by now could be called standard zeroing complaints: the EC made claims against 52 specific instances of zeroing. We have previously stated our legal and economic perspective on the practice of zeroing and we see no reason to repeat those

7 *US–Continued Zeroing* (EC), AB, para. 1.

Table 1. Excerpt from annex to EC's Panel request

	ADMINISTRATIVE REVIEWS					
CASE XIII	Period covered by the review	Final results (unless otherwise specified)	Amended final results	Company	Dumping margin	No.
Certain Pasta – Italy US DOC NO A-475-818	1 July 2004– 30 June 2005	72 FR 7011, 14 February 2007		Atar Corticella/ Combattenti	18.18 % 1.95 %	43
	1 July 2003– 30 June 2004	70 FR 71464, 29 November 2005		Barilla	20.68 %	44
				Corticella/ Combattenti	3.41 %	
				Indalco	2.59 %	
				Pagani	2.76 %	
				Riscossa	2.03 %	
	1 July 2002– 30 June 2003	70 FR 6832, 9 February 2005		Barilla	7.25 %	45
				Corticella/ Combattenti	4 %	
				Indalco	6.03 %	
				PAM	4.78 %	
				Riscossa	1.05 %	
				Russo	7.36 %	
	1 July 2001– 30 June 2002	69 FR 6255, 10 February 2004	69 FR 81, 27 April 2004	Garofalo	2.57 %	46
				Indalco	2.85 %	
				PAM	45.49 %	
				Tomasello	4.59 %	
				Zaffiri	7.23 %	
	SUNSET REVIEWS					
	DOC Final determ.	ITC Case number	ITC Determ.	Continuation order		
	72 FR 5266, 5 February 2007	731-TA-734				47

arguments here. For those interested in details, we include a summary table of the Panel and AB decisions in an appendix.

Instead, we proceed by discussing several other issues that emerged in the dispute. Two are particularly significant. The first involves the issue of what constitutes a zeroing measure. To our knowledge, this case is the first time it has surfaced in the zeroing context. The second issue concerns the role of precedent; this was also discussed extensively in *US–Stainless Steel (Mexico)*. The other issues likely have less consequence for future AB jurisprudence but deserve some brief comments.

3.1 'Cases' versus 'proceedings'

In its request for establishment of the Panel (REP)[8] the EC had made a distinction between the (continued) application of specific anti-dumping duties resulting from

8 *United States – Continued Existence and Application of Zeroing Methodology*, request for the establishment of a Panel by the European Communities, WT/DS350/6 (11 May 2007).

18 anti-dumping orders and – more specifically – administrative determinations pertaining to these 18 orders in which it considered that the US authorities had applied zeroing.

The Panel had found that the EC had failed to identify in the REP the specific measures at issue within the meaning of Article 6.2 DSU[9] with respect to the (continued) application of the 18 orders. The Panel had considered that, in this regard, the REP had not been specific enough and that the (continued) application did not represent a measure in and of itself. On appeal, the EC explained that its objective in challenging the 18 orders as measures was to 'apprehend the *root* of the WTO inconsistency as it relates to a particular anti-dumping duty'.[10]

According to the consistent case law of the AB, it has to be clear from the REP which measures are challenged because the REP establishes both the jurisdiction of the Panel and notifies the respondent and possible third parties of the content and the parameters of the dispute.[11] Where jurisdictional objections are raised, as was the case here, the Panel must examine whether the REP, read as a whole, on its face complies with these requirements.

The AB considered that the REP linked (1) the duties resulting from the 18 anti-dumping duty orders, (2) their most recent periodic or sunset review, and (3) the use of the zeroing methodology, and that, consequently, the United States could reasonably have expected to understand the nature of the challenges. Therefore, the AB concluded that the REP was specific enough. The AB rejected that the Panel examination at this stage would need to encompass a substantive assessment of whether a claimed measure constituted a challengeable measure. Such analysis comes into play only in the course of a Panel proceeding and is not a prerequisite for the establishment of the Panel.[12]

Nor did the AB consider relevant the Panel's argument that to accept the EC's claims with respect to the continued application of the 18 orders would amount to an acceptance of prospective remedies. On the contrary, the AB considered it logical in light of the nature of the EC's challenge of ongoing measures that the remedy sought was prospective. Furthermore, prospective remedies were common in other areas of WTO dispute settlement as well, for example in case of 'as such' claims or claims related to recurring subsidies.[13]

The AB then proceeded to examine whether these measures were susceptible to a WTO challenge. It reiterated that any act or omission attributable to a WTO

9 Article 6.2 DSU provides, in relevant part, that the REP shall identify the specific measure at issue and provide a brief summary of the legal basis of the complaint sufficient to present the problem clearly. These two elements together constitute the 'matter' that forms the basis for the terms of reference of the Panel, see AB Report, para. 160.

10 *US–Continued Zeroing* (*EC*), AB, para. 16.

11 Ibid., para. 161.

12 Ibid., para. 169.

13 Ibid., para. 171.

Table 2. Decisions regarding continued application of zeroing in 18 AD cases

	Decision	Rationale
Panel	Rejected EC claims	Lack of specificity makes claims 'outside terms of reference'
AB	Reversed Panel; completed analysis • 4 cases inconsistent • 14 cases excluded	Continued use of zeroing within a case can be challenged • ADA Article 9.3; GATT Article VI.2; ADA Article 11.3 • Repeated instances of zeroing were not presented (6 cases) • Partial evidence inconclusive (8 cases)

member may qualify as a measure[14] and considered the distinction between 'as such' and 'as applied' claims not relevant for the dispute at issue. In other words, the fact that the continued-application claims of the EC fit in neither of the two categories had no bearing on their ability to be challenged.[15] The AB considered that ongoing conduct could form the basis for a WTO challenge and that, in fact, the EC 'in seeking an effective resolution ... is entitled to frame the subject of its challenge in such a way as to bring the ongoing conduct, regarding the use of the zeroing methodology in these 18 cases, under the scrutiny of WTO dispute settlement'.[16]

The AB then completed the analysis in the cases where it considered that there was sufficient factual evidence available to conclude that zeroing would likely continue to be applied in successive future determinations. The results regarding these cases are given in Table 2. The AB proceeded very cautiously at this point, stating 'we must ascertain whether the factual findings made by the Panel and undisputed facts in the record show that the zeroing methodology has been used repeatedly in successive proceedings, in each of the 18 cases, by which the duties are maintained'.[17]

In four of the 18 cases, the AB found a 'density of factual findings ... regarding the continued use of the zeroing methodology in a string of successive proceedings pertaining to the same anti-dumping duty order', sufficient to provide a basis for concluding that 'the zeroing methodology would likely continue to be applied in successive proceedings whereby the duties in these four cases are maintained'.[18]

Six of the cases concerned only a single proceeding in each case where duties were applied with zeroing. The AB did not find the single instance sufficient to

14 Ibid., para. 176.
15 Ibid., paras. 178–180.
16 Ibid., para. 181.
17 Ibid., paras. 187–189.
18 Ibid., paras. 191–192.

conclude ongoing conduct in those cases.[19] In the other eight cases, the AB found the Panel's factual findings inconclusive with respect to the use of zeroing in successive proceedings – either evidence was missing or incomplete from the record.[20] As a result, the AB opted to proceed extremely cautiously and declared the evidence was inconclusive to render a decision.

We believe that the AB's adoption of a broad definition of 'measures' so as to encompass ongoing illegal conduct was the only way in which the ongoing cat-and-mouse game could effectively be sanctioned. As a matter of law, we see no problem with the AB's broad definition of a 'measure'. In anti-dumping proceedings, the basic calculation methodologies are often established in the course of the original investigation. In subsequent review investigations, the same methodologies are then applied. In the US retrospective system, the original investigation culminates in the publication of the anti-dumping duty order, for example, on pasta. As of this moment, an anti-dumping measure applies to pasta. The fact that, in the US system, the actual rate of the duty to be paid is only determined subsequently in the course of the annual reviews seems irrelevant.

We do feel that the terminology used by not only the AB and the Panel, but also by the parties remains confusing. While the ADA is not clear either, one could envisage a relatively simple distinction between a 'proceeding' and an 'investigation'. Under this terminology, in the example above the proceeding would be 'Certain Pasta from Italy'. A proceeding continues as long as it is not terminated. In the course of a proceeding, various investigations may be conducted, starting with the original Article 5 investigation. Assuming that the initial Article 5 investigation leads to the imposition of anti-dumping measures, such measures may then be subject to, for example, periodic review investigations (in the US retrospective system), interim, expiry, and newcomer review investigations, and anti-circumvention and (in the EC) anti-absorption investigations. Depending on the type of investigation, the measure, as originally imposed in the Article 5 investigation, may then be confirmed, amended, or terminated, which ends the investigation. However, as long as the measure is not terminated in the course of a review investigation, the proceeding continues.

3.2 *The role of precedent: simple zeroing as applied in 29 periodic reviews*

The Panel was well aware that the prior AB Reports had consistently reversed the findings in prior Panel Reports that simple zeroing in periodic reviews is not WTO-inconsistent. Seemingly with great reluctance, the Panel acknowledged it needed to consider the role of jurisprudence in the WTO dispute-settlement system, in particular the 'role of adopted Appellate Body reports'.[21] Particular weight was given

19 Ibid., para. 193.
20 Ibid., para. 194.
21 *US–Continued Zeroing (EC)*, Panel, para. 7.170.

to the AB Report in *US–Stainless Steel* (*Mexico*)[22] wherein the Panel did not follow prior AB Reports and was subsequently overturned and rebuked by the AB.

In light of the *Stainless Steel* Report, the Panel agreed with the view that 'security and predictability in the dispute settlement system *per se* is a purpose served by the development of a consistent body of case law based on panels following the reasoning of adopted Appellate Body reports'.[23] The Panel then stated that (1) 'it is obviously incumbent upon any panel to consider prior adopted Appellate Body reports, as well as adopted panel reports, and adopted GATT panel reports, in undertaking the objective assessment required by Article 11',[24] and (2) 'prior adopted reports form part of the GATT/WTO *acquis*, and, as stated by the Appellate Body, create legitimate expectations among WTO Members, and, therefore, should be taken into account where they are relevant'.[25]

However, the Panel was not about to go quietly into the night. Countering the above discussion, the Panel stated that it did 'not consider that the development of binding jurisprudence is a contemplated element to enable the dispute settlement system to provide security and predictability to the multilateral trading system'[26] and that 'a panel cannot simply follow the adopted report of another panel, or of the Appellate Body, without careful consideration of the facts and arguments made by the parties in the dispute before it'.[27]

In effect, the Panel is saying that it would be perfectly legitimate for it to deviate from the AB's jurisprudence. However, since the AB would almost surely overrule the Panel, the only consequence of such a decision would be to delay a final settlement of the dispute, which thus would be at odds with the goal of promptly settling the dispute. One gets the very real sense that the Panel cannot accept that the AB has some superior authority in its role as interpreter of the law.

Ultimately, a clearly conflicted Panel grudgingly accepted the findings of the AB Report in *US–Stainless Steel* (*Mexico*)[28] and accordingly found that the United States' use of simple zeroing in 29 periodic reviews had violated Article 9.3 ADA and Article VI:2 GATT 1994.

On appeal, the United States essentially rehashed its traditional argumentation that simple zeroing in periodic reviews constitutes a permissible interpretation of the ADA.

The AB started its analysis with examination of Article 17(6)(ii) and reiterated that, on the basis of the first sentence, Panels adjudicating disputes under the ADA

22 *US–Stainless Steel* (*Mexico*), discussed in Crowley and Howse (2010), '*US–Stainless Steel* (*Mexico*)'.

23 *US–Continued Zeroing* (*EC*), Panel, para. 7.179.

24 Ibid.

25 Ibid.

26 Ibid.

27 Ibid., para. 7.180.

28 *US–Stainless Steel* (*Mexico*), discussed in Crowley and Howse (2010), '*US–Stainless Steel* (*Mexico*)'.

must apply Articles 31 and 32 of the *Vienna Convention on the Law of Treaties* (VCLT):

> The principles of interpretation that are set out in Articles 31 and 32 are to be followed in a holistic fashion. The interpretative exercise is engaged so as to yield an interpretation that is harmonious and coherent and fits comfortably in the treaty as a whole so as to render the treaty provision legally effective. A word or term may have more than one meaning or shade of meaning, but the identification of such meanings in isolation only commences the process of interpretation, it does not conclude it.[29]

The AB then emphasized that the first and second sentence of Article 17(6)(ii) have to be applied sequentially, meaning that the second sentence ('more than one permissible interpretation') will need to be applied only if there is room for that after proper application of Articles 31 and 32 VCLT under the first sentence. On the other hand, these articles also apply to the interpretation of the second sentence itself, so that it cannot be interpreted in a manner which makes it redundant or which derogates from Articles 31 and 32. The AB considered that the second sentence therefore envisages the possibility that application of Articles 31 and 32 may give rise to an 'interpretative range'.

The AB then consecutively considered and rejected US arguments with respect to the concept of 'dumping' and 'margins of dumping' in the ADA, implications for importer-specific duty assessment in periodic reviews, discrimination between prospective normal value systems and the US retrospective duty-assessment system, 'mathematical equivalence' and the historical background of the dumping concept. It concluded that zeroing is inconsistent with Article 9.3 ADA on the basis of the application of Article 17(6)(ii), first sentence. The second sentence therefore did not come into play:

> A holding that zeroing is also consistent with Article 9.3 would be flatly contradictory. Such contradiction would be repugnant to the customary rules of treaty interpretation ... Consequently, it is not a permissible interpretation.[30]

In a concurring opinion, one Member of the Division further noted that:

> The range of meanings that may constitute a permissible interpretation does not encompass meanings of such wide variability, and even contradiction, so as to accommodate the two rival interpretations. One must prevail. The Appellate Body has decided the matter. At a point in every debate, there comes a time when it is more important for the system of dispute resolution to have a definitive outcome, than further to pick over the entrails of battles past. With respect to zeroing, that time has come.[31]

29 *US–Continued Zeroing* (*EC*), AB, para. 268.
30 Ibid., para. 317.
31 Ibid., para. 312.

In this context, it is also noted that in one of its conditional appeals, the EC had – somewhat gratuitously – requested that, if the Panel Report were to be construed as finding that a Panel can invoke 'cogent reasons' for departing from previous AB rulings on the same issue of legal interpretation, the AB modify or reverse such a Panel finding.[32] In the view of the EC, only the AB itself should have the power to invoke such cogent reasons.

The AB considered that it did not have to rule on the conditional appeal because, although the Panel Report was at places ambiguous, in the end the Panel followed the previous AB Reports and therefore appeared 'to have acceded to the hierarchical structure contemplated in the DSU'.[33]

Crowley and Howse (2010) offer an excellent discussion of the role of precedent at the WTO.[34] In particular, they argue that while the original agreement may contain vague language (because it is impossible for negotiators to include all possible developments in the text), economic efficiency can be enhanced with specificity that comes from legal challenges. Not only does precedent reduce uncertainty but it also can induce welfare-enhancing changes in behavior. The cost of precedent is the loss of flexibility. We agree with Crowley and Howse's analysis and also with their conclusion that, in the case of zeroing, the benefits of precedent outweigh the costs.

We find the Panel's discussion has again added unneeded ambiguity to the zeroing saga. The Panel argues that it must evaluate each case on its own merits. But this 'evaluation' need not involve the issue of whether the practice is consistent. The Panel's discussion misrepresents the AB's basis for finding zeroing inconsistent and also suggests that the practice of zeroing varies from case to case. One can read the Panel Report and get the impression that zeroing is less like an explicit violation such as levying tariffs beyond bound rates and more akin to a phytosanitary dispute where (in most cases) the basis for the restriction must be carefully evaluated.

We entirely agree that the Panel must confirm that zeroing was conducted in each case. That being said, the United States has never provided evidence of any challenged measure where the zeroing methodology was not performed. The best the United States has ever argued is that zeroing might not affect the calculated duty for a particular set of pricing data, e.g. when the export price is always lower than the home-market price. While the Panel must conduct its review, it also must recognize that the zeroing method is a standard part of the computer code that the US Department of Commerce uses in every case.

Moreover, while we agree with the Panel's view that its finding that zeroing is permitted would simply delay a final settlement of the dispute (because the AB would surely overrule the Panel) and therefore is at odds with the goal of promptly

32 Ibid., para. 358.

33 Ibid., para. 365.

34 Crowley and Howse (2010), '*US–Stainless Steel (Mexico)*'.

settling the dispute, we consider there are additional costs to such an opinion. To begin with, it undermines the legitimacy of the prior AB decisions. Ambiguity in the face of clear AB language to the contrary fosters ongoing disputes over zeroing. The United States can quote Panel decisions that support the current practice.

In addition, the Panel's discussion suggests that the basis for the previous AB decisions is something that it is not. The AB has not said that the inconsistency lies in a particular application; rather the AB has repeatedly said that zeroing is inconsistent with Article 2.4.2 AD Agreement – it violates the notion of 'fair comparison'.

We are also troubled by what the lack of consistent AB decisionmaking would mean for the two important GATT/WTO principles: predictability and non-discrimination. Said differently, the Panel's suggestion that the consistency of zeroing might vary from case to case would create a serious time-consistency problem for WTO members. Under the Panel's view, it is quite possible that the United States could practice zeroing when computing margins for a pasta producer from Italy but be prohibited from using zeroing when computing margins for a pasta producer from Japan. As a result, two firms with identical home and export prices could have dramatically different margins. Furthermore, not every WTO member may be willing to spend money and/or political capital in challenging the United States on zeroing in the WTO.

3.3 *Challenging preliminary determinations*

Four of the 52 administrative determinations challenged by the EC were preliminary determinations in periodic or sunset reviews. The Panel had considered these claims to be outside its terms of reference because the EC had not claimed a violation of Article 7.1 ADA while Article 17.4 ADA provides that a provisional anti-dumping measure may be challenged only if it has a significant impact and if the complainant considers that the provisional measure was taken contrary to the provisions of Article 7.1.[35]

The EC appealed this decision, arguing that it had not challenged preliminary determinations within the meaning of Article 7.1 ADA. The AB agreed with the EC's contention. The AB considered Article 7 only applicable to provisional measures taken in the context of an original Article 5 investigation and therefore overturned the Panel's finding.

However, the AB declined to complete the analysis on the grounds that the two preliminary DOC determinations could still be modified by the final results while the other two final DOC determinations had still been pending before the USITC at the time the Panel was established.[36] The fact that one of these latter two cases

35 *US–Continued Zeroing (EC)*, Panel, para. 7.158.

36 *US–Continued Zeroing (EC)*, AB, paras. 209–211.

was ultimately revoked[37] further convinced the AB that the EC's challenge was premature.

The AB's refusal to complete the analysis seems based on the logic that the various preparatory steps in an investigation are not final yet and may still be changed at the definitive stage. While the AB rightly concluded that the EU's challenge was not based on Article 7.1 ADA, in effect its refusal to complete the analysis would appear to indicate that it is even harder to challenge a preliminary review determination than it would be to challenge a preliminary determination in an original investigation based on Article 7.1.

3.4 *Linkage between request for consultations and REP*

During the Panel proceeding, the United States had requested a preliminary ruling that 14 of the 52 determinations listed in the annex to the REP were outside the Panel's terms of reference because they had not been identified in the request for consultations (RfC). The Panel had rejected this request on the ground that the RfC and the REP covered the same subject matter and the same dispute.

The AB upheld the Panel findings on the basis of its previous case law that Articles 4 and 6 DSU do not require a precise and exact identity between the specific measures that were the subject of the consultations and those identified in the REP, as long as the REP does not expand the scope of the dispute.[38]

The AB also found as a factual matter that the EC *had* identified the 18 cases in the RfC.[39]

The AB's findings on this issue confirm that there does not necessarily need to be complete synchronicity between the contents of the RfC and the REP, as long as the REP does not broaden the scope of the dispute. As consultations are merely a preparatory, albeit mandatory, step in the WTO dispute-settlement process, and amicable settlement as a result of consultations is relatively rare, the AB's relatively relaxed position on this procedural issue seems justified.

3.5 *Mathematical equivalence*

One ongoing argument made by the United States justifying zeroing is that prohibiting zeroing implies that the two methods for calculating margins in Article 2.4.2, weighted average-weighted average (WW) and weighted average-transaction (WT), yield identical results. As a result, according to the United States prohibiting zeroing makes one of the methods redundant and hence meaningless.[40] By inference, this means that zeroing was anticipated by the negotiating parties, for what other reason would have the ADA mentioned two methods that yield identical results?

37 The revocation was the result of a negative ITC sunset injury determination.
38 *US–Continued Zeroing* (*EC*), AB, paras. 222 and 235.
39 Ibid., paras. 237–241.
40 *US–Continued Zeroing* (*EC*), Panel, para. 7.125.

The United States' argument has never garnered any support at the AB. The AB has repeatedly stated that one method of calculation cannot be used to interpret other methodologies. In addition, the AB has questioned the generality of the mathematical equivalence.

Previously we have discussed the mathematical equivalent issue.[41] We mention two important results. First, as we explain, the two methods do produce equivalent margins without zeroing under certain circumstances. Namely, all transactions must be used to compute the weighted-average price. While that sounds simple enough, the United States generally does not calculate the WT margins this way. Rather, the United States will divide the transactions by time period or exporter and then calculate the comparison margin. As shown in Prusa and Vermulst (2009), this can produce different margins.

Second, we are troubled by the argument that the WTO AB should not restrict zeroing if doing so means two methods produce identical outcomes. According to the United States, why would the treaty mention two methods for calculating margins if they produce the same margin? From an economic perspective, the US argument is problematic. There are many policies that produce identical results; some are allowed under the WTO, some are not. Does the United States' 'potentially equivalent' argument apply to all such policies? Tariffs and quotas can have the exact same impact on exporters. One of the more celebrated theorems in international economics, the Lerner symmetry theorem, states that an ad valorem tariff will have the same effect as an export tax. Tariffs are subject to countless WTO rules but export taxes are permitted. It is the United States' position that the possible equivalence between export taxes and tariffs means the WTO should not negotiate reductions to tariffs. What about ad valorem and specific tariffs? They too can be designed to have the same impact. Does the United States believe that negotiators did not know of their equivalence during the Uruguay Round talks?

If the AB upheld the United States' position that the potential equivalence could not have been what negotiators meant, then all sorts of WTO provisions could be potentially challenged. We do believe this would neither be good for the system nor what negotiators actually intended. Alternative methods can be mentioned in the text to give countries flexibility in implementing policy. In cases with tens of thousands of individual transactions (e.g., semiconductors) one method might be preferred, while in a case with only a handful of sales (e.g., large printing presses) another method might be preferred. We believe this is why the negotiators offered several methods for calculating margins.

3.6 *Evidence*

The Panel had found that the EC had not been able to show that the United States had actually zeroed in seven of the 37 challenged periodic reviews. The main

41 Prusa and Vermulst (2009), 'A One–Two Punch on Zeroing: *US–Zeroing* (*EC*) and *US–Zeroing* (*Japan*)'.

reason was that in these seven reviews, the United States had not explicitly mentioned that it had used zeroing. However, the EC had submitted various types of evidence to the Panel which, in its view, established that the DOC had employed zeroing. The Panel had examined this evidence type by type and determined that none of them conclusively showed that zeroing had been used. On appeal, the EC claimed that the Panel had not made an objective assessment of the matter before it, including an objective assessment of the facts of the case, within the meaning of Article 11 DSU.

The AB noted in general terms that a Panel has to 'consider evidence before it in its totality, which includes consideration of submitted evidence in relation to other evidence'.[42] The AB considered that, in this case, the type-by-type approach taken by the Panel failed to consider the evidence in its totality. The AB further considered that the Panel had failed to assess the probative value of individual pieces of evidence in relation to other evidence.[43] Last, the AB found that the Panel's insistence on authenticated DOC margin-calculation programs to show the use of zeroing (rather than printed copies provided by the EC), amounted to a failure to make an objective assessment.

Under Article 13, DSU Panels have the right to seek information from any individual or body that it deems appropriate. During the Panel proceeding, the EC had noted that 'should the Panel consider further corroboration appropriate, the Panel should request the United States to provide copies of the detailed margin calculations for each of the seven administrative reviews at issue'.[44] However, the Panel had declined to do so. The AB did not find fault with the Panel's refusal to do so as such, because the Panel has discretion to exercise its Article 13 right. However, the AB emphasized that Article 13 and Article 11 are linked and that Panels have an important investigative function to request information, for example, to evaluate evidence already before it. In light of the importance that the Panel had attached to the evidentiary value of authenticated DOC margin-calculation programs, the Panel had not taken the necessary steps to elicit such information.[45]

The AB then tried to complete the analysis on the basis of the factual findings and uncontested facts on the Panel record and found that it could do so for five of the seven periodic reviews. By looking at the totality of the evidence and effectively taking into account the printouts of the DOC margin calculations provided by the EC to the Panel, the AB concluded that the DOC had applied zeroing in five of the seven reviews.[46]

42 *US–Continued Zeroing* (*EC*), AB, para. 331.
43 Ibid., paras. 336–338.
44 Ibid., para. 344.
45 Ibid., paras. 345–347.
46 Ibid., paras. 349–357.

4. Concluding comments

All in all, the AB's ruling in this case is a decisive rejection of the US practice. When considered alongside two other very broad rulings, *US–Zeroing* (*EC*)[47] and *US–Zeroing* (*Japan*),[48] it is becoming increasingly unlikely that the United States can ever succeed in a WTO dispute involving zeroing.

The most significant issue in the case involved the concept of a 'measure'. The standard classification of claims as either 'as such' (measures of general and prospective application) or 'as applied' (acts that apply to specific situations) was not adequate in this case. While the Panel struggled with the EC's identification of the precise content of the measures, the AB argued that the 'as such-as applied' distinction was only an 'analytical tool to facilitate the understanding of the nature of a measure at issue'[49] and did 'not define exhaustively the types of measures that may be subject to challenge in WTO dispute settlement'.[50] In this case, the AB stated that 'the measures at issue consist of the use of the zeroing methodology in a string of connected and sequential determinations'[51] and it saw 'no reason to exclude ongoing conduct that consists of the use of the zeroing methodology from challenge in WTO dispute settlement'.[52]

With this decision, the ability for the United States to continually use successive administrative reviews to avoid sanctionable violations appears to have come to an end. The question remains whether this will force the United States to alter its zeroing policy.

47 *US–Zeroing* (*EC*) (also WT/DS294/AB/Corr.1, 20 August 2007; WT/DS294/R, 31 October 2005).
48 *US–Zeroing* (*Japan*)] (also WT/DS322/R, 20 September 2006).
49 *US–Continued Zeroing* (*EC*), AB, para. 179.
50 Ibid.
51 Ibid., para. 181.
52 Ibid.

Appendix: Summary of Panel and AB Decisions regarding 52 specific instances of zeroing

	Panel		AB	
	Decision	Rationale	Decision	Rationale
Model Zeroing in 4 original investigations	4 inconsistent	ADA Article 2.4.2	US did not appeal	
Simple Zeroing in 37 periodic reviews	29 inconsistent	ADA Article 9.3; GATT Article VI.2	Upheld	
	7 measures excluded	EC had not showed zeroing had been used	Reversed Panel; completed analysis for 5 measures; 5 measures inconsistent	ADA Article 9.3; GATT Article VI.2
	1 preliminary measure excluded	'outside terms of reference'	Reversed Panel's basis for decision but did not find the measure inconsistent	EC challenge 'premature'
Model Zeroing in 11 sunset reviews	8 inconsistent	ADA Article 11.3	Upheld	
	3 preliminary measures excluded	'outside terms of reference'	Reversed Panel's basis for decision but did not find the measures inconsistent	EC challenge 'premature'

Incomplete Harmonization Contracts in International Economic Law: Report of the Panel, *China – Measures Affecting the Protection and Enforcement of Intellectual Property Rights*, WT/DS362/R, adopted 20 March 2009

KAMAL SAGGI

Dedman Distinguished Collegiate Professor of Economics Southern Methodist University, Dallas, TX

JOEL P. TRACHTMAN

Professor of International Law, The Fletcher School of Law and Diplomacy, Tufts University, Medford, MA

Abstract: In *China – Measures Affecting the Protection and Enforcement of Intellectual Property Rights*, the Panel addressed three main issues:

1. the relationship between China's censorship laws and its obligations to protect copyright under the WTO Agreement on Trade Related Intellectual Property Rights ('TRIPS');
2. China's obligations under TRIPS to ensure that its customs authorities be empowered to dispose properly of confiscated goods that infringe intellectual property rights;
3. whether China's volume and value of goods thresholds for application of criminal procedures and penalties with respect to trademark counterfeiting or copyright piracy comply with TRIPS requirements for application of criminal procedures and penalties.

International trade agreements are generally intended to cause states to internalize policy externalities. The policy externalities that arise from domestic decisions regarding intellectual property protection may deprive foreign intellectual property owners of the monopoly profits that they would otherwise derive from intellectual property protection. In connection with intellectual property protection, even a state that lacks 'traditional' market power on world markets may be able to impose terms-of-trade externalities on other states by reducing its protection of intellectual property below the global optimum. For this reason, and because of the international public-goods aspects of intellectual property, states have incentives to undersupply intellectual property protection. At least in part, TRIPS seems to be an attempt to reduce these policy externalities. All contracts, and all international treaties, are incomplete. This case involves some good examples of treaty incompleteness. Incompleteness can arise from circumstances of uncertainty regarding the possible tradeoffs, and the optimal balance, between different goals, including state autonomy in censorship on the one hand and internalizing policy externalities in intellectual property protection on the other. We analyze the possibility that it might be efficient to allow states broad discretion over censorship. Alternatively, in connection with the requirement for criminal penalties, incompleteness can arise from uncertainty regarding the particular industry structure that might be involved, and what would constitute production of 'commercial scale' for that industry. We also question the rationale for the limitation on the use of nonviolation complaints in connection with the TRIPS, since non-violation complaints may be used to reduce the possibility that states will use discretion, such as that granted with respect to censorship, in a manner that is inconsistent with the rationale for that discretion so as to defect from the general commitment to provide copyright or other intellectual property rights.

Introduction

In *China – Measures Affecting the Protection and Enforcement of Intellectual Property Rights* ('*China–IP Rights*'),[1] which was not appealed, and therefore was adopted without an Appellate Body review, the Panel addressed three main issues:

1. the relationship between China's censorship laws and its obligations to protect copyright under the WTO Agreement on Trade Related Intellectual Property Rights ('TRIPS');
2. China's obligations under TRIPS to ensure that its customs authorities be empowered to dispose properly of confiscated goods that infringe intellectual property rights;
3. whether China's volume and value of goods thresholds for application of criminal procedures and penalties with respect to trademark counterfeiting or copyright piracy comply with TRIPS requirements for application of criminal procedures and penalties.

This case is not directly about trade in goods or services. Rather, it is about the extent to which China was required to harmonize and enforce its intellectual property law for the benefit of persons of other WTO member states. The TRIPS Agreement, which was part of the WTO single undertaking agreed in 1994, provides for a minimum level of protection of intellectual property rights and enforcement of those rights. Each of the US claims in this case involves a challenge to the implementation by China of its obligations under the TRIPS Agreement; each involves a question of interpretation of the scope of protection required under the TRIPS Agreement. However, these TRIPS claims can be understood in terms of

1 Hereinafter Panel Report.

concerns regarding policy externalities – harm to US firms – and more specifically regarding terms-of-trade externalities.

The establishment of certain minimum levels of IPR protection might be seen as a third level of discipline on domestic, or 'behind the border', regulation. The first level of discipline is a requirement of national treatment, as discussed in Horn.[2] A second level of discipline is a proportionality requirement, as discussed and compared to national treatment in Hoekman and Trachtman.[3] A third level is a requirement for harmonization of IPRs that basically resulted in a significant increase in the degree of IPR protection available in most of the developing world. These three levels do not neatly map into either magnitudes of discipline or degree of specificity of obligation. However, all three may be understood, like much international law in this area, as addressing policy externalities that may arise from actions of the regulating state. National-treatment requirements may be understood as protecting imports from differential treatment motivated by protectionist goals, and proportionality might be understood either as supplementing national treatment or as imposing an additional requirement of rationality in regulation as applied to imports. These disciplines can be understood as 'negative integration' in the sense that they prohibit certain types of national measures. On the other hand, the establishment of minimum levels of IPRs under TRIPS recognizes that each state may have an incentive to enact a level of regulation that falls below the globally efficient level. But the fact that nations have incentives to under-protect intellectual property does not necessarily imply that it is efficient to *equalize* the degree of IPR protection in all nations. Indeed, while such harmonization of IPRs is called for under TRIPS, Grossman and Lai[4] have argued convincingly that such harmonization is neither necessary nor sufficient for achieving global efficiency. In other words, in an open global economy, while each nation will generally undersupply IPR protection and attempt to free-ride on the protection provided by other countries, efficient IPR reform does not require all nations to adopt the same set of IPR policies, since nations are heterogeneous with respect to innovative capacity, market size, and a variety of other relevant variables. Nevertheless, the strengthening of IPR protection in many developing countries that was called for under TRIPS can be viewed as a type of 'positive integration'.

To varying degrees, both negative integration and positive integration can be seen as attempts to internalize what would otherwise be policy externalities imposed by the pursuit of policies based purely on national interest. However, in the case of each of national treatment, proportionality, and harmonization there is always a degree of contractual incompleteness: it is impossible to specify

2 Henrik Horn (2006), 'National Treatment in the GATT', 96 : 1 *The American Economic Review*, 394–404.

3 Bernard Hoekman and Joel P. Trachtman (2010), 'Continued Suspense: *EC–Hormones* and WTO Disciplines on Discrimination and Domestic Regulation', 9 : 01 *World Trade Review*, 151–180.

4 Gene M. Grossman and Edwin L.-C. Lai (2004), 'International Protection of Intellectual Property', 94 : 5 *The American Economic Review*, 1635–1653.

explicitly the treatment of every anticipated circumstance, and it is also impossible *ex ante* to anticipate every possible circumstance. Each of the United States's three claims in the *China–IP* case involves a TRIPS provision that could have been drafted more specifically, with more precision. How can we explain the existing level of incompleteness of the WTO 'contract' with respect to the establishment of minimum standards for enforcement of IPR law? What are the implications of this incompleteness?

Horn, Maggi, and Staiger (referred to as 'HMS')[5] have argued that the WTO can be viewed as an incomplete contract whose form is endogenously determined. They note that the WTO agreement displays both rigidity as well as discretion: while trade instruments are largely bound (and therefore rigid), domestic instruments are largely left to the discretion of governments except that they have to abide by the principle of national treatment. Can this approach be applied to shed some light on the present case?

In Sections 1, 2, and 3, we describe the Panel's analysis in each of the three major issues addressed in this decision. In Section 4, we suggest an incomplete contracts analysis of these issues.

1. Copyright and censorship

As to the first issue of this case, the main question, in summary, is whether China is permitted to deny copyright protection to works that are not permitted to be published in China due to censorship. To some extent, as China argues, it is a moot point: if you lack the right to publish in China, and for reasons of censorship China also prevents others from publishing your work, why would you need copyright protection?[6]

In any event, TRIPS incorporates by reference Article 17 of the Berne Convention, which provides for broad rights for governments to censor. But TRIPS also contains very specific formal obligations to accord copyright protection to works, and to enforce copyright protection, and Article 17 is not structured as an exception to these obligations but as an independent right of states. So, the Panel is called upon to reconcile within TRIPS this set of possibly inconsistent norms. One type of contractual incompleteness is incomplete reconciliation of different values within the WTO treaty.

While this case could be understood as a conflict between the permissive approach (as to state action) to censorship of Article 17 of the Berne Convention and the restrictive approach of human-rights law, the Panel did not mention the

5 Henrik Horn, Giovanni Maggi, and Robert W. Staiger (2010), 'Trade Agreements as Endogenously Incomplete Contracts', 100: 1 *The American Economic Review*, 394–419.

6 On the other hand, perhaps copyright protection would protect authors' rights against unauthorized edited versions, or in circumstances in which the censorship is not as fully enforced as copyright would be. Copyright would often be enforced through private claims, whereas censorship is based on government enforcement.

possible application of human-rights norms to limit the scope of censorship by states.[7] Another type of contractual incompleteness is incomplete reconciliation of different values between one treaty regime and another.

The applicable WTO law – the TRIPS Agreement – incorporates by reference certain provisions of the 1971 Berne Convention on Copyright. The relevant portion of the Berne Convention, Article 5(1), protects the rights of authors 'in countries ... other than their country of origin'. Other provisions of the TRIPS Agreement and the Berne Convention set minimum standards for protection of copyright. This harmonization was intended to enhance the protection of the intellectual property rights of foreign persons, not to enhance either the protection of intellectual property rights of domestic persons, or the freedom of expression of anyone. Of course, as a collateral matter, the protection of rights of foreign authors could enhance freedom of expression for domestic persons, and it might be that harmonization for the benefit of foreign authors would naturally lead to a decision to conform national rules for the benefit of domestic authors.

The facts

This case, brought by the United States, did not involve a particular copyright that China was alleged not to have recognized or protected. Rather, it was an 'as such' case, in which the United States claimed that China's copyright law did not, as such, comply with WTO law. Since this is an 'as such' case, the only relevant 'facts' are those about what the Chinese law provides and how it is applied – there was no concrete case before the Panel to assess.[8] So it was incumbent upon the Panel to make an objective assessment of the relevant Chinese law.

Article 4(1) of the Chinese Copyright Law ('CCL'), according to the agreed translation in this case, reads as follows: 'Works the publication and/or dissemination of which are prohibited by law shall not be protected by this Law.' So, the US concern was that this provision would deny copyright protection to works that, under WTO law, are required to be protected. The United States was concerned both about (i) grant of copyright status, and (ii) enforcement of copyright law to protect the copyrighted work.

While Article 4(1) of the CCL on its face seems clear, there were substantial arguments regarding its interpretation and application. China acknowledged that Article 4(1) of the CCL denies protection to certain works due to their content.[9] The Panel found that Article 4(1) denies the protection of Article 10 of the CCL to

7 See Tomer Broude (2009), 'It's Easily Done: The China-Intellectual Property Rights Enforcement Dispute and the Freedom of Expression', Hebrew University International Law Forum Research Paper No. 22-09, October.

8 The Panel referred to the statement by the Appellate Body in *US – Corrosion-Resistant Steel Sunset Review* (WT/DS244/AB/R, adopted 9 January 2004) to the effect that 'When a measure is challenged "as such", the starting point for an analysis must be the measure on its face. If the meaning and content of the measure are clear on its face, then the consistency of the measure *as such* can be assessed on that basis alone' (para. 168).

9 Panel Report, para. 7.30.

certain works.[10] Article 10 of the CCL sets forth the four moral rights and 13 economic rights of copyright holders. Relying on a letter authored by the Chinese Supreme People's Court in connection with the so-called '*Inside Story*' case, the Panel found that Article 4 of the CCL denies copyright protection when the publication or dissemination of a work is prohibited due to its content.[11] However, China argued that only works affirmatively found to be illegal are unprotected.[12] China argued that denial of copyright protection under Article 4(1) requires determination by a court or the National Copyright Administration of China ('NCAC') during enforcement proceedings.[13]

China's first written submission argued that 'illegal' referred to works that are 'completely unconstitutional or immoral'.[14] The NCAC, in a letter to the Supreme People's Court in connection with the *Inside Story* case, had stated that the 'works the publication and dissemination of which are prohibited by law' in Article 4 of the CCL 'refer only to works whose contents are illegal (reactionary, pornographic, or superstitious contents)'. However, China's content review regulations list a number of additional categories of works that are censored, including those that incite hatred, propagate cults, disrupt public order and undermine social stability, propagate obscenity, gambling, or violence, insult or slander others, or infringe upon legitimate rights and interests of others, jeopardize social ethics, and other contents banned by laws.[15] The Panel understood that the NCAC statement referring to 'reactionary, pornographic, or superstitious contents' was a summary reference to this broader list.[16]

The Panel found that works denied protection are those that have already failed content review, and deleted portions of works edited to satisfy content review.[17] It determined that the United States had not made a prima facie case with respect to works never submitted, works awaiting results, and unedited versions of works for which an edited version had been approved.

Legal analysis

The dispute in this case was about the relationship between (i) the obligation to protect the intellectual property rights of foreign authors, on the one hand, and (ii) the scope of discretion of the obligor state to censor that work, on the other hand. The United States claimed that the discretion of the state to censor could not limit the obligation to protect intellectual property rights of foreign authors. China argued first factually that the relevant Chinese law did not restrict the protection of

10 Ibid., para. 7.50.
11 Ibid., para. 7.52.
12 Ibid., para. 7.55.
13 Ibid., paras. 7.64, 7.66.
14 Ibid., para. 7.78, quoting China's first written submission.
15 Ibid., para. 7.79.
16 Ibid., para. 7.81.
17 Ibid., para. 7.103.

these rights, and second that the right to censor either fully satisfied the obligation to protect these rights, or made it moot.

From a broadly theoretical perspective, this dispute demonstrates the difficulty of limiting any legal rule to its intended purpose, and the impossibility of specifying a particular category of obligation so as to isolate its effects from other areas of law or policy. It also shows the difficulty of anticipating and addressing these types of extensions or collisions. International lawyers refer to this problem as the problem of fragmentation, but it can be understood within a broader set of problems categorized by economists as the problem of incomplete contracts.[18]

The United States claimed that under the CCL, authors of unauthorized works do not enjoy minimum rights granted by the Berne Convention, inconsistently with Article 5(1) of the Berne Convention, which is incorporated by reference in the TRIPS via Article 9.1 of TRIPS. Article 5(1) provides as follows:

> Authors shall enjoy, in respect of works for which they are protected under this Convention, in countries of the Union other than the country of origin, the rights which their respective laws do now or may hereafter grant to their nationals, as well as the rights specially granted by this Convention.

The US claim was predicated on the last clause of this provision – the United States argued that the CCL denies 'rights specially granted by [the Berne] Convention'. The Panel found that China's law violated Article 5(1) of the Berne Convention, as incorporated pursuant to Article 9.1 of TRIPS, as to works that have already failed content review, and also as to deleted portions of works edited to satisfy content review.[19]

China offered a defense based on Art. 17 of the Berne Convention, which also is incorporated in TRIPS via Article 9.1 thereof, and provides as follows:

> The provisions of this Convention cannot in any way affect the right of the Government of each country of the Union to permit, to control, or to prohibit, by legislation or regulation, the circulation, presentation, or exhibition of any work or production in regard to which the competent authority may find it necessary to exercise that right.

China understood this provision as broadly ensuring the sovereignty of the state to censor. China claimed that this broad language 'effectively denies WTO jurisdiction in this area'.[20] Indeed, the reference to the determination of the competent authority may be understood as providing a 'self-judging' right to censor, similar to the portion of Article XXI(b) of GATT that has been understood to be 'self-judging' as to the necessity of security measures. The Panel agreed that Article 17

18 For an effort to do so, see Joel P. Trachtman (1999), 'The Domain of WTO Dispute Resolution', 40 *Harvard International Law Journal*, 333.

19 Panel Report, para. 7.117.

20 Ibid., para. 7.120, quoting China's rebuttal submission, paras. 286–287.

of the Berne Convention allows censorship for public-order purposes.[21] Note that, within an incomplete contracts framework, China may be viewed as arguing either that (i) the contract authorizes the obligor state itself to determine the level of protection, or (ii) that there is no effective obligation in this context.

However, while there is broad authority for censorship, this authority does not, according to the Panel, extend to denying copyright protections. The right reserved for states under Article 17 to control 'circulation, presentation, or exhibition' does not include a number of rights granted to copyright holders by the Berne Convention.[22] Furthermore, according to the Panel, censorship may allow governments to interfere with the *exercise* of copyright rights, but not with the *existence* of these rights.[23] This distinction may have limited practical effect.

Indeed, China argued that copyright protection is a 'legal and material nullity' because economic rights are preempted by censorship.[24] In response, the Panel referred to the fact that Article 3.8 of the WTO Dispute Settlement Understanding provides for prima facie nullification or impairment, and that therefore there is no need to show actual economic effects.[25] China argued that public censorship renders private enforcement unnecessary. Again, the problem with this argument is that there is more to copyright than the right to publish. The Panel found assertions by China that it enforces *censorship* against copyright violations in respect of censored works unsubstantiated. It is procedurally interesting, and perhaps questionable that, in an 'as such' case, where there is no actual instance of application of the allegedly illegal national measure, the defending state is required to show actual instances of measures that would obviate the alleged illegality.

The United States made an additional claim that China also violated its obligations to provide enforcement mechanisms for copyright under Article 41.1 of TRIPS. In response, China argued that its censorial ban on publication is a form of 'effective action' – an 'alternative form of enforcement against infringement'. The Panel rejected this argument, finding that Part III of TRIPS requires a broader minimum set of enforcement procedures.[26] This finding is important as it suggests that the existence of alternative forms of protection against violation of IPRs – such as that provided for by the use of censorship – does not mean that a country need not set up the enforcement procedures called for under TRIPS. Thus, the Panel concluded that 'the Copyright Law, specifically the first sentence of Article 4, is inconsistent with China's obligations under Article 41.1 of the TRIPS Agreement'.[27]

21 Ibid., para. 7.126.
22 Ibid., para. 7.127.
23 Ibid., para. 7.132.
24 Ibid., para. 7.134.
25 Ibid., para. 7.138.
26 Ibid., para. 7.180.
27 Ibid., paras. 7.179–7.181.

2. Disposal of infringing goods

The United States claimed that certain Chinese measures relating to customs procedures on the import or export of infringing goods violated TRIPS Articles 46 and 59. Article 59, addressing 'special requirements relating to border measures', provides that 'competent authorities shall have the authority to order the destruction or disposal of infringing goods in accordance with the principles set out in Article 46'.

The Panel found that Article 59, included in Section 4 of TRIPS, only addresses infringing imports, and not exports.[28] While the US claim referred generally to infringing goods, the United States took no position with respect to the question of whether the first sentence of Article 59 also applies to exports, and the Panel found that it did not. The Panel examined Article 51 of TRIPS, as context for Article 59. Article 51 provides states with an option to provide similar procedures to those contained in Section 4 with respect to *exports*, suggesting that the required procedures do not otherwise apply to exports.

Article 46 provides in relevant part as follows:

> In order to create an effective deterrent to infringement, the judicial authorities shall have the authority to order that goods that they have found to be infringing be, without compensation of any sort, disposed of outside the channels of commerce in such a manner as to avoid any harm caused to the right holder, or, unless this would be contrary to existing constitutional requirements, destroyed.

The United States claimed that the relevant authorities lacked the requisite authority to order the destruction or disposal of infringing goods in accordance with the principles set out in Article 46.

The Chinese regulations at issue provided as follows:

> Where the confiscated goods which infringe on intellectual property rights can be used for the social public welfare undertakings, Customs shall hand such goods over to relevant public welfare bodies for the use in social public welfare undertakings. Where the holder of the intellectual property rights intends to buy them, Customs can assign them to the holder of the intellectual property rights with compensation. Where the confiscated goods infringing on intellectual property rights cannot be used for social public welfare undertakings and the holder of the intellectual property rights has no intention to buy them, Customs can, after eradicating the infringing features, auction them off according to law. Where the infringing features are impossible to eradicate, Customs shall destroy the goods.

The United States criticized these regulations as follows:

> *Donation to social welfare bodies* can be harmful to a right holder and nothing appears to prevent such bodies from selling the infringing goods; *sale to the right holder* harms the right holder in the amount that the right holder pays for the

28 Ibid., para. 7.231.

> infringing goods; and *auction* does not constitute disposal outside the channels of commerce and, absent his consent, may harm the right holder. Where any of these three options is available, the authorities are not authorized to order *destruction* of the infringing goods.[29]

The United States argued that the measures at issue created a 'compulsory scheme' limiting the authority of customs officials to destroy infringing goods, and requiring them to give priority to disposal options that allow the infringing goods to enter commerce or otherwise harm the right holder. The focus of the argument, therefore, was on the extent to which China was entitled to condition or prioritize the action of its authorities. In simple terms, where Article 46 says that the 'competent authorities shall have the authority' to take specified actions, (i) are the competent authorities required to take those actions, and (ii) can any conditions be imposed on the ability of the competent authorities to take those actions?

Facts

This also was a challenge of the Chinese measures 'as such', and therefore no specific case of application of these measures was pleaded by the United States.

However, interestingly, the Panel found that during the period 2005–2007, 'all confiscated infringing imports were either donated to the Red Cross Society of China (0.12 %) or destroyed (0.02 %). The volume of infringing imports that was sold to the right holder, or auctioned, was zero.'[30] The percentages in parentheses are calculated against a base of all goods disposed of or destroyed under China's measures at issue; 99.85 % of infringing goods disposed of or destroyed were destined for exportation.[31] Recall that the Panel found that the first sentence of Article 59 of TRIPS only applies to imports, not exports.

Legal analysis

The Panel found that the terms of Article 59 do not indicate that the authority to order the specified types of remedies must be exclusive.[32] The list of remedies is not exhaustive.[33] National authorities are required to be granted certain authority, but are permitted to be accorded the discretion to make other dispositions. Nor does the requirement for the grant of authority imply a requirement that such authority be exercised.[34] Nor does the requirement for the grant of authority imply that conditions cannot be set for the exercise of that authority.[35] Furthermore, the Panel found that the requirement in Article 46 that authority to order a remedy be

29 Ibid., para. 7.197 (emphasis in original).
30 Ibid., para. 7.232.
31 Ibid., para. 7.228.
32 Ibid., para. 7.240.
33 Ibid., para. 7.239.
34 Ibid., para. 7.236.
35 Ibid., para. 7.246.

exercised 'in such a manner as to avoid any harm caused to the right holder' is applicable only to the remedy of disposal outside the channels of commerce.[36]

However, the United States argued that by establishing a mandatory sequence of possible remedies, the Chinese measure denied Chinese authorities the required authority. The Panel agreed that if a different method of disposition is *mandatory*, then this may preclude authority that is required by Article 59.[37]

As noted above, the Chinese measure provided for three disposal methods besides destruction: (i) donation to social-welfare bodies, (ii) sale to the right holder, and (iii) auction.

As to donation to social-welfare bodies, the United States claimed that this method of disposal might cause harm to rights holders, including by virtue of subsequent sale by the social-welfare bodies. The Panel found that if the social-welfare bodies sell the infringing goods into ordinary commerce, this would not constitute disposal outside the channels of commerce.[38]

The United States argued that the Chinese measures failed to provide discretion to the Chinese customs authorities to determine that transfer to a social-welfare body might harm the right holder, and therefore failed to comply with the principles of Article 46, as required by Article 59 of TRIPS. Interestingly, in this 'as such' case, the Panel relied on the fact that 'nothing in the evidence suggests that any harm has ever been caused, or is likely to be caused, to right holders' reputations due to donation of infringing goods under the measures at issue'.[39] Therefore, the Panel found that the United States failed to demonstrate that the Chinese customs officials lacked the requisite authority to dispose of the goods in such a manner as to avoid harm to the right holder.

As to the risk of sale by social-welfare bodies, China pointed out that the implementing measures for the Chinese regulations provide that the customs authorities shall 'carry out necessary supervision'.[40] The Panel found that the United States failed to show that customs authorities lacked the requisite authority in this context to ensure that the right holder is not harmed.[41]

As to sale to the right holder, the Panel found that, since there are always other options available, and sale to the right holder only takes place with the consent of the right holder, 'there appear to be no circumstances in which sale to the right holder is the only option available and could preclude any authority required by Article 59'.[42]

As to the authority of Chinese customs authorities to auction infringing goods, the Panel observed that this is not a method of disposal that is required to be

36 Ibid., para. 7.244.
37 Ibid., para. 7.252.
38 Ibid., para. 7.279.
39 Ibid., para. 7.297.
40 Ibid., para. 7.299.
41 Ibid., para. 7.324.
42 Ibid., para. 7.326.

authorized under Article 59, but recalled its findings that the remedies specified in Article 59 are not required to be exclusive. Therefore, the authorization for auction is not itself inconsistent with Article 59.[43] The United States argued that the Chinese measures treated auction as a 'compulsory prerequisite' to destruction, thereby precluding authority for destruction, in violation of Article 59. However, the Panel found that the Chinese measures only provided authority for auction, rather than a requirement.[44]

Finally, the Panel found that in regard to counterfeit trademark goods, China's measures allow that the 'simple removal' of the trademark unlawfully affixed is sufficient to permit release of the goods into commerce in more than just exceptional cases, and therefore violates the principle stated in the last sentence of Article 46.

3. Thresholds for criminal procedures and penalties

The United States also argued that China had failed to provide appropriate criminal penalties for certain trademark and copyright infringement, as required by the first sentence of Article 61 of TRIPS, which provides as follows: 'Members shall provide for criminal procedures and penalties to be applied at least in cases of wilful trademark counterfeiting or copyright piracy on a commercial scale.' This was another claim regarding the quality of China's implementation of its TRIPS obligations, in which the United States argued that the Chinese thresholds for criminal penalties were higher than those permitted by Article 61.

At stake again was the degree of discretion retained by member states of the WTO under the TRIPS. China argued that the ostensible principle of *in dubio mitius* applies to protect the discretion of member states in the special field of criminal law.[45] The Panel noted that its interpretative mandate is set by Article 3.2 of the WTO Dispute Settlement Understanding. While recognizing 'the sensitive nature of criminal matters and attendant concerns regarding sovereignty', the Panel stated that 'these concerns may be expected to find reflection in the text and scope of treaty obligations regarding such matters as negotiated by States and other Members'.[46] This seems to be an implicit rejection of the argument for special deference, suggesting that to the extent that member states determine that deference is appropriate, they would express the requirement for deference in the specific terms of the treaty text.

China further argued that Article 61 is too general to create legally enforceable obligations,[47] and further asserted that it retains unfettered discretion under Article 1.1 of TRIPS, which provides that 'Members shall be free to determine the

43 Ibid., para. 7.327.
44 Ibid., para. 7.343.
45 Ibid., para. 7.497.
46 Ibid., para. 7.501 (citation omitted).
47 Ibid., paras. 7.508–7.513.

appropriate method of implementing the provisions of this Agreement within their own legal system and practice.' The Panel rejected this argument.

Facts

Here again, the United States challenged China's measures 'as such'. Thus, in order for China to be in breach of the first sentence of Article 61, in this 'as such' case, the United States would be required to show that there is a class of cases of counterfeiting or piracy that are (i) willful, and (ii) of a commercial scale, for which China does not provide criminal penalties. The United States was unable to bear this burden. In particular, the United States offered much evidence in the form of newspaper articles, and the Panel found this evidence to lack sufficient credibility.[48]

The basis for this US complaint was China's Criminal Law, Judicial Interpretation No. 19, and Judicial Interpretation No. 16 – measures that established specific thresholds that had to be met in order for criminal punishments to be imposed. For example, under Judicial Interpretation No. 19, forging of registered trademarks can result in criminal punishments only when the number of forged units is not less than 20,000 pieces or if the 'illegal business operation volume' is not less than 50,000 Yuan, or if the amount of illegal gains is less than 30,000 Yuan.

Legal analysis

The first interpretative question for the Panel involved the determination of the meaning of 'commercial scale' in the first sentence of Article 61. The United States argued that the Chinese thresholds were quantitatively too low, and that, qualitatively, they failed to take into account certain necessary factors. However, the United States accepted that, in principle, numerical thresholds could be acceptable without more.[49]

The essence of the US complaint here was that the use of such thresholds necessarily implied that any act of trademark counterfeiting or copyright piracy that fell below these thresholds was free from the risk of criminal prosecution. The Panel noted that the US complaint with respect to Article 61 had 'two limbs'. The first limb concerned the level and the method of calculating thresholds wherein the threshold levels were argued to eliminate whole classes of criminal activities from risk of prosecution. The second aspect of the complaint was that the use of specific numerical thresholds basically required law-enforcement officials to 'disregard other indicia of counterfeiting and piracy', such as the presence of unfinished products and fake packaging.

The first limb of the US complaint received careful scrutiny from the Panel, whereas the second limb was dismissed summarily on the grounds that the

48 Ibid., para. 7.629.
49 Ibid., para. 7.495.

United States had not made a prima facie case with respect to other indicia of infringement.

It is worth noting that, in and of itself, the use of thresholds by China can hardly be problematic. After all, enforcement costs for criminal prosecution are nontrivial and, either implicitly or explicitly, thresholds are bound to guide enforcement efforts. Indeed, efficiency requires turning a blind eye to trivial occurrences of counterfeiting and piracy. For example, few would argue that photocopying of a few pages (but exceeding an amount considered 'fair use') from a copyrighted textbook for personal use by a student should be subject to criminal prosecution. But, on the other hand, if a student undertook such illegal copying *on a large enough scale* for selling them to classmates, the question becomes more serious. The use of a threshold as guiding principle cannot be avoided: only if the level of copyright piracy exceeds a certain amount would criminal prosecution appear to make legal and economic sense. Indeed, as the Panel Report notes, the United States conceded as much since it did not object to the use of thresholds per se, although it did argue that the fact that China uses thresholds across a range of commercial crimes ought to have no bearing on the Panel's 'assessment of whether China meets its international obligations under the first sentence of Article 61' of TRIPS.[50]

The first limb of the US complaint brought the concept of 'commercial scale' to the forefront, and the Panel Report devoted much space to it. Indeed, from an economic viewpoint, this is a reasonably important aspect of this case and is therefore worth discussing in some detail.

The Panel noted that TRIPS Article 61(1) creates an *obligation* to provide for criminal procedures for all willful acts of counterfeiting and piracy on a commercial scale. In other words, only those acts of piracy and counterfeiting that occur on a 'commercial scale' must be subject to criminal prosecution. Indeed, the Panel clarified the scope of the obligation created by Article 61(1) by noting that it is subject to four different limitations, an emphasis that is likely to prove important for future TRIPS related disputes at the WTO. First, the Panel noted that:

> the obligation applies to trademarks and copyright *rather than to all intellectual property rights* covered by the TRIPS Agreement. The fourth sentence of Article 61 gives Members the *option to criminalize* other infringements of intellectual property rights, in particular where they are committed wilfully and on a

50 See Gene M. Grossman and Petros C. Mavroidis (2003), 'United States – Section 110(5) of the US Copyright Act, Recourse to Arbitration under Article 25 of the DSU: Would've or Should've? Impaired Benefits Due to Copyright Infringement', 2:2 *World Trade Review*, 233–249. Grossman and Mavroidis note that the optimal enforcement policy is not one that ensures 100% compliance (i.e., zero copyright violations in our context) since the costs of enforcing such perfect compliance would far outweigh the benefits. In other words, below some level of thresholds, it would be globally optimal to let IPR violations occur.

commercial scale. Despite the potential gravity of such infringements, Article 61 creates no obligation to criminalize them.[51]

The fact that the obligation applies only to trademarks and copyrights means that there exists a wedge between the degree of protection available under TRIPS to different types of IPRs, with somewhat stronger protection afforded to copyrights and trademarks relative to other IPRs, such as patents. This obviously raises the question of why this might be so. One potential answer is that, with the exception of pharmaceuticals, violations of patents in the form of illegal imitation of products and technologies are relatively costlier to commit than violations of copyrights and trademarks. If so, the legal deterrent required in order to provide equivalent protection to copyrights and trademarks might be greater.

The second limitation of Article 61 noted by the Panel was that the obligation to provide for criminal procedures 'applies to counterfeiting and piracy rather than to all infringements of trademarks and copyright'.[52] Indeed, the Panel went so far as to note that 'the records of the negotiation of the TRIPS Agreement confirm that the term "infringements of trademarks and copyright" on a commercial scale was considered in the draft provision on criminal procedures but ultimately rejected'. In other words, the negotiators found it useful to single out counterfeiting and piracy as serious enough violations worthy of criminal prosecution, although the terms 'counterfeiting' and 'piracy' are not themselves defined under TRIPS.

The third limitation of the obligation singled out by the Panel was that the use of the word 'willful' implies that infringement ought to have been 'intentional' so that there was no obligation 'to make such penalties available with respect to acts of infringement committed without the requisite intent'. In the Panel's view, this focus on intent reflected the criminal nature of enforcement procedures under consideration.

The fourth limitation, and easily the most important one from an economic perspective, is indicated by the use of the words 'commercial scale'. Indeed, the Panel noted that

> The *principal interpretative point in dispute* is the meaning of the phrase 'on a commercial scale'. This phrase functions in context as a qualifier, indicating that wilful trademark counterfeiting or copyright piracy is included in the scope of the obligation provided that it also satisfies the condition of being 'on a commercial scale'. Accordingly, *certain acts of wilful trademark counterfeiting or copyright piracy are excluded from the scope of the first sentence of Article 61.*[53]

After an extensive review of dictionary definitions, and other uses of the terms in the WTO treaties and in other related contexts, the Panel found that '"commercial scale" is the magnitude or extent of typical or usual commercial activity'.

51 Panel Report, para. 7.518 (emphasis added).
52 Ibid., para. 7.519.
53 Ibid., para. 7.525 (emphasis added).

'Therefore, counterfeiting or piracy "on a commercial scale" refers to counterfeiting or piracy carried on at the magnitude or extent of typical or usual commercial activity with respect to a given product in a given market.'[54]

The Panel emphasized that while 'commercial' is a qualitative concept, 'scale' is a quantitative one, noting that it referred to the size of counterfeiting and piracy. The Panel's position was quite different from that of the United States, which initially insisted that any infringer pursuing financial gain in the market was acting on a commercial scale. The Panel also did not agree to the Chinese position that commercial scale was equivalent to 'industrial scale activity'. Instead, *the Panel noted that what constitutes commercial scale depends upon the product or market in question.* This necessarily implies that the Chinese thresholds for criminal prosecution could indeed be too high for certain markets, but the Panel noted that the United States had not provided any hard evidence demonstrating this was the case for any specific market or product in China.

Indeed, the evidence provided by the United States was rather thin in that it was comprised of a few newspaper and magazine articles. Furthermore, the Panel correctly rejected the use of GDP per capita as a measure of commercial scale, since it is too broad a measure that may or may not be relevant for any specific market. Characterizing the evidence submitted by the United States as anecdotal in nature, the Panel ruled that the United States had failed to establish that China's criminal thresholds were inconsistent with its obligations under TRIPS Article 61(1).

While it is easy to fault the United States for not providing sufficient evidence in support of its position that Chinese thresholds were allowing counterfeiting and piracy to occur on a commercial scale in certain markets, it is worth bearing in mind that violations of 'behind the border' rules and commitments are not easy to prove. The collection of such evidence would require the cooperation of Chinese officials responsible for enforcing the law. If such officials enforce TRIPS fully, there would be little evidence to collect. However, if they do not, they certainly have no incentive to cooperate with the United States and provide incriminating evidence against themselves! Indeed, this basic dilemma might partly explain why the United States submitted so little hard evidence in support of its position, choosing to rely more on explicit statements contained in Chinese laws as opposed to the lack of 'enforcement' of those laws.

A potential interpretation of the Panel's definition of 'commercial scale' is that it is a general 'standard', compliance with which is to be determined by dispute-settlement bodies on a case-by-case basis. This standard may be understood as a kind of delegation to Panels to evaluate facts to determine whether they meet the standard's requirements. The Panel noted that, 'what constitutes a commercial scale for counterfeiting or piracy of a particular product in a particular market will

54 Ibid., para. 7.577.

depend on the magnitude or extent that is typical or usual with respect to such a product in such a market, which may be small or large'.[55] In this way, the use of a standard may be seen as a special type of contractual incompleteness, with a special type of institutional mechanism to provide for *ex post* completion. Thus, the Panel noted that the determination of 'commercial scale' cannot be rigidly fixed *ex ante*.

Given that commercial scale is context specific, whether a certain level of illegal copying is deemed to occur on a commercial scale or not is a judgment regarding an appropriate standard that can be made only with the requisite market data in hand for a given work. Thus, the TRIPS contract is incomplete in that it does not include a specific definition of 'commercial scale'. With the Panel's decision, it can be argued that commercial scale is a context-specific standard that is to be determined by future WTO Panels on a case-by-case basis. What this implies, of course, is that the explicit numerical thresholds specified in Chinese law cannot, in and of themselves, be considered too high or too low. Indeed, as we have argued above, even from an efficiency perspective, the existence and use of such thresholds are not inherently problematic.

4. Economic and policy analysis

China has always guarded its sovereignty vigorously. With respect to the claims in the present case regarding copyright protection for prohibited works, and with respect to the claims regarding criminal penalties, China made explicit arguments that the sovereign right to censor, and to determine its own criminal laws, dominates review under WTO law. With respect to the claims regarding disposal of infringing goods, the core argument was also about retained autonomy after harmonization under TRIPS, and in particular the retained discretion to exercise authority that is required to be made available to national authorities under TRIPS. The TRIPS agreement can be characterized in these three contexts as incomplete in its specification of the relationship between the relevant harmonization obligations, and certain areas of retained national autonomy.

Policy externalities in connection with intellectual property rights

Of course, all international law restricts the autonomy of states, and all international trade law may be understood in terms of management of policy

55 The Panel is quite sensible to say that thresholds have to be specific to the context. So in this sense, the Chinese law's specification of rigid thresholds might be a bit odd: infringing sales of 50,000 Yuan might be astronomical (and therefore on a commercial scale) in one market while trivial in another. Furthermore, it is worth noting that the sales revenue lost by the IPR holder and the sales revenue gained by an infringer need not always correlate perfectly. Only when the sales revenue of infringers exceeds that which the IPR holder *would have earned* if infringement were absent does the use of thresholds based on infringing sales work in favor of the rights holder.

externalities. The TRIPS is no exception. As pointed out by Grossman and Mavroidis:

> In a non-cooperative world regime of intellectual property protection, externalities might come in two main forms. *First*, governments may have a national incentive to discriminate against the intellectual property rights of foreign citizens. This explains the requirements for national treatment that are included in *TRIPs*, and in the *Berne Convention* and *Paris Treaty* before it. *Second*, even with national treatment, national governments may choose to provide insufficient protection for intellectual property relative to the strength of protection that would be globally efficient.[56]

The basic calculus of optimal patent protection in a closed economy has been well understood since Nordhaus, who argued that the optimal policy must balance the marginal benefit of inducing more innovation against the marginal static loss imposed by extending monopoly power.[57] More recently, Grossman and Lai[58] have provided a thorough analysis of optimal patent policies in a two-region (North–South) open-economy context. It turns out that the presence of international trade matters a great deal. More specifically, they highlight two reasons why patent protection will be too weak in an open-economy setting when countries choose policies to maximize their own welfare. As was also noted by Grossman and Mavroidis, these two reasons are as follows:

> *First*, national governments do not take into account in their cost–benefit calculus the benefits that accrue to foreign citizens when protection induces additional investments in intellectual property. *Second*, national governments do not consider as an offset to the static cost of granting patent and copyright protection the monopoly profits that accrue to foreign rights holders. For both these reasons, a global regime of independently chosen patent and copyright policies will provide too little incentive for investment in intellectual property relative to the aggregate reward that would maximize world welfare. In effect, countries have an incentive to free ride on the intellectual property rights protection provided by their trading partners.[59]

This is a public-goods problem. Importantly in the present case, it may be that states differ in the extent to which their citizens are benefited by either investment in intellectual property or monopoly profits of rights holders. Importantly also, the magnitudes of (i) the benefits to foreign citizens from investment induced by protection, and (ii) the monopoly profits that accrue to foreign rights holders, are uncertain.

56 See Gene M. Grossman and Petros C. Mavroidis (2003), 'United States – Section 110(5) of the US Copyright Act, Recourse to Arbitration under Article 25 of the DSU: Would've or Should've? Impaired Benefits Due to Copyright Infringement', 2:2 *World Trade Review*, 233–249 (citations omitted).

57 William D. Nordhaus (1969), *Invention, Growth, and Welfare: A Theoretical Treatment of Technological Change*, Cambridge, MA: MIT Press.

58 Grossman and Lai, 'International Protection of Intellectual Property'.

59 Grossman and Mavroidis, 'United States – Section 110(5) of the US Copyright Act'.

To some extent, intellectual property protection below the globally efficient level would impose its policy externality in a way similar to a tariff, although the market mechanism can be rather different. By their very nature, IPRs bestow market power on rights holders. Therefore, any meaningful discussion of the effects of IPR enforcement (or the lack of it) has to recognize the market power of rights holders. This is important because all countries have the ability to affect the degree to which rights holders can exercise their market power locally by controlling the degree of IPR protection available in their respective markets. In other words, the presence of intellectual property-based market power makes the standard distinction between 'small' and 'large' countries somewhat superfluous.

For example, when faced with an import tariff in a foreign market, a monopolist will typically find it optimal to absorb some of the tariff and not pass it on entirely to foreign consumers. While a tariff directly affects the effective price collected by a monopolist or a right holder, the lack of IPR protection can lower the market price for the right holder's good by creating competition in the local market. Sometimes such competition can occur in the form of a lower-quality version of the original good, while at other times the copied version (such as in software or books) might work just as effectively as the original. Regardless, the competition created by the infringing product necessarily implies a reduction in the price of imports, allowing domestic infringers to profit at the expense of foreign intellectual property owners. Indeed, the competition created by the failure to protect IPRs benefits local consumers in the short run and is one reason many analyses of IPR protection in a global economy find that allowing for *some* level of imitative activities can be in the interest of countries that do not possess significant innovative capacity themselves.[60]

Furthermore, for a state like China in which the government continues to own a significant portion of the means of production, the benefits to domestic infringers would in part be captured by the government. Of the two reasons identified by Grossman and Lai[61] as to why IPR protection will generally be too weak, perhaps the second reason is more applicable in the present context since US consumption of Chinese goods that require IPR protection is not nearly as large as the Chinese consumption of US goods that require such protection. The harm inflicted by its weaker IPR protection on US producers would not be internalized by China through narrow reciprocity, resulting in a level of protection that is too low from a global-welfare perspective.

TRIPS as an incomplete contract

TRIPS requires a certain degree of harmonization of intellectual property rights across member countries of the WTO. It sets minimum standards for various types of IPRs, but, as demonstrated in the case at hand, provides a rather incomplete

60 Elhanan Helpman (1993), 'Innovation, Imitation, and Intellectual Property Rights', 61:6 *Econometrica*, 1247–1280.

61 Grossman and Lai, 'International Protection of Intellectual Property'.

specification[62] of its requirements. TRIPS is internally incomplete, but it is also incomplete in an external sense: the relationship between TRIPS and other (incomplete) law – such as on the one hand the human right of expression,[63] and on the other hand the sovereign right to restrict expression – is incompletely specified. In the present case, there is a moderate degree of consistency between the relevant WTO law and human-rights law,[64] but the relevant WTO law was argued by China to be inconsistent with China's sovereign right to restrict expression. Thus, it might be that the incompleteness of TRIPS allows TRIPS rights to be obviated, or nullified or impaired, by a broad national discretion to censor. Furthermore, this is an asymmetric discretion, (i) since the United States censors less than China does, and (ii) to the extent that the United States has more intellectual property to protect than China does.

HMS examine the GATT, finding that it includes an interesting combination of '*rigidity*, in the sense that contractual obligations are largely insensitive to changes in economic (and political) conditions, and *discretion*, in the sense that governments have substantial leeway in the setting of many policies. They observe that 'there is a *wide array of policy instruments* – border measures and especially "domestic" measures – that should be constrained to keep in check each government's incentives to act opportunistically'.[65]

HMS argue that national discretion is likely to be increased where domestic instruments are less available to manipulate the terms of trade, or where the importing country has less market power in connection with the imported good. Under these circumstances, we would expect less use of domestic measures to manipulate the terms of trade.

Intellectual property protection is one type of 'domestic' measure. Interestingly, intellectual property rights protection is different from normal trade measures, insofar as any state, even a state without conventional market power, can impose terms-of-trade externalities on exporters from other states by declining to protect their intellectual property rights. As noted above, this is because IPRs create market power that gives individual sellers the ability to influence prices, and this ability can be manipulated by importing countries by altering the product market

62 Incompleteness is a concept of limited analytical power, insofar as, in effect, all contracts are *completed* by default by letting the costs remain where they fall *except* to the extent that the contract shifts them. The more appropriate concept to refer to is actually specificity: contracts, and treaties, can be expected to vary in their specificity. States may be expected to establish treaties of varying specificity depending on the costs and benefits of specification. One alternative to specificity is implicit delegation to dispute settlement of decisionmaking authority. This institutional alternative can provide *ex post* contract completion, or specification. Considering the role of precedent, it can also, over time, provide greater *ex ante* specification.

63 See, e.g., Article 19 of the International Covenant on Civil and Political Rights, Article 10 of the European Convention on Human Rights, Article 13 of the American Convention on Human Rights, and Article 9 of the African Charter on Human and Peoples' Rights.

64 See Broude, 'It's Easily Done'.

65 Horn, Maggi, and Staiger (2010), 'Trade Agreements as Endogenously Incomplete Contracts', 394.

conditions faced by such sellers in their markets. This fact seems to accentuate the observation of HMS to the effect that, with rising volumes of trade, and consequent increasing costs of allowing discretion, there is an increasing need to constrain domestic policies.[66]

This accentuation would seem to be especially likely in the case of China, which generally has world-class manufacturing capabilities, allowing it to compete with imported intellectual property-based goods. A state without local manufacturing capabilities would not be able to impose terms-of-trade externalities on exporters from other states since it would lack the means of changing market conditions faced by rights holders. In other words, if local providers are incapable of producing competing goods that violate copyrights or trademarks, the lack of local IPR enforcement would not create any competition for rights holders and therefore would not affect their prices. The criminal penalties 'commercial scale' threshold in the present case may be understood as an example of a state contingency related to the question of sufficient manufacturing capabilities – or at least sufficient manufacturing.

Under significant uncertainty as to the future state of affairs, states would wish to establish complex state-contingent contracts. As noted above, the magnitudes of (i) the benefits to foreign citizens from investment induced by protection, and (ii) the monopoly profits that accrue to foreign rights holders, are uncertain. However, contracting is costly, limiting the ability to specify state-contingencies. On the other hand, by specifying general 'standards', and delegating to dispute-settlement bodies the responsibility to apply these standards, states are able to include complex state-contingency in their contracts, with significantly less variable contracting costs. This is a design feature that is not addressed in HMS, but it was clearly at work in the present case.[67]

Consider a simplified version of the HMS model. Suppose an import creates a local externality (like the consumption externality of HMS) that serves to directly lower the government's objective function. In connection with the first claim in this case, that relevant externality could arise because (the government believes) the consumption of the import – such as a novel or an artistic work critical of centralized power – reduces its ability to govern effectively by fomenting dissent or forces it to allocate resources away from other pursuits toward maintaining 'law and order'. Further, assume that the extent of the externality imposed by the import is uncertain and the transactions costs of contracting over censorship are quite large. This is a reasonable assumption in the present context given the long list of types of works that can be potentially subject to censorship and the fact that countries might (and often do) have very different views regarding

66 Ibid., at 406.

67 Ibid., at 416, referring to Giovanni Maggi and Robert W. Staiger (2008), 'On the Role and Design of Dispute Settlement Procedures in International Trade Agreements', National Bureau of Economic Research Working Paper 14067. See Joel P. Trachtman (1999), 'The Domain of WTO Dispute Resolution', 40 *Harvard International Law Journal*, 333.

censorship: what is deemed immoral or worthy of censorship is likely to vary across nations due to very different cultures, religions, and social norms regarding the freedom of expression.[68]

Under such circumstances, the exclusion from the trade agreement of disciplines on the degree of censorship would be optimal, providing governments with a high degree of discretion regarding its use. Indeed, Article 17 of the Berne Convention, incorporated by reference in the TRIPS, permits censorship without detailing any constraints on how and when it can be used.

Nonviolation claims

An alternative mechanism by which to address uncertainty and contracting costs is through a mechanism such as the remedy for nonviolation nullification or impairment developed in the GATT context. We may evaluate the utility of nonviolation nullification or impairment (NV) doctrine to complete the WTO contract in areas beyond tariff concessions. We note that WTO member states have determined that, for the time being, member states will not exercise the right to bring NV complaints in connection with TRIPS.[69]

As applied more specifically to the *China–IP Rights* case, the question is whether NV should apply to the obligation of intellectual property protection under TRIPS. If NV claims become available under TRIPS, would it be possible for the United States to make an NV claim against China, on the basis that China's censorship, authorized by Article 17 of the Berne Convention, nullifies or impairs US copyright rights under other provisions of TRIPS? Interestingly, in the *Asbestos* case,[70] the Appellate Body suggested that even where a state took advantage of a policy exception – Article XX of GATT – it might be required to compensate the complainant for nullification or impairment of the complainant's rights. Of course, in the context of the present case, the extent of Chinese censorship was well known prior to China's accession to the WTO, and so it would be difficult for the United States to argue formally that it had 'legitimate expectations' of a noncensorship state of affairs, as required by existing doctrine. But would the availability of a general NV claim in TRIPS otherwise be appropriate?

The case for extending TRIPS to include the possibility of NV claims would appear to be no weaker than that for the original inclusion of NV claims in Article XXIII in GATT. After all, the point of this article under GATT is to prevent the erosion of previously granted market access. The question posed by Bagwell and

68 Recall, for example, that Salman Rushdie's novel *The Satanic Verses* met with critical acclaim in the West but was considered offensive enough by Islamic fundamentalists to have earned him a *fatwā* from Ayatollah Khomeini of Iran in 1989. Indeed, the novel was even banned in India, a secular democracy with a large Muslim population.

69 Article 64.2 of TRIPS specified that NV would not be available with respect to TRIPS for the first five years from the date of entry into force of the WTO Agreement. Paragraph 45 of the 2005 Hong Kong Ministerial Declaration seems to have extended the period of nonapplication of NV indefinitely.

70 Appellate Body Report, *European Communities – Measures Affecting Asbestos and Asbestos-Containing Products* (WT/DS135/AB/R, adopted 5 April 2001).

Staiger is of immediate relevance here.[71] They ask: to what extent must nations cede control over domestic policies (that only affect other countries in a pecuniary manner) in order to achieve economic efficiency in an interdependent world? While their analysis is motivated by the interaction between trade policies (such as tariffs) and domestic policies (such as labor and environmental standards), their findings have implications for the present context as well.

One could view the extent of censorship practiced by a country as a domestic standard that has *no direct economic impact* on its trading partners except for its effects on prices of copyrighted works (i.e., the terms of trade). If so, Bagwell and Staiger's analysis implies that tariff negotiations (analogous to negotiations over the degree of IPR protection in our context) would not be sufficient to achieve efficiency, since each government has an incentive to reclaim a portion of the market access granted under such negotiations via manipulating its domestic standard. In the present context, this result means that TRIPS negotiations regarding copyright protection (i.e., market access) could be undone by the strategic use of censorship.

Perhaps more importantly, Bagwell and Staiger go on to show that an NV complaint procedure (such as that provided for under GATT Article XXIII) that either requires compensation for the trade effects of domestic-policy changes or permits the complainant to withdraw an equivalent market concession of its own can play an important role in helping achieve global efficiency by ensuring that previously granted market-access commitments remain intact. As noted above, while the sovereign right to censor may trump market-access commitments made under TRIPS, the availability of an NV complaint can help ensure that governments do not use this right in an opportunistic manner.

5. Conclusion

International trade agreements are generally intended to cause states to internalize policy externalities. The policy externalities that arise from domestic decisions regarding intellectual property protection may deprive foreign intellectual property owners of the monopoly profits that they would otherwise derive from intellectual property protection. In connection with intellectual property protection, even a state that lacks 'traditional' market power on world markets may be able to impose terms-of-trade externalities on other states by reducing its protection of intellectual property below the global optimum. For this reason, and because of the international public-goods aspects of intellectual property, states have incentives to undersupply intellectual property protection. At least in part, TRIPS seems to be an attempt to reduce these policy externalities, since it basically requires all WTO members to adopt the same level of IPR protection as that which prevails in the

71 Kyle Bagwell and Robert W. Staiger (2001), 'Domestic Policies, National Sovereignty, and International Economic Institutions', 116 : 2 *The Quarterly Journal of Economics*, 519–562.

industrialized world. As noted earlier, the literature has shown that the global harmonization of IPRs is neither necessary nor sufficient to achieve efficiency, even though individual nations have an incentive to undersupply IPR protection.

All contracts, and all international treaties, are incomplete. This case involves some good examples of treaty incompleteness. Incompleteness can arise from circumstances of uncertainty regarding the possible tradeoffs, and the optimal balance, between different goals, including state autonomy in censorship on the one hand and internalizing policy externalities in intellectual property protection on the other. Following HMS, we analyze the possibility that it might be efficient to allow states broad discretion over censorship. Alternatively, in connection with the requirement for criminal penalties, incompleteness can arise from uncertainty regarding the particular industry structure that might be involved, and what would constitute production of 'commercial scale' for that industry.

We have also questioned the rationale for the limitation on the use of NV complaints in connection with the TRIPS, since NV complaints may be used to reduce the possibility that states will use discretion, such as that granted with respect to censorship, in a manner that is inconsistent with the rationale for that discretion so as to defect from the general commitment to provide copyright or other intellectual property rights.

Comment

China – Measures Affecting the Protection and Enforcement of Intellectual Property Rights

ROBERT HOWSE
New York University School of Law

The fundamental premise of Saggi's and Trachtman's analysis of this dispute is that the WTO TRIPs agreement should be viewed as an 'incomplete contract'. Should multilateral treaties be analogized to incomplete contracts? What are implications of doing so for the proper approach to treaty interpretation? We have to begin with the theory of incomplete contracts, which is not really explained in Saggi's and Trachtman's report. As developed by Hart and Moore (1988), the notion of 'incomplete contracts' represents the intuition that, while a large number of possible future states of the world may affect the value and cost of performance of a contract, the transaction costs of the parties bargaining *ex ante* about the legal consequences of all of these possible eventualities are prohibitive. Therefore, taking account of transaction costs, we will expect 'incomplete contracts' to be efficient; these contracts generally will either provide various mechanisms for renegotiation triggered by the occurrence of certain future events or allow for the application by an adjudicator or arbitrator of default or background rules to 'complete' the contractual bargaining in the face of such eventualities. Equally important to contract theory is the problem of moral hazard: a party to a contract may have incentives to engage in behavior *ex post* the bargain that increases the riskiness of the contract to the other party. A classic example is insurance contracts. Effective *ex ante* mechanisms for controlling moral hazard often entail effective means of monitoring the behavior of contracting parties *ex post*. Although the concept of 'incomplete contract' and that of moral hazard have in common that both are concerned with the transaction costs of addressing future events that can affect the cost and value of contractual performance, moral hazard deals specifically with what might be called a form of opportunistic behavior by one of the parties. Unfortunately, these concepts are often (implicitly) blurred in the analysis of Saggi and Trachtman, as I shall go on to explain.

I agree with those trade economists and lawyer economists who find both these concepts useful for understanding specific features of bargaining in the GATT/WTO and specific features of the covered Agreements. For example, 'incomplete contract' is a powerful concept for understanding those provisions of the GATT that provide a structure for renegotiation of a Member's tariff concessions (GATT Article XXVIII) and of the GATS that address renegotiation of a Member's specific commitments (GATS Article XXI). Contract theory makes sense of these provisions, which could actually allow for renegotiation upwards of particular trade barriers (with compensation), whereas a constitutionalist view of the WTO as a regime progressively moving towards complete removal of all such barriers could not easily do so. Along similar lines, the notion of moral hazard is powerful in understanding the concept of nonviolation nullification and impairment. This entails that a Member that has acted in such a way as to undermine the expected benefit to another Member of a specific negotiated concession provide compensation to the latter.

But it does not follow that because these ideas of contract theory (which are really an application of broader conceptions of information and transactions costs, useful in bargaining contexts far removed from contractual bargaining between private parties, such as political bargaining) necessarily explain or illuminate *all* kinds of WTO obligations, and, much less, that because these insights are, as a matter of intellectual history, closely connected to the emergence of contract theory in law and economics, the canons of treaty construction should be replaced by canons of contract interpretation. What conceptual tools are appropriate with respect to particular provisions, and how the resulting understanding of 'object and purpose' relates to the other relevant canons in Vienna Convention 31 and 32 are separate, if obviously interconnected, questions.

Do incomplete contract (and/or moral hazard) properly illuminate the functionality of the provisions of TRIPs at issue in the dispute?

The specific feature common to some of the provisions in TRIPs in question that cause the authors to have recourse to the incomplete-contract concept is that these provisions are 'incomplete' in the sense that they articulate an international legal obligation while not fully specifying what exact domestic measures will satisfy that obligation. I do not believe that the incomplete-contract concept is necessarily the most powerful analytical tool for understanding this kind of structure. There are simply more plausible explanations than the transaction costs of bargaining in light of uncertainty about many possible future states of the world. I begin with a very elementary legal observation: as a matter of background norms of state responsibility, states are generally understood to be able to choose the domestic instrumentalities that will implement a given international legal obligation. This background norm may be associated with Westphalian assumptions of the kind we see in play in the *Lotus* case[1] and in the *in dubito mitius* canon of interpretation. International law is understood as something less hegemonic and more compatible with Westphalian understandings of sovereignty than for instance would be the law of a world state or world federation. An alternative way of formulating this norm, in terms of democracy and related political values rather than Westphalian sovereignty, has been articulated by Kalypso Nicolaidis and myself as global subsidiarity (Howse and Nicolaidis, 2003).

But there are also various other conceptual tools that would illuminate a structure of obligation that leaves choices about implementation to the state. One is the notion, common to many regulatory approaches influenced by law and economics, that it is more efficient to specify regulatory requirements in terms of performance or results rather than specific means or modalities. This is based in part on the notion that the most efficient means of achieving a given regulatory result will vary from one regulatory entity to another and also over time. Indeed, this concept even finds explicit expression in one WTO treaty, the TBT (Technical Barriers to Trade) Agreements, which provides that, in general, WTO Members should express their domestic regulatory requirements in terms of performance. A further possible conceptual framework would derive from the recognition that the TRIPs Agreement represents a highly contested and controversial limit on regulatory diversity. The resulting text embodies a balance of competing values and interests. One legal instrumentality for expressing or protecting this balance is to entrench a large measure of deference to the choices of states as to the modalities for implementing TRIPs obligations, which are understood as carefully bargained and bounded constraints on regulatory diversity. This is broadly consistent with the views of many economists that regulatory diversity is efficient in the case of intellectual property protection, and that while policy externalities of the kind identified by Saggi and Trachtman might exist, harmonization may entail considerable costs to domestic welfare, thus suggesting the need to manage complex welfare trade-offs between harmonization and regulatory diversity (see Trebilcock and Howse, 1998: 5). These various possibilities are more or less implicitly or obscurely alluded to by Saggi and Trachtman, but there is a certain lack of conceptual clarity or a *glissage* that occurs by assimilating them to the incomplete-contract concept, just because (it seems) there is *some* kind of incompleteness.

Now I want to turn to the interaction of these various possible analytics, for understanding the objective and purpose, or functionality, of the kind of legal provisions, with the other interpretative elements in Vienna Convention 31. These include the preamble of the treaty and other provisions of it and other relevant rules of international law applicable between the parties.

Article I of TRIPS is fundamental to understanding the nature and scope of the legal obligations it creates. It provides an essential part of the 'context' within the meaning of Vienna Convention 31. Article I provides: 'Members shall give effect

1 The Case of the S.S. 'Lotus,' Judgment 9, 1927, PCIJ, Series A, No. 10, p. 19.

to the provisions of this Agreement. Members may, but shall not be obliged to, implement in their law more extensive protection than is required by this Agreement, provided that such protection does not contravene the provisions of this Agreement. Members shall be free to determine the appropriate method of implementing the provisions of this Agreement within their own legal system and practice.' It seems very clear from this provision that the parties did not intend the dispute-settlement organs to complete the contract in the sense of extending intellectual property protection beyond what is manifestly required on the face of the Agreement, regardless of how any future states of the world might affect value or the cost of the performance of the terms of the 'contract'. Instead, the notion of Members being free to determine the method of implementation is consistent with the alternative analytic frames discussed above. In sum, what Saggi and Trachtman term 'incompleteness' does not represent a *grant* of discretion to the dispute-settlement organs, but *retention* of sovereignty by Members. Of course, as the Appellate Body emphasized in the early *India–Patents* ruling,[2] the required deference to Members' regulatory choices is not by any means absolute: those choices must ensure the requisite state responsibility for fulfilling the obligation. But in determining this, *the dispute-settlement organs should start from the assumption that there may be many different and permissible domestic legislative, judicial, and regulatory options for doing so*. Above all, and especially where the defending state is a developing one such as China with a very different legal system in general, the dispute-settlement organs must avoid judging the domestic implementation choices against the implicit norm of domestic intellectual property laws in for instance the United States or the European Union.

Contrary to what Saggi and Trachtman suggest, the Panel was not so much implicitly rejecting the 'argument for *special* deference' (emphasis added) as indicating in the case of TRIPs that the required deference is to be found in the language and structure of the obligations themselves. Since the protection of regulatory diversity is built into the obligations, as is explained or affirmed by Article I, the Panel would not need to refer to some nontextual canon or principle related to deference such as *in dubio mitius* (as did the AB in the first *Hormones*[3] ruling, applying the Precautionary Principle as an interpretative canon, although not as a rule of customary law or a general principle of international law).

Thus, when faced with a provision of TRIPs requiring that judicial authorities have the legal capacity to order the destruction or disposal outside the channels of commerce of copyright-infringing goods so as to avoid harm to the rights holder, the Panel correctly held that this provision in no way limited the discretion of

2 Appellate Body Report, *India – Patent Protection for Pharmaceutical and Agricultural Chemical Products*, WT/DS50/AB/R, adopted 16 January 1998, DSR 1998:I, 9.

3 Appellate Body Report, *United States – Continued Suspension of Obligations in the EC – Hormones Dispute*, DS320, adopted 14 November 2008.

member-state authorities to provide remedies other than destruction, or to choose those other remedies in any given case. When the Panel was faced with interpreting the provision of TRIPs calling for criminal procedures and penalties in 'cases of willful trademark counterfeiting or copyright piracy on a commercial scale', it found that the Chinese authorities had the discretion to establish a minimum quantitative threshold below which no prosecutions would be required. In other words, the expression 'commercial scale' was for the domestic authorities to interpret. However, this interpretative discretion was not unbounded; any such threshold would need to take account of the product or market in question. Rejecting the US claim of a violation, the Panel noted the United States had not offered any evidence that the thresholds chosen failed appropriately to take into account the nature of the product or market. Saggi and Trachtman speculate that 'With the Panel's decision, it can be argued that commercial scale is a context-specific standard that is to be determined by future WTO Panels on a case-by-case basis.' While consistent with their 'complete the contract' approach, this reading is I believe erroneous. Instead, along the lines of Article I of TRIPs, the Panel is interpreting the relevant provision of the TRIPs Agreement as giving the WTO Member in question discretion to determine the kind of legal threshold that expresses the notion of commercial scale, provided that the Member takes into account, in an appropriate way, the nature of the product and the market. Since the Panel does not have institutional competence to second-guess on its own such determinations, it will give the regulating Member the benefit of the doubt unless the complaining Member provides convincing evidence that the threshold actually chosen does *not* reflect the nature of the product and the market.

Censorship, human rights, and TRIPs

In their discussion of censorship, human rights, and TRIPs, the authors refer to a kind of 'incompleteness' that is even more removed from the 'incomplete contract' concept than the examples discussed above. They invoke a notion of 'external' incompleteness to describe the situation where more than one set of international legal norms or more than one international legal regime governs some particular situation or particular behavior of a state. Before the Panel, China defended its denial of copyright protection to prohibited products on the grounds that the provisions of the Berne Union, as incorporated into TRIPs, gave it broad authority to prohibit copyrighted material on public-order grounds. In order properly to adjudicate the United States' claim of a failure to extend copyright protection to prohibited works and China's defense, was it necessary to consider the conformity of China's censorship laws and practices with its international human rights obligations? The answer is quite simply, no. The Panel rightly held that Article 17 of the Berne Convention merely indicated that states could interfere with the *exercise* of intellectual property rights through 'control' or 'prohibition' of the 'circulation, presentation, or exhibition' of a work on their territory. This is *not* the same thing as being permitted to deny copyright protection as such. Could Article 17 really be used for instance to justify failing to prosecute piracy of domestically prohibited works for purposes of *export*? Having found that Article 17 of the Berne Convention as such did not provide a defense to the denial of copyright protection under TRIPs, the Panel simply did not need to reach the issue of the interaction of Article 17 and international human rights norms in relation to China's censorship policies. Matters might have been different had the Panel found that Article 17 was an applicable defense. In that case, the Panel might well have had to consider how Article 17, as incorporated into TRIPs, had been affected by the evolution of international human rights law. In this respect, I think it is somewhat misleading for the authors to characterize Article 17 as 'permissive' towards censorship. Article 17 merely states that *copyright* is not an inherent protection against certain forms of censorship. It is not clear that control or prohibition of circulation, presentation, or exhibition would allow a state to eviscerate, for instance, the moral rights in the Berne Convention (these are not incorporated into TRIPs) through bowdlerizing or sanitizing the work in question or changing its content in a manner contrary to moral rights. Since Article 17 was drafted prior to the evolution of international human rights law, it could not be plausibly interpreted as a limitation on, or contracting out of, customary norms of human rights. (As far as treaty law is concerned, China has signed but not ratified the International Covenant on Civil and Political Rights.) While I have argued that WTO dispute-settlement organs should *interpret* WTO law in a manner informed by and consistent with international human rights law (Howse and Teitel, 2006), one should be mindful of the Appellate Body's caution in *Mexico–Soft Drinks*[4] that the dispute-settlement system of the WTO is not designed for the *determination* or *enforcement* of legal norms in other international regimes. In the dispute at issue, the Panel was able adequately to *interpret* the provisions of the WTO law at issue without recourse to international human rights norms, as these norms would not affect the essential issue of whether Article 17 is an applicable defense to the denial of copyright protection as such (rather than *what other kinds of acts* might be rendered permissible by Article 17). Of course, in no case could a Panel authorize activity in contravention of *jus cogens*,[5] but freedom of expression or information is not, in the current state of the law, *jus cogens*.

4 Appellate Body Report, *Mexico – Tax Measures on Soft Drinks and Other Beverages*, WT/DS308/AB/R, adopted 24 March 2006, DSR 2006:I, 3.

5 See Case Concerning Oil Platforms (*Islamic Republic of Iran* v. *United States of America*), merits [2003] ICJ Rep 161.

References

Hart, Oliver and John Moore (1988), 'Incomplete Contracts and Renegotiation', *Econometrica*, **56**(4): 755–785.

Howse, Robert and Kalypso Nicolaidis (2003), 'Enhancing WTO Legitimacy: Constitutionalization or Global Subsidiarity?', in Marco Verweij and Tim Josling (eds.), *Deliberately Democratizing Multilateral Organization*, special issue of *Governance*, **16**(1).

Howse, Robert and Ruti Teitel (2006), 'Beyond the Divide: The Covenant on Economic, Social and Cultural Rights and the World Trade Organization', Occasional Paper No. 30, Friedrich Ebert Stiftung, Geneva.

Trebilcock, Michael and Robert Howse (1998), 'Trade Liberalization and Regulatory Diversity: Reconciling Competitive Markets with Competitive Politics', *European Journal of Law and Economics*, **6**, 5.

Trading Cultures: Appellate Body Report on *China–Audiovisuals*

(WT/DS363/AB/R, adopted 19 January 2010)

PAOLA CONCONI

Université Libre de Bruxelles (ECARES) and CEPR

JOOST PAUWELYN

Graduate Institute of International and Development Studies, Geneva

Abstract: In *China–Audiovisuals*, a series of Chinese restrictions on the importation and distribution of certain 'cultural' or 'content' goods and services were found to violate GATT, GATS, and China's Accession Protocol. This paper reviews the definition of what is a 'good' (is a 'film' a good or a service?) and the extent to which GATT Article XX exceptions can justify violations under WTO instruments other than the GATT itself. We argue that trade volumes are unlikely to significantly rise as a result of this ruling as it does not affect China's right to keep out foreign films and publications if China finds them objectionable. However, foreign producers of audiovisuals can now gain potentially large economic rents, by being able to export and distribute their products into the Chinese market. Finally, we discuss the issue of the protection of cultural goods and review the recent literature on trade and culture that has put forward economic arguments to justify, under some conditions, the protection of cultural goods.

Summary of the dispute

China–Audiovisuals[1] is a complex and broad-based dispute filed by the United States in April 2007 against a series of Chinese restrictions on the importation and distribution of certain 'cultural' or 'content' goods and services: (i) reading materials such as books, periodicals, and electronic publications; (ii) audiovisual home-entertainment products such as DVDs; (iii) sound recordings; and (iv) films for theatrical release. More particularly, the dispute concerns problems faced by the US 'content' industry trying to obtain the right to import and distribute within China on a nondiscriminatory basis. This dispute is closely related to the one on

1 Appellate Body Report, *China – Measures Affecting Trading Rights and Distribution Services for Certain Publications and Audiovisual Entertainment Products*, WT/DS363/AB/R, adopted 19 January 2010.

China–IP Rights[2] where the issue at stake was the protection and enforcement within China of intellectual property rights, in particular copyrights, linked to cultural goods and services. Indeed, the United States argued that the fact that China was controlling which companies could import audiovisual items and which ones could distribute these items raised prices and opened up the market to piracy and counterfeits.

As a preliminary matter, the Panel found that certain measures and products complained about fell outside its terms of reference. The Chinese measures it did examine, however, were almost all (15 out of 17 measures[3]) found to violate one or more of the following WTO commitments: (i) China's commitment to grant the right to trade (in particular, import) to all enterprises in China including foreign-invested enterprises and individuals, under China's Protocol of Accession; (ii) GATS market-access and national-treatment obligations towards foreign (US) suppliers of distribution services operating within China; and (iii) GATT national treatment in respect of measures that affect the distribution of imported reading materials.

The Panel Report was circulated in August 2009. Most Panel findings were not appealed. China only appealed three elements. First, it appealed the Panel's finding that China's trading-rights commitments apply to Chinese measures concerning *films for theatrical release* and *unfinished audiovisual products*, on the ground that, according to China, these measures regulate 'services' and content, not 'goods'. Second, China appealed the Panel's analysis and conclusion under GATT Article XX(a) (public morals), an exception that China had unsuccessfully invoked to justify violations of its Accession Protocol with reference to China's censorship regime allegedly imposed to protect public morals against sensitive cultural imports.[4] Third, China appealed the Panel's finding that '*Sound recording distribution services*' in China's GATS Schedule cover the electronic distribution of sound recordings in nonphysical form, notably over the Internet. The Appellate Body upheld all of the Panel's conclusions and confirmed that China had violated its Protocol of Accession in a way that cannot be justified under GATT Article XX(a). The Appellate Body also confirmed the Panel's findings of GATS violation. The Panel's findings of violation under GATT had not been appealed. Both the Panel and the Appellate Body Reports were adopted by the WTO Dispute Settlement Body on 19 January 2010.

In what follows, we discuss what we believe to be the most interesting legal and economic issues raised by the Appellate Body's ruling on

2 Panel Report, *China – Measures Affecting the Protection and Enforcement of Intellectual Property Rights*, WT/DS362/R, adopted 20 March 2009.

3 Appellate Body Report, *China–Audiovisuals*, paras. 129–130.

4 In this respect, the United States also filed an appeal against an intermediate finding by the Panel that one of China's restrictions (the so-called 'State plan requirement') can be seen as 'necessary' to protect public morals in China (even if the Panel ultimately found that this was not the case).

China–Audiovisuals.[5] The legal analysis is divided in two parts. First, we review the Appellate Body's approach to, and definition of, what is a 'good' (is a 'film' a good or a service?). Second, we discuss the extent to which GATT Article XX exceptions can justify violations under WTO agreements or instruments other than the GATT itself. In this case, China was allowed to invoke 'public morals' under GATT Article XX(a) to justify violations under its Protocol of Accession. In future cases, the issue may well be whether a health or environmental regulation, anti-dumping duty, safeguard, or subsidy that violates the SPS, TBT, AD, SG, or SCM agreement can be justified under GATT Article XX (or XXIV) exceptions.

The economic analysis will also be divided in two parts. First, we review the economic implications of the Appellate Body's ruling in *China–Audiovisuals*. We argue that trade volumes are unlikely to significantly rise as a result of this ruling as it does not affect China's right to keep out foreign films and publications if China finds them objectionable. However, foreign producers of audiovisuals can now gain potentially large economic rents, by being able to export and distribute their products into the Chinese market. Second, we discuss the issue of the protection of cultural goods. In *China–Audiovisuals*, China argued that reading materials and finished audiovisual products are so-called 'cultural goods' and as such have a potentially serious negative impact on public morals. However, this dispute left open the question of whether the protection of cultural goods can or should actually be justified under GATT/WTO rules. We briefly review the recent literature on trade and culture, which has put forward economic arguments to justify, under some conditions, the protection of cultural goods.

1. Legal analysis

1.1 *Is a film a 'good' or a 'service'?*

In *China–Audiovisuals*, the United States invoked market-access and trading rights under the GATT, GATS, and China's Accession Protocol. It complained that China's distribution system discriminates imports as compared to domestic, Chinese goods or service suppliers in violation of national treatment, a cornerstone of both GATT and GATS agreements.[6]

Faced with such choice between GATT and GATS in the context of today's sophisticated 'content' industry that often has goods-and-services components (a newspaper is made of paper, but its content is a bundle of services that are by far the most important added value; moreover, newspapers can now also be read and traded online), a question that arises is whether a product is a 'good' or a 'service'

5 Parts of this contribution draw upon Pauwelyn (2010: 119), which includes a more expansive discussion of the good versus service distinction with reference also to EU and US law.

6 See Broude and Hestermeyer (2009).

and whether a particular measure is subject to the GATT as a restriction on trade in goods or the GATS as a restriction on trade in services, or both. This classification may be rather academic in a legal system (such as the EU) where free movement of goods and free movement of services are by now subject to more or less the same commitments. In other situations, in contrast, the goods and the services regimes may impose radically different obligations. In such cases, drawing the line between goods and services can make or break a dispute. This is the situation in the WTO, where GATT is over 60 years old with a complete ban on all quantitative restrictions and discriminatory regulations unless justified under limited exceptions (in particular GATT Article XX). The GATS, in contrast, is only 15 years old and composed mainly of country-specific commitments carefully bound (or not bound, depending on the services sector in question) so that national-treatment or market-access obligations only exist if and to the extent that a particular member made a specific commitment for the particular sector in question. These obligations are subject to general exceptions, particularly, in GATS Article XIV, which is similar to GATT Article XX. A similarly divergent regulation of goods as opposed to services can be found in anti-dumping rules. Such rules permit the imposition of anti-dumping duties on imports of goods below fair or normal value. In cases where an import is classified as a 'service' (instead of a 'good') no anti-dumping duties can be imposed.[7]

So how does the WTO proceed in its application of the GATT and/or the GATS in situations of doubt? Firstly, and most importantly, nowhere does GATT define what a 'good' or 'product' is. GATS, in turn, does not define the concept of a 'service' either. Instead, the GATT Secretariat issued an indicative list of service activities or sectors that most WTO members have used as a template when making GATS commitments.[8] GATS Article I:1 does, however, state broadly that it applies to any measure by any WTO member 'affecting' trade in services. Secondly, and largely as a consequence, in *EC–Bananas* the Appellate Body found that the GATT and the GATS are *not* mutually exclusive so that one and the same measure can be subject to both GATT and GATS.[9] In *Canada–Periodicals*, for example, the Appellate Body found that 'a periodical is a good comprised of two components: editorial content and advertising content. Both components can be viewed as having services attributes, but they combine to form a physical product – the periodical itself'.[10] In *US–Lumber CVDs Final*, the Appellate Body found that standing timber, even before it is harvested (that is, trees attached to the land but severable from it), is a 'good' even if it is not tradable as

7 The distinction between goods and services in the anti-dumping context was at the center of a recent US Supreme Court opinion, *United States* v. *Eurodif SA*, 129 S. Ct. 878 (2009).

8 *Services Sectoral Classification List*, GATT Document, MTN.GNS/W/120, 10 July 1991.

9 Appellate Body Report, *European Communities – Regime for the Importation, Sale and Distribution of Bananas*, WT/DS27/AB/R (DSR 1997:II, 591), para. 221.

10 Appellate Body Report, *Canada – Certain Measures Concerning Periodicals*, WT/DS31/AB/R (DSR 1997:I, 449), p. 17.

such.[11] The Appellate Body rejected Canada's argument that the term 'goods' must be read as limited to 'tradable items with an actual or potential tariff classification'[12] but added that important *caveat* that '"[g]oods" in ... the *SCM Agreement* and "products" in ... the GATT 1994 are different words that need not necessarily bear the same meanings in the different contexts in which they are used'.[13]

That set the stage for a jurisprudence that focuses on the *measure* in question and whether it has an *effect* or *impact* on trade in goods and/or services, with *physical* or *material* nature being a decisive criterion for something to be a good.

China–Audiovisuals follows this line. In China, only certain state-approved entities may engage in the business of importing films into China. These entities enter into a licensing or distribution agreement with a foreign-film producer or licensor and, after content review, import certain delivery materials including hard-copy cinematographic films. In paragraph 5.1 of its Accession Protocol, however, China committed to phase out state trading three years after its accession (with limited exceptions) and that, after three years, 'all enterprises in China shall have the right to trade in all goods throughout the customs territory of China'. The Protocol defines the right to trade as 'the right to import and export goods'. According to China, this right to trade in goods does not apply to measures pertaining to films for theatrical release since such measures 'do not regulate the importation of goods, but, rather, regulate the content of films and the services associated with the importation of such content'.[14] For China, 'films for theatrical release are not goods because they are exploited through a series of services; because the commercial value of films for theatrical release lies in the revenue generated by these services; and because the delivery materials containing the content of films are mere accessories of such services and have no commercial value of their own'.[15]

In response, the United States argued that 'the vast majority of goods are commercially exploited through a series of associated services and that China's argument would transform virtually all goods into services'.[16] The United States added that 'Articles III:10 and IV of the GATT 1994, which deal with cinematographic films, confirm that films for theatrical release are goods'.[17] The United States also referred to the international classification of products under the Harmonized Commodity Description and Coding System of the World Customs

11 Appellate Body Report, *United States – Final Countervailing Duty Determination with Respect to Certain Softwood Lumber from Canada*, WT/DS257/AB/R (DSR 2004:II, 571), para. 67.

12 Ibid., para. 61.

13 Ibid., para. 63.

14 Appellate Body Report, *China–Audiovisuals*, para. 169.

15 Ibid., para. 173.

16 Ibid.

17 Ibid.

Organization and China's WTO Schedule of Concession for goods, both of which contain a heading for 'cinematographic film' with embedded content.

In line with the abovementioned focus on *measures* (and their effect) rather than *products as such* (is a film a good or a service?), the Appellate Body focused on the Chinese regulation setting out the restriction, including a detailed analysis of the term '*Dian Ying*' used in that regulation and its English translation ('motion picture'). The Appellate Body concluded that 'where the content of a film is carried by physical delivery materials, [the Chinese restriction] will *inevitably* regulate who may import goods for the plain reason that the content of a film is expressed through, and embedded in, a physical good'.[18] For the Appellate Body, this effect on goods (i.e. the physical film reel that crosses the border) is '*inevitable*, rather than "*incidental*"' and 'the mere fact that the import transaction involving hard-copy cinematographic films may not be the "essential feature" of the exploitation of the relevant film does not preclude the application of China's trading-rights commitments to the *Film Regulation*'.[19] The Appellate Body reached the same conclusion in respect of restrictions on unfinished audiovisual products or master copies to be used to publish and manufacture copies for sale in China.[20]

Several lessons can be drawn from this ruling. First, the Appellate Body confirms that a given product can have both a goods and a services component and that a given measure can be subject to both GATT and GATS where it 'affects' both goods and services. The two universes are not mutually exclusive. Crucially, the Appellate Body did *not* find that a film 'is' a good, but rather that it has a good's 'component' or 'includes' a good, to the extent the film is carried on a film reel or other physical material and that, as a result, a regulation which affects such film 'inevitably' affects a good. This means that regulators, when enacting a rule, must be aware that the new rule may have to comply with both GATT and GATS. This approach cumulates WTO obligations and may not make it easier to figure out which GATT or GATS discipline applies. The safest move may then be to comply with the strictest discipline be it under GATT or GATS. For complainants, including countries that want to challenge China's censorship regime, this approach is positive news: they do not have to limit themselves to GATT or GATS claims; they can submit and prevail under both. For regulating countries, such as China, the cumulative application of GATT and GATS is, obviously, less appealing.

Second, as in *Canada–Periodicals*, the Appellate Body's definition of a good focuses on the tangible or material nature of the product, i.e. the film reel or hard-copy films, and this irrespective of whether this tangible component represents only a minor fraction of the value or economic reality of the product. This, in

18 Ibid., para. 188.
19 Ibid., para. 196.
20 Ibid., para. 204.

turn, raises two questions. First, will the Appellate Body automatically find a good whenever it sees tangible material? Is, for example, a paper lottery ticket automatically a good – so that cross-border restrictions on lottery activities affect trade in goods? – or merely an element in the supply of (lottery) services, making the entire activity subject only to GATS? What about coins or paper money in the context, for example, of allegations of currency undervaluation or subsidization?[21] Would the Appellate Body consider paper money to be a 'good' provided by the government ('financial contribution') or rather as falling under the free movement of capital and, therefore, neither subject to GATT/SCM nor GATS rules on free movement of goods or services? What about paper carbon-emission allowances or permits which, under EU law, companies can trade and must submit when emitting CO2? Are these goods or services, or neither?[22]

A second question that arises from the Appellate Body's focus on tangible material is this: does it suffice for a traded product to be intangible for that product to be regarded only as a service?[23] For example, if US film producers would stop physically shipping film reels or master copies to China for reproduction within China, and rather send the material electronically over the Internet, would that automatically imply that we can no longer talk of trade in goods and trading rights, and must examine the transaction exclusively under GATS (say, as a cross-border supply of 'entertainment services')? If so, China would then no longer violate its Accession Protocol (trading rights only apply in respect of goods) and the United States would have to rely exclusively on, for example, Chinese GATS commitments in entertainment or distribution services (which may well be below China's commitments in GATT). Should the mere method of delivery (tangible or over the Internet) bring about this drastic change in legal regime? If so, the GATT could be said to be technologically biased (unlike the GATS which, as discussed below, is technologically neutral). Should the law follow economic reality (in business terms little changes when sending the film on a reel or over the Internet, assuming the quality is the same), or should the law stick to physics (tangible is GATT, intangible is GATS)? Making tangibility a necessary condition for something to be a good may also mean that, for example, in the trade-in-energy

21 An unadopted GATT Panel found that gold coins are 'products' and that Canada violated national treatment by imposing a retail tax on the South African Krugerrand which it was not imposing on the Canadian Maple Leaf (Panel on *Canada – Measures Affecting the Sale of Gold Coins*, L/5863, 1985).

22 Note, in this respect, that the Appellate Body in *Canada–Lumber CVDs Final*, para. 66, found that standing timber is a 'good' even if 'specific trees' are not 'identified' in stumpage contracts: 'we do not see the relevance, for an assessment of whether trees are goods, of the fact that each individual tree within the specified area of land covered by a stumpage contract may not be identified at the time the contract is made ... We see no reason why disciplines on subsidies that regulate the provision of non-monetary resources should focus on identifiable physical objects and not on tangible, but fungible, input material' (underlining added).

23 Note, in this respect, that the Appellate Body in *Canada–Lumber CVDs Final*, para. 59, found that 'the ordinary meaning of the term "goods" [in the SCM Agreement] ... *includes* items that are tangible and capable of being possessed' (emphasis added). This could hint at the universe of goods being broader than just tangible products.

context electricity cannot be classified as a good. Similarly, is a carbon-emissions allowance a good as long as it is traded in paper form or sufficiently linked to a 'tangible, but fungible, input material'[24] (e.g., carbon emitted during production), but does it become a service, or otherwise stop being a good, when traded and registered electronically? The same conclusion could then be drawn in respect of intellectual property rights – which are intangible and arguably, on that basis, not a good – and this even though they are now commonly protected as 'assets' or 'investments' under bilateral investment treaties and the IP value (e.g., copyright) of a film is by far the most valuable component of the film. In contrast, if IP rights as such were to be seen as 'goods', major questions of GATT-TRIPS overlap would arise.

Interestingly, when interpreting the phrase '[s]ound recording distribution services' in China's *GATS Schedule*, the Appellate Body found that this includes not only distribution of tangible products (such as CDs) as China had argued, but also distribution of intangibles over the Internet, as submitted by the United States.[25] It did so based on a textual and contextual interpretation of the words in this phrase, rather than with reference to broader criteria of 'services' or 'goods' definitions. Crucially, the Appellate Body confirmed its evolutionary approach to treaty interpretation, finding that the terms in China's *GATS Schedule* 'are sufficiently generic that what they apply to may change over time',[26] and that limiting their meaning to 'the time the Schedule was concluded' would mean that 'very similar or identically worded commitments could be given different meanings … depending on the date of their adoption', which would 'undermine the predictability, security, and clarity of GATS'.[27]

As a result, it is interesting to point out that the Appellate Body interpreted *services* commitments in a technologically neutral way (distribution covers both old-style physical delivery and new-style delivery over the Internet, unless otherwise specified), but limited *goods* commitments and the right to import goods to restrictions affecting material or tangible products (thereby, as noted earlier, apparently excluding films traded intangibly over the Internet). In other words, method of delivery (tangible or over the Internet) matters for goods, but not for services. In this sense, *GATS* is technologically neutral, *GATT* technologically biased.

From an economic perspective, it should be pointed out that the fine legal distinctions made in the WTO between goods and services, and the often crucial regulatory consequences that come with it, find little or no support in the economic literature. In general, there should be no reason why basic trade effects and welfare

24 See footnote 22 above.
25 Appellate Body Report, *China–Audiovisuals*, para. 412.
26 Ibid., para. 396.
27 Ibid., para. 397.

calculations should apply differently to, for example, tangible versus intangible products or to distribution by mail or over the Internet.

1.2 Can GATT exceptions justify breach under all WTO agreements?

Important issues are raised by the finding of the Appellate Body that a GATT exception can, in principle, justify a violation of China's Accession Protocol. Interestingly enough, in *China–Audiovisuals*, China did not invoke any *GATS* or *GATT* exception to justify the abovementioned *GATS* and *GATT* violations found by the Panel (but not appealed). In particular, although it could have done so, China did not invoke 'public morals' so as to justify some of these violations with reference to its censorship regime. In contrast, China did invoke *GATT* art. XX(a) ('public morals') to justify certain (but not all) restrictions on trading rights found to be in violation of China's *Accession Protocol*.[28]

GATT Article XX is entitled 'General Exceptions' and states that 'nothing in this Agreement shall be construed to prevent the adoption or enforcement' of certain measures, including those 'necessary to protect public morals'. Paragraph 5.1 of China's Accession Protocol, in turn, explicitly states that the right to trade that China committed to is '[w]ithout prejudice to China's right to regulate trade in a manner consistent with the WTO Agreement'. For GATT Article XX to justify a Protocol breach raises two hurdles. First, given that Article XX explicitly refers back to 'nothing in this Agreement', i.e. GATT, how can Article XX justify breaches outside the GATT? Second, and related, given that the Appellate Body had not made any prior finding of violation under GATT (say, a national-treatment violation under GATT Article III) how could China even rely on, or the Panel turn to, GATT Article XX exceptions?

The Appellate Body skillfully jumped over both hurdles. It found that China's obligation to grant the 'right to trade' under the Protocol may not impair China's 'right to regulate trade' in the sense of both (i) measures that other WTO agreements 'affirmatively recognize' provided they 'satisfy prescribed disciplines and meet specified conditions' (think of WTO-consistent import licensing, TBT, or SPS measures), and (ii) regulatory action that derogates from WTO obligations but 'may be justified under an applicable exception'.[29] For the Appellate Body, the fact that the United States had not made a claim of violation under GATT to begin with (it only claimed a violation of the Protocol) should not 'deny China access to a defence'. What matters, according to the Appellate Body, is the existence of a 'clearly discernable, objective link' or relationship between (i) the restriction on *who* may trade (breach of the right to trade) and (ii) China's regulation of *what*

28 Panel Report, *China – Measures Affecting Trading Rights and Distribution Services for Certain Publications and Audiovisual Entertainment Products*, WT/DS363/R, para. 4.112.

29 Appellate Body Report, *China–Audiovisuals*, para. 223.

may be traded (China's right to regulate trade).[30] Since the regulation of trade or *what* can be traded (here, content review) may restrict or require regulation of *who* may import or trade (here, only selected state enterprises), the Appellate Body found that China's breach of the right to trade under the Protocol could possibly be justified by China's right to regulate trade pursuant to GATT Article XX(a).

This approach raises a fundamental question of WTO law. Must the 'right to regulate trade' as a possible defense be explicitly provided for in the violated provision that needs justification? Put differently, would China have been able to rely on GATT Article XX(a) even if paragraph 5.1 of China's Accession Protocol had not stated that the right to trade is '[w]ithout prejudice to China's right to regulate trade in a manner consistent with the WTO Agreement'? The Appellate Body's close textual analysis of this phrase and its context in China's Protocol may lead some to conclude that without this savings clause, GATT Article XX(a) would not have been available. On the other hand, one could argue that adding this savings clause was not strictly necessary in the first place and that all WTO obligations must be interpreted in the context of a WTO member's background or default 'right to regulate trade consistent with the WTO Agreement'. In this direction, the Appellate Body saw 'the "right to regulate", in the abstract, as an inherent power enjoyed by a Member's government, rather than a right bestowed by international treaties such as the *WTO Agreement*'.[31] On this view, even without the savings clause in the Protocol, China could have relied on its 'inherent power' to regulate trade and, as a result, have justified its breach with reference to GATT Article XX(a). If so, what matters is not an explicit savings clause or reference back to GATT Article XX – nor the fact that the text of GATT Article XX itself is limited to 'this Agreement' (i.e., GATT) – but that the trade restriction or WTO violation in question may, as a *regulatory* or *factual* matter, result from, and be justified by, a GATT Article XX type regulation to protect public morals, health, or the environment. This relates to what the Appellate Body referred to as the 'clearly discernable, objective link' between, on the one hand, the breach and, on the other hand, a legitimate regulation of trade (consistent with specific WTO rules or exceptions).

That this question is of the utmost importance for WTO law is illustrated by the following examples. Can an environmental subsidy inconsistent with the SCM Agreement (be it a prohibited or actionable subsidy) on this ground be justified under GATT Article XX(g) as a measure 'relating to the conservation of exhaustible natural resources'? Similarly, can a health or safety restriction

30 Ibid., para. 230 (adding that this link must be 'established through careful scrutiny of the nature, design, structure, and function of the measure, often in conjunction with an examination of the regulatory context within which it is situated').

31 Appellate Body Report, *China–Audiovisuals*, para. 222.

inconsistent with the SPS or TBT Agreement on this ground be excused as a 'public morals' measure in line with GATT Article XX(a)?[32] Can an anti-dumping duty inconsistent with the AD Agreement be justified under GATT Article XX(d) as a measure 'necessary to ensure compliance with laws or regulations which are not inconsistent with' GATT?[33] Can a safeguard that carves out regional partners in violation of the Safeguards Agreement be justified under GATT Article XXIV allowing for preferential agreements?[34] Finally, can a measure in violation of TRIPS be excused as the exercise of the right to regulate so as to protect health in line with GATT Article XX(b)?

The above reasoning in *China–Audiovisuals* may support such general, fall-back right to regulate. Although these other WTO agreements do not include a general 'without prejudice clause' as set out in China's Protocol, there is a clear, *legal* relationship between these other agreements and GATT provisions (e.g., between GATT Articles VI and XVI and the SCM and AD agreements; GATT Article XIX and the Safeguards Agreement; GATT Article XX(b)/(g) and the SPS and TBT agreements; and GATT Article XX(d) and TRIPS). Moreover, as a *regulatory* or *factual* matter, there may also be a 'discernable, objective link' between the trade restriction or breach and the exception invoked, in that the breach sufficiently relates to, or results from, a legitimate exercise of the right to regulate consistent with other WTO rules or exceptions (the way Chinese censorship on *what* can be traded may require restrictions on *who* can trade).

Such approach would certainly harness the regulatory autonomy of WTO members. At the same time, it risks a considerable reduction of WTO obligations. It would also create tension with the Appellate Body's approach of applying WTO

32 In this respect, see Panel Report, *European Communities – Measures Affecting the Approval and Marketing of Biotech Products*, WT/DS291/R, WT/DS292/R, WT/DS293/R, Add.1 to Add.9, and Corr.1, adopted 21 November 2006, DSR 2006:III–VIII, 847, which found that one single measure can be considered and justified under different agreements so that even if it violates the SPS Agreement as a health measure, it could still be justified under GATT Article XX(a) as a public-morals measure.

33 In *United States – Customs Bond Directive for Merchandise Subject to Anti-Dumping/Countervailing Duties*, WT/DS345/R, para. 310, the Appellate Body 'assumed *arguendo*', without deciding the matter, that a measure in violation with the AD Agreement can be justified under GATT Article XX(d).

34 Note, in this respect, that the Appellate Body has found that the 'unforeseen development' condition in GATT Article XIX, though not incorporated into the Safeguards Agreement, continues to apply for safeguard measures to be WTO-consistent (Appellate Body Report on *Argentina – Safeguard Measures on Imports of Footwear*, WT/DS121/AB/R (DSR 2000:I, 515), para. 83: 'Article XIX continues in full force and effect, and, in fact, establishes certain prerequisites for the imposition of safeguard measures'). Although the Appellate Body has condemned members for having investigated all imports and then applying a safeguard only on imports from outside, for example, NAFTA or MERCOSUR (see, for example, Appellate Body Report, *United States – Definitive Safeguard Measures on Imports of Circular Welded Carbon Quality Line Pipe from Korea*, WT/DS202/AB/R, adopted 8 March 2002), the Appellate Body has so far not decided the question of whether investigating and applying a safeguard only against third countries, in violation of Article 2 of the Safeguards Agreement, could be justified under GATT Article XXIV.

agreements and obligations cumulatively,[35] as well as with the principle that, in the event of conflict, GATT (including presumably GATT Article XX) must give way to more specialized WTO agreements on trade in goods such as obligations in the SCM, AD, SPS, or TBT agreements.[36] Finally, allowing GATT Article XX to be invoked to justify any WTO violation could well mean that any WTO dispute will ultimately be decided on whether the measure is 'necessary' to pursue an Article XX objective and nondiscriminatory under the chapeau of Article XX. This would both confer considerable power and discretion to the Appellate Body in its 'weighing and balancing exercise' under Article XX as well as highlight the limited list of objectives that can be pursued under Article XX (should, indeed, the fall-back 'right to regulate' not extend beyond the exhaustive list of objectives mentioned in GATT Article XX, a provision written in 1947 essentially with quantitative border restrictions in mind?).

From an economic perspective, if there are reasons to justify the use of protectionist measures on the ground of environmental externalities (under the GATT and Article XX), then similar arguments could in principle be used to justify exceptions when it comes to, for example, the use of subsidies (under the SCM Agreement, where no environmental exception is available). Indeed, if traditionally more harmful distortions such as a full ban on imports can be justified on environmental grounds under GATT, why not the normally less harmful distortion of a production subsidy under the SCM Agreement?

35 See, for example, Appellate Body Report on *European Communities – Measures Affecting Asbestos and Asbestos-Containing Products*, WT/DS135/AB/R (DSR 2001:VII, 3243), para. 80 ('although the *TBT Agreement* is intended to 'further the objectives of GATT 1994', it does so through a specialized legal regime that applies solely to a limited class of measures. For these measures, the *TBT Agreement* imposes obligations on Members that seem to be *different* from, and *additional* to, the obligations imposed on Members under the GATT 1994' (underlining added). But see Appellate Body Report, *Brazil – Measures Affecting Desiccated Coconut*, WT/DS22/AB/R (DSR 1997:I, 167), adopted 20 March 1997, p. 14: 'The relationship between the GATT 1994 and the other goods agreements in Annex 1A is complex and must be examined on a case-by-case basis. Although the provisions of the GATT 1947 were incorporated into, and became a part of the GATT 1994, they are not the sum total of the rights and obligations of WTO Members concerning a particular matter. For example, with respect to subsidies on agricultural products, Articles II, VI and XVI of the GATT 1994 alone do not represent the total rights and obligations of WTO Members. The *Agreement on Agriculture* and the *SCM Agreement* reflect the latest statement of WTO Members as to their rights and obligations concerning agricultural subsidies. The general interpretative note to Annex 1A was added to reflect that the other goods agreements in Annex 1A, in many ways, represent a substantial elaboration of the provisions of the GATT 1994, and to the extent that the provisions of the other goods agreements conflict with the provisions of the GATT 1994, the provisions of the other goods agreements prevail. This does not mean, however, that the other goods agreements in Annex 1A, such as the *SCM Agreement*, supersede the GATT 1994' (underlining added).

36 See *General interpretative note to Annex 1A* of the WTO Agreement: 'In the event of conflict between a provision of the [GATT 1994] and a provision of another agreement in Annex 1A to the [WTO] Agreement … the provision of the other agreement shall prevail to the extent of the conflict.' The question remains, of course, when there is such a 'conflict' and when exactly this *lex specialis* rule is triggered.

2. Economic analysis

In *China–Audiovisuals*, the United States has obtained certain rights to import and distribute within China on a nondiscriminatory basis. In what follows, we briefly review the main economic implications of the Appellate Body's ruling on this dispute and discuss the economic arguments that could be used for the protection of audiovisual products and other cultural goods.

2.1 *Economic implications of the Appellate Body's ruling*

Audiovisuals have for the most part been excluded from the progress in trade liberalization that has occurred in other sectors. Indeed, they are the object of an explicit exception concerning internal film quotas in Article IV of GATT 1994.[37] Countries such as Korea, Brazil, Venezuela, Italy, and Spain, have taken advantage of this exception to institute screening quotas for domestic (or EU) film exhibition (Bernier, 2003). Within China, there is a similar screening quota, pursuant to which two-thirds of films projected must be made in China.

In the case of China, foreign films must, in addition, be deemed suitable for all audiences. Under an elaborate censorship mechanism, China prohibits all content that, in its view, would have a negative impact on 'public morals'. The list of materials banned includes, for example, material that 'injures the national glory', 'undermines the solidarity of the nationalities', 'propagates evil cults or superstition', 'destroys social stability', or 'jeopardizes social morality or fine cultural traditions of the nationalities'.[38] For foreign-made films, this sometimes means controversial footage must be cut before such films can play in Chinese cinemas.[39]

Regardless of the screening quota and the censorship, China permits only 20 foreign films per year for theatrical release on a revenue-sharing basis (of which 14–16 are usually Hollywood releases).[40] This means that only 20 foreign films per year get a (small) percentage of what they earn in the country instead of selling distribution rights for a flat fee.[41]

China's internal screening quota, censorship policy, and quota on foreign movies that can be imported on a revenue-sharing basis were not at issue in

37 Article IV of the GATT 1994 is an exception to Article III, which prohibits any form of discrimination between domestic and foreign products. It stipulates that a Member may maintain domestic quotas including the obligation to show, for a specified amount of time, films of domestic origin for a minimum fraction of the overall time of projection actually used; however, it also specifies that screen quotas remain the subject of negotiations aiming to limit their scope or to eliminate them.

38 Panel Report, *China–Audiovisuals*, and Corr.1, para. 7.760.

39 An example is the removal of a footage that 'vilifies and humiliates the Chinese' in *Pirates of the Caribbean: At World's End* (BBC news, 12 June 2007).

40 The quota doubled in 2001 from the original ten in 1994, thanks to China's WTO accession. Sector 2.D of China's GATS Schedule reads: 'China will allow the importation of motion pictures for theatrical release on a revenue-sharing basis and the number of such imports shall be 20 on an annual basis.'

41 The revenue-sharing deal is reportedly one of the worst in the world for film studios. Foreign films earn about 13% of ticket sales in China (see http://www.chinabusinessreview.com/public/0703/miller.html (last visited 30 September 2010)).

China–Audiovisuals. The dispute was instead over the fact that imported audiovisual products could only be distributed by Chinese state-owned enterprises.[42]

China–Audiovisuals has been hailed as a big victory for US movie producers. On the day when the Appellate Body Report was circulated, the US Trade Representative Ron Kirk announced: 'Today America got a big win ... The Appellate Body's findings are key to ensuring full market access in China for legitimate, high-quality entertainment products and the exporters and distributors of those products.'[43]

Yet, the WTO ruling did not affect China's right to keep out foreign films and publications if it finds them objectionable. It also left in place the existing screening and import quotas. Therefore, sales of US audiovisuals in China are unlikely to increase as a result of this dispute. The WTO basically said that foreign audiovisuals can no longer be distributed only by Chinese state-owned enterprises. This implies that, even if market access is unaffected, foreign companies will be able to earn potentially very large economic rents when now allowed to import and distribute their entertainment products into the Chinese market.[44] Distribution by US companies (instead of Chinese state-owned companies) could also mean that more Chinese consumers watch the (still limited amount of) US movies allowed for screening in China. In other words, more transparent or efficient distribution may lead to more sales of particular imports that do pass China's quotas and censorship.

The Chinese government restricts the volume of cultural goods imported through strict censorship and explicit import quotas. Both kinds of policies are equivalent to quantitative restrictions of imports. In what follows, we examine the economic implications of such restrictions, distinguishing between two scenarios: (a) if China is a small country, i.e., takes the world price of cultural goods as given; (b) if China is a large country, which can affect the price of cultural goods in the world market. In both scenarios, we examine the welfare effects of a quantitative restriction (compared to free trade) and discuss the implications of the Appellate Body's ruling in *China–Audiovisuals*.

42 In the case of films, China Film Group and Huaxia Film Distribution Co. were the two state-owned enterprises allowed to distribute foreign movies. China Film controlled most of the 20 import licenses. For more details, see Jennifer M. Freedman, *China Appeals WTO Ruling on Book, Film, Music Imports (Update 3)*, BLOOMBERG.CO.JP, http://www.bloomberg.co.jp/apps/news?pid=conewsstory&tkr=DIS:US&sid=aMgqddJ_22DQ (22 September 2009) (last visited 30 September 2010).

43 See press release of 21 December 2009, 'WTO Appellate Body Confirms Finding Against China's Treatment Of Certain Copyright-Intensive Products', on http://www.ustr.gov (last visited 30 September 2010).

44 In addition, what used to be a discriminatory and opaque distribution network run by Chinese state-enterprises should now be left to US companies or their affiliates themselves. This may mean that even if the number of movies stays capped at 20, a more efficient and competitive distribution network may lead to more tickets sold per movie.

Figure 1.

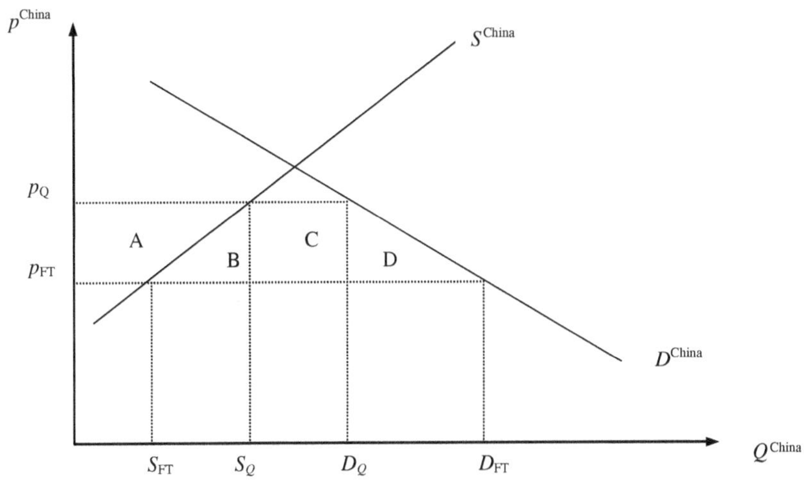

Small-country case

Assume that China is a small country importing cultural goods and facing a world price equal to p_{FT}. At this price, domestic demand in China is given by D_{FT}, domestic supply by S_{FT}, and imports by the difference $D_{FT} - S_{FT}$.

Now suppose that the Chinese government desires to reduce the volume of cultural goods imported to an amount Q, which is below the free-trade level. It can do so by censoring some foreign goods or by explicitly introducing an import quota. The welfare effects of a quantitative restriction on imports can be described with the use of Figure 1. A reduction in imports will lower the supply in the domestic market and raise the domestic price.[45] In the new equilibrium, the domestic price will rise to the level p_Q, where import demand equals the value of the quota, i.e. $Q = D_Q - S_Q$. Since the country is 'small', there will be no effect on the world price, which will remain at p_{FT}.

Table 1 provides a summary of the welfare effects of the quota on cultural goods on the Chinese economy compared to free trade. The left panel and right panel of the table consider, respectively, the welfare implications of quantitative restrictions before and after the Appellate Body's ruling on *China–Audiovisuals*. Notice that, since quantitative restrictions on foreign cultural goods (through *de facto* censorship quotas or import quotas) are still in place after the ruling, equilibrium quantities and prices are unaffected and so are Chinese consumers and

45 Depending on the city and theater, movie-ticket prices in China currently range from ¥30 to ¥80 ($3.90–$10). In 2006, China's annual urban per capita disposable income hit $1,517, and the annual rural per capita net income reached only $463, making a $10 ticket an expensive outing for most Chinese (see http://www.chinabusinessreview.com/public/0703/miller.html).

Table 1. Welfare effects of a quota on cultural goods compared to free trade

	Before *China–Audiovisuals*	After *China–Audiovisuals*
Consumer surplus	−(A+B+C+D)	−(A+B+C+D)
Producer surplus	+A	+A
Quota rents	+C	0
National welfare	−(B+D)	−(B+C+D)

producers: compared to free trade, consumers continue to experience a loss equivalent to the area A+B+C+D, while producers continue to gain A. However, the WTO ruling has a crucial impact on who receives the *quota rents*. These are given by area C, which is equivalent to the domestic price of the imported good, minus the world price, times the quantity of imports. Before the ruling, the permit to import and distribute foreign cultural goods was given by the Chinese government to state-owned companies; after the ruling, such right will be given to foreign producers.

Compared to free trade, a quota on cultural goods unambiguously hurts the Chinese economy. Compared to the previous policy regime, the Appellate Body's ruling on *China–Audiovisuals* leads to a net welfare loss for China, equivalent to area C, and to a corresponding gain for the United States.

The above analysis of the economic implications of *China–Audiovisuals* could have a potentially crucial impact on the calculation of US-authorized retaliation in the event China does not implement the Appellate Body ruling within the prescribed period. Traditionally, annual retaliation rights are set by the WTO at the annual *value of trade* that is kept out by the WTO-inconsistent measure. In the present case, China's restriction on *who* may import is unlikely to impact the *amount* of audiovisual products that can be imported, since this is limited by government censorship (and, in the case of films, by the quota of 20 foreign movies on a revenue-sharing basis per year). Hence, there may be no trade value linked to the violation. Yet, if welfare effects were used to calculate retaliation rights, the shift in quota rents could be used to fix the 'nullification or impairment' linked to the violation and with it the authorized level of US retaliation.[46]

Large-country case

In our analysis above, we have examined the welfare implications of China's quantitative restrictions on cultural goods assuming that such restrictions have no impact on world prices. However, with just over 1.3 billion people, China is the world's largest and most populous country, representing a full 20 % of the world's population, and has thus the potential to affect world prices in many sectors. As shown below, this can change some of the welfare implications of its policies on imported cultural goods.

46 To this, one would then have to add any negative effects linked to China's discriminatory distribution system (see Bown and Pauwelyn, 2010).

Figure 2.

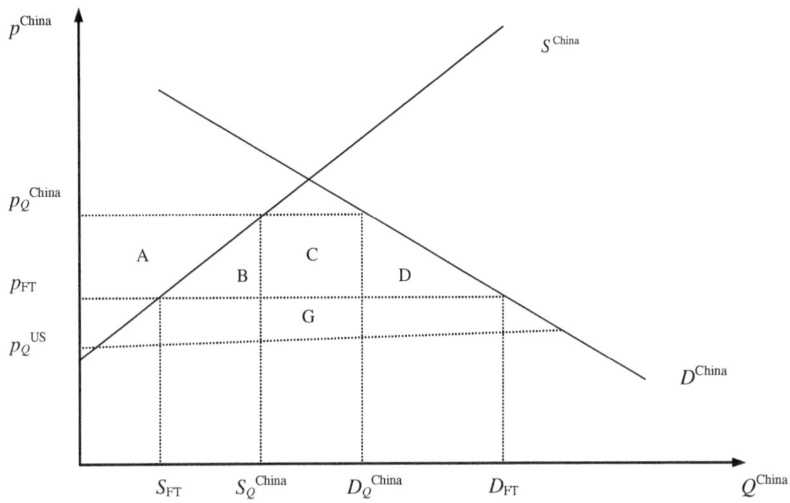

To illustrate the large-country case, consider two trading countries, one importing (China) and one exporting (United States) cultural goods. At the free-trade equilibrium price, denoted by p_{FT}, the excess demand by the importing country equals excess supply by the exporter

$$D^{China}(p_{FT}) - S^{China}(p_{FT}) = S^{US}(p_{FT}) - D^{US}(p_{FT})$$

Suppose now that China introduces a quantitative import restriction, allowing only an amount Q of cultural goods to be imported from the United States. As a result, the supply of cultural goods in the Chinese market will fall and, if the price remained at p_{FT}, there would be excess demand for these goods in the market. The excess demand will induce an increase in the price; in turn, this will reduce demand and increase domestic supply causing a reduction in China's import demand.

Since China is a 'large' importer, the fall in its demand for cultural goods will cause excess supply in the US market at the original price, leading to a reduction in the US price. The lower price will, in turn, reduce US supply and raise US demand, causing a reduction in US export supply. The price in China will rise to the level at which import demand is equal to the quota level; the price in the United States will fall until export supply is equal to the quota level. A new equilibrium will be reached when the following two conditions are satisfied

$$D^{China}(p_Q^{China}) - S^{China}(p_Q^{China}) = Q$$

$$S^{US}(p_Q^{US}) - D^{US}(p_Q^{US}) = Q$$

where p_Q^{China} is the price in China after the quota, and p_Q^{US} is the price in the US after the quota. Figure 2 depicts the welfare effects of the introduction of a quantitative

Table 2. Welfare effects of a quota on cultural goods compared to free trade

	Before *China–Audiovisuals*	After *China–Audiovisuals*
Consumer surplus	−(A+B+C+D)	−(A+B+C+D)
Producer surplus	+A	+A
Quota rents	+ (C+G)	0
National welfare	+ G − (B+D)	−(B+C+D)

restriction on imports of cultural goods for the Chinese economy, while Table 2 distinguishes between the effects on producers, consumers, and the government (before and after the WTO ruling).

Notice that, in the large-country case, the quota rents gained by those individuals or firms that are allowed to sell foreign cultural goods in China are larger than in the small-country case (they are equal to C+G rather than C). As discussed below, this implies that, if China is able to affect world prices, the WTO ruling leads to a larger loss in terms of quota rents for the Chinese government (and to a correspondingly larger gain for US content producers).

The Appellate Body's ruling in *China–Audiovisuals* implies that the quota rents (C+G) are transferred from Chinese state-owned enterprises to foreign-content producers. It is also interesting to compare Table 1 with Table 2 above. Notice that, if China is able to affect its terms of trade, the introduction of a quota on cultural goods can potentially be beneficial compared to free trade. However, for this to be the case, the quota rents must be sufficiently large (i.e. G must exceed B+D) and the right to sell foreign cultural products must be given to Chinese firms. This implies that, following the ruling on *China–Audiovisuals*, China would unambiguously gain by removing restrictions on the number of foreign movies that can be imported into its market. Of course, this assumes that the Chinese government makes decisions with respect to cultural goods based on national welfare rather than internal politics. That said, the recent literature on trade and culture has shown that, even from an economic perspective, there can be arguments for restricting imports of cultural goods. It is to these arguments that we turn next.

2.2 *Economic arguments for the protection of cultural goods*

In *China–Audiovisuals*, China argued that reading materials and finished audiovisual products are so-called 'cultural goods' and as such have a potentially serious negative impact on public morals. Referring to the UNESCO Universal Declaration on Cultural Diversity – which defines cultural goods as 'vectors of identity, values and meaning' – China explained that cultural goods play an essential role in the evolution and definition of elements such as societal features, values, ways of living together, ethics, and behaviors. It then argued that restrictions on cultural products are needed to prevent the dissemination of cultural goods with a content that could have a negative impact on public morals in China. The Panel and Appellate Body in *China–Audiovisuals* ultimately rejected this defense, finding that China could pursue its censorship regime and the 'public morals' it is allegedly protecting in a less-trade-restrictive manner, for example, by letting the Chinese government itself do the censorship and then granting the right to import the approved goods to all companies, be they Chinese or foreign, on a nondiscriminatory basis.

Both the Panel and the Appellate Body simply 'assumed' that all of the censorship by the Chinese government is driven by the need to protect 'public morals', an assumption that is, given the above examples of censored content, not easy to make. The Panel recalled that in *US–Gambling* the term 'public morals' was found to denote 'standards of right and wrong conduct maintained by or on behalf of a community or nation' and that 'content of these concepts for Members can vary in time and space, depending upon a range of factors, including prevailing social, cultural, ethical and religious values'.[47] Given the absence of US protest on the matter, the Panel simply 'assumed that each of the types of prohibited content in China's measures could, if it were brought into China, have a negative impact on "public morals" in China within the meaning of Article XX(a)'.[48]

While accepting the Panel's 'assumption' on this question, the Appellate Body had, however, a few pages earlier (in respect of another assumption that it found unacceptable) stressed that assumptions may 'not always provide a solid foundation upon which to rest legal conclusions' and 'detract from a clear enunciation of the relevant WTO law and create difficulties for implementation'.[49] Indeed, now that the Appellate Body found that China's trading-rights restrictions are not 'necessary' to protect public morals because, as explained earlier, there are less-trade-restrictive alternatives (e.g., the government rather than importers could do the censorship), what if China now implements such alternative but still restricts trading rights? Given that the Appellate Body merely 'assumed' that public morals are at issue, nothing guarantees China that such less-trade-restrictive alternatives would actually comply with Article XX.

China–Audiovisuals leaves open the question of whether the protection of cultural goods can or should actually be justified under GATT/WTO rules. This is the question that we address in the remainder of this section.[50]

47 Panel Report, *China–Audiovisuals*, para. 7.759, referring to Panel Report on *United States – Measures Affecting the Cross-Border Supply of Gambling and Betting Services*, WT/DS285/R (DSR 2005:XII, 5797), para. 6.465 and 6.461.

48 Appellate Body Report, *China–Audiovisuals*, para. 243, referring to Panel Report, *China–Audiovisuals*, para. 7.763.

49 Appellate Body Report, *China–Audiovisuals*, para. 213.

50 China and the United States avoided arguments on this issue. Only Australia argued that 'in seeking to rely on the public morals exception of Article XX(a), China needs to have demonstrated the contribution the measure at issue brings to the achievement of its objective' (Third Participant Submission of Australia on 19 October 2009, page 6).

For many years, concerns have been expressed about the possible detrimental effects of globalization on cultural diversity. In some countries, policymakers have taken these concerns very seriously. For example, Canada and France have implemented policies to prevent the possible loss of cultural identity that might result from free trade. France has restrictions on foreign films and television programs from English-speaking countries, while Canada requires minimum levels of Canadian content in radio and television broadcasts.

Does the economic literature support these concerns? In recent years, various papers have attempted to model the effects of trade on culture. In what follows, we briefly review some of the economic arguments developed in this literature to justify the use of protectionist measures in the case of cultural goods.

Many of these theories develop the idea that consumers have *heterogeneous preferences* and that an individual's decision to consume foreign cultural goods imposes a *negative externality* on other consumers. Below we will distinguish between two classes of such models: those in which the externality is due to increasing returns in the production of cultural goods, and those in which it is directly built in consumers' preferences.[51]

Economies of scale in the production of cultural goods

One of the first papers to examine the link between trade and culture is by Francois and van Ypersele (2002), who show that losses from trade may occur when cultural goods are characterized by fixed costs and heterogeneous valuations.

To fix ideas, they describe a simple model of trade between two countries, denoted by France and the United States. Both countries can produce their 'auteur' (or locally flavored) cinema, which is valued differentially by their own consumers.[52] In addition, the United States can produce Hollywood movies, a homogeneous good that is valued equally by all consumers in both countries. There are important economies of scale in the movie industry: producers must sell enough units, at relatively low marginal costs, to cover the high fixed costs.

Trade leads to greater production of a 'culturally homogeneous' good at the expense of culturally specific goods, since with the homogeneous good fixed costs can be spread out across countries. In their example, the Hollywood blockbuster can drive out independent films in both France and the United States. Depending on parameters, trade restrictions on Hollywood movies may be Pareto improving because it makes local movies viable in both markets.

The intuition for their result is that, if price discrimination is not possible (for example, cinema tickets must, by law, be priced the same irrespective of the movie watched), high consumer valuation cannot be captured in the heterogeneous case.

51 The emerging theoretical literature on trade and culture has some empirical work on this relationship. See, for example, the paper by Disdier *et al.* (2010), which uses a long panel of French birth registries to assess the link between foreign media and culture using name frequencies as a measure of tastes.

52 In the model by Francois and van Ypersele (2002), individuals are interested only in the local movies produced in their own country.

In contrast, the social benefit of a homogeneously valued good can be effectively captured by the producers setting one price. This can lead to inefficiently low production of the heterogeneous good, even when welfare would be higher with it.

The paper by Francois and van Ypersele (2002) demonstrates that restrictions on trade of cultural goods (for instance by a tariff or quota) can be welfare improving. The two main assumptions that are required for their argument to hold are: (1) cultural goods must be produced using increasing-returns-to-scale technologies; (2) for some cultural goods, there is high variation in valuation amongst consumers, while for others valuations are relatively homogeneous.

The authors argue that these conditions seem to be satisfied by the film-industry example, but possibly also by other cultural goods (for example radio and television programming, literature, or print media). However, they also stress that their analysis does not definitively favor protection over free trade in cultural goods. It only suggests that protection *may* be justified when consumers have heterogeneous tastes and cultural goods are produced under increasing returns to scale.

Network externalities in the consumption of cultural goods

A second stream of the literature on trade and culture provides a rationale for the protection of cultural goods based on the existence of consumption externalities.

Seminal contributions to this literature are by Janeba (2004, 2007), who formalizes the notion of cultural identity and incorporates it in a Ricardian model of trade. To define culture, he adopts the 'identity function' of Akerlof and Kranton (2000), whereby a person suffers a utility loss if some individuals in his country deviate from social norms, and an individual who deviates from social norms incurs a direct utility loss for the self-inflicted loss of identity.

In Janeba's model, an individual's utility for a cultural good is based in part on how many others are also consuming it. He argues that consumers often face the choice between differentiated products that are characterized by network externalities. One notable example is the choice of a computer operating system. Similarly, in the context of cultural goods people may have an additional benefit from consuming a certain good when others do the same. For example, watching a movie when others see it as well allows consumers to share their experience.

This interdependence of preferences can be used to study how a country's cultural identity is affected by trade liberalization. In this framework, 'cultural goods differ from other goods in that they create an interdependence among individual consumption decisions, like a network externality, and thus generate cultural identity ... the more consumers buy the same good the lower is the loss in identity for existing consumers and the more attractive becomes the consumption of such good for other consumers' (Janeba, 2004: 25).

The analysis of Janeba points out that trade can be welfare reducing when a country is culturally homogeneous. In particular, he shows that free trade is not always Pareto superior to autarky because individuals can suffer a negative externality when others have different consumption patterns.

Janeba studies the welfare effects of trade openness on welfare for a given and *exogenous* population of cultural agents.[53] Olivier *et al.* (2008), on the other hand, do not derive welfare results but focus on the impact of trade openness on *endogenous* cultural identity. In particular, they highlight the disutility experienced by the parent generation as their children adopt new cultures. In their model, cultural identity comes as the outcome of a dynamic process of transmission of preferences as micro-founded for instance by Bisin and Verdier (2000), in which preferences of children are acquired through an adaptation and imitation process that depends on their parents' decisions and on the environment in which they live.

A dynamic analysis of culture is also presented in Bala and Van Long (2005). They develop an evolutionary model of preferences in which cultural dynamics are driven by an *exogenous* process directly imported from the Darwinian literature in biology. They show that a large country may be able to overrun the indigenous preferences of a smaller country through trade.

Where does this leave the WTO and possible exceptions based on culture or cultural diversity? First, it must be noted that apart from GATT Article IV on internal film or screening quotas, there is no explicit cultural exception in the GATT or GATS. Second, in *China–Audiovisuals*, the cultural exception was channeled into GATT through the backdoor of 'public morals'. However, nowhere under this exception of GATT Article XX(a) is reference made to any of the criteria referred to in the economics literature. What matters under Article XX(a) is whether the measure does, indeed, protect public morals and, if so, whether the measure is 'necessary' to achieve its objective. Third, when it comes to China's censorship it is far from clear whether all of it is related to public morals, let alone culture. Moreover, even to the extent that it is related to culture, further examination would be needed to see whether any of China's measures are welfare enhancing. The only aim of the above survey is to indicate that, in some cases, and under certain assumptions, trade restrictions on cultural goods can be welfare enhancing and can, therefore, be justifiable.

3. Conclusions

No head-on collision occurred in *China–Audiovisuals* between, on the one hand, free trade in cultural goods and services and, on the other hand, China's censorship regime. The main parties involved went to great pains to avoid such clash: China, by only invoking GATT's public-morals exception for Protocol violations (not for GATT/GATS violations); the United States, by not contesting that all of the content prohibited by China harms 'public morals'; and, finally, the Panel and

53 Rauch and Trindade (2009) extend Janeba's setup and allow for imperfect competition and innovation in the cultural sector.

Appellate Body by simply assuming that China's censorship does, indeed, promote 'public morals', without making a definitive finding on the matter.

In future disputes, governments may be required to justify the use of measures to protect cultural goods. To do so, they may be able to use different economic arguments that have been developed in the recent literature on trade and culture, which we have reviewed in Section 2.2 above. However, it is important to stress that the arguments developed in this literature do not unambiguously favor protection over free trade in cultural goods. They merely suggest that protection *may* be justified when (a) consumers have heterogeneous preferences over cultural goods and (b) there are economies of scale in the production and/or network effects in the consumption of cultural goods.

The Appellate Body's ruling clarified crucial questions on how to distinguish between goods and services when it comes to today's 'content' industry. For the application of WTO rules on trade in 'goods' the Appellate Body focused on whether Chinese restrictions have an *effect* or *impact* on a material or physical product, even if this tangible product was only a minor element in the economic value of the transaction (e.g., a physical film reel when it comes to movies). This implies a technological bias requiring a physical product before WTO rules on trade in goods can be applied (not, for example, when a film is transferred over the Internet). When it comes to services, in contrast, the Appellate Body approached GATS in a technologically neutral fashion, covering under 'distribution services' both the physical transfer of CDs and distribution of music over the Internet. It remains to be seen whether tangibility or material nature is a *sufficient* condition for something to be a 'good' and whether it is, conversely, a *necessary* condition (can intangible assets, such as IP, electricity, or films over the Internet never be 'goods'?).

The Appellate Body also confirmed a general 'right to regulate' (e.g., pursuant to GATT Article XX) and found that the right to regulate *what* can be traded can, in principle, excuse violations or restrictions on *who* can trade or import. The exact scope of this 'right to regulate' and whether it must be explicitly referred to in the text of WTO obligations remains unclear. It is sure to animate many WTO disputes ahead.

Finally, the Appellate Body found that, even assuming that China's censorship regime promotes public morals, China's approach of limiting the right to import cultural goods to certain state-owned enterprises is not 'necessary' to protect public morals since less-trade-restrictive alternatives are available – for example, letting the Chinese government itself do the censorship and then granting the right to import the approved goods to all companies, including US companies established in China.

The ruling does not restrict censorship by the Chinese government and keeps the existing quota on foreign movies in place. However, it allows producers to import and distribute audiovisual products that pass China's censorship without discrimination. Even if their sales may be unaffected by the ruling, US producers can now obtain potentially large rents in the Chinese market. In addition, more efficient or transparent distribution by US companies (rather than state-owned Chinese) may lead to more sales of particular imports that do pass China's quotas and censorship.

References

Akerlof, George A. and Rachel E. Kranton (2000), 'Economics and Identity', *The Quarterly Journal of Economics*, **115**(3): 715–753.

Bala, Venkatesh and Ngo Van Long (2005), 'International Trade and Cultural Diversity with Preference Selection', *European Journal of Political Economy*, **21**(1): 143–162.

Bernier, Ivan (2003), 'Local Content Requirements for Film, Radio, and Television as a Means of Protecting Cultural Diversity: Theory and Reality', Mimeo, http://www.diversite-culturelle.qc.ca/fileadmin/documents/pdf/update031112section1.pdf.

Bisin, Alberto and Thierry Verdier (2000), '"Beyond the Melting Pot": Cultural Transmission, Marriage, and the Evolution of Ethnic and Religious Traits', *The Quarterly Journal of Economics*, **115**(3): 955–988.

Bown, Chad P. and Joost Pauwelyn (eds.) (2010), *The Law, Economics and Politics of Retaliation in WTO Dispute Settlement*, Cambridge: Cambridge University Press.

Broude, Tomer and Holger Hestermeyer, 'The First Condition of Progress – The Limits of International Trade Law as a Promoter of Freedom of Speech', Research Showcase, Poster Session, 103rd Annual Meeting of the American Society of International Law, 27 March 2009.

Disdier, Anne-Célia, Keith Head, and Thierry Mayer (2010), 'Exposure to Foreign Media and Changes in Cultural Traits: Evidence from Naming Patterns in France', *Journal of International Economics*, **80**(2): 226–238.

Francois, Patrick and Tanguy van Ypersele (2002), 'On the Protection of Cultural Goods', *Journal of International Economics*, **56**(2): 359–369.

Janeba, Eckhard (2004), 'International Trade and Cultural Identity', NBER Working Paper No. 10426.

Janeba, Eckhard (2007), 'International Trade and Consumption Network Externalities', *European Economic Review*, **51**(4): 781–803.

Olivier, Jacques, Mathias Thoenig, and Thierry Verdier (2008), 'Globalization and the Dynamics of Cultural Identity', *Journal of International Economics*, **76**(2): 356–370.

Pauwelyn, Joost (2010), 'Squaring Free Trade in Culture with Chinese Censorship: The WTO Appellate Body Report on *China – Audiovisuals*', *Melbourne Journal of International Law*, **11**(1): 119–140.

Rauch, James E. and Vitor Trindade (2009), 'Neckties in the Tropics: A Model of International Trade and Cultural Diversity', *Canadian Journal of Economics*, **42**(3): 809–843.

Comment

Appellate Body Ruling in *China–Publications and Audiovisual Products*

FRIEDER ROESSLER
Executive Director, Advisory Centre on WTO Law

I would like to add to the analyses of the authors comments on two questions: First, how should measures falling under the GATT be distinguished from those falling under the GATS? Second, could a measure inconsistent with one WTO agreement be justified by an exception contained in another?

1. How should measures falling under the GATT be distinguished from those falling under the GATS?

The Appellate Body concluded in *China–Publications and Audiovisual Products* that 'where the content of a film is carried by physical delivery materials, [the Chinese restriction] will *inevitably* regulate who may import goods for the plain reason that the content of a film is expressed through, and embedded in, a physical good'.[1] For the Appellate Body, this effect on goods (i.e., the physical film reel that crosses the border) is '*inevitable*, rather than "*incidental*"' and 'the mere fact that the import transaction involving hard-copy cinematographic films may not be the "essential feature" of the exploitation of the relevant film does not preclude the application of China's trading rights commitments to the *Film Regulation*'.[2]

The authors ask whether the Appellate Body will 'automatically find a good whenever it sees tangible material? Is, for example, a paper lottery ticket automatically a good – so that cross-border restrictions on lottery activities affect trade in goods? – or merely an element in the supply of (lottery) services, making the entire activity subject only to GATS?' They further ask whether it suffices 'for a

The views expressed are those of the author and should not be attributed to the ACWL.

1 Appellate Body Report, *China – Measures Affecting Trading Rights and Distribution Services for Certain Publications and Audiovisual Entertainment Products*, WT/DS363/AB/R, adopted 19 January 2010 ('*China–Publications and Audiovisual Products*'), para. 188.

2 Ibid., para. 196.

traded product to be intangible for that product to be regarded only as a service? For example, if US film producers would stop physically shipping film reels or master copies to China for reproduction within China, and rather send the material electronically over the Internet, would that automatically imply that we can no longer talk of trade in goods and trading rights, and must examine the transaction exclusively under GATS (say, as a cross-border supply of 'entertainment services')? ... Should the law follow economic reality ... or should the law stick to physics (tangible is GATT, intangible is GATS)?'

I would like to add to the authors' analysis of these issues some general observations on the criteria that, in my view, should be used to determine whether a measure falls under the GATT or the GATS.

A product is a tangible object, a service an observable action. Put simply, what is regulated by the GATT can be touched, what is covered by the GATS can only be observed. Given the ease with which products and services can normally be distinguished, GATT and WTO jurisprudence and decision making have had no difficulty segregating the two, even though neither the GATT nor the GATS provides a definition of the terms 'product' and 'service'. The only case that gave rise to debate was the case of electricity because it is not clear whether electricity is a physical object. In practice, electricity has been treated as a product, presumably because the rules governing trade in products can easily be extended to electricity.[3]

While it is generally easy to distinguish between products and services, it can be very difficult to determine whether a measure applies to products or services or both. To take an example used by the authors: it is clear that a lottery ticket is a product and a lottery a service, but it may be very difficult to determine whether a specific measure regulates lottery tickets or lotteries or both. The legally relevant question is therefore not: 'Is a lottery ticket a good?' but: 'Does the measure at issue regulate lottery tickets?' The national-treatment provision of Article III:4 of the GATT applies to internal regulations 'affecting' the sale of products. Article I of the GATS provides that the GATS applies to measures 'affecting' trade in services. Thus, the key term that the judicial organs of the WTO must interpret when deciding whether internal regulations fall under the GATT or the GATS is the term 'affecting'.

The ordinary meaning of the verb 'to affect' is 'to make a difference to'. Theoretically, there are three different methods of determining whether a measure 'makes a difference to' trade in goods or trade in services:

- First, one could look at the policy objective that the government pursues through the measure: Is it the government's *intention* to regulate trade in goods or trade in services?

3 For an extensive discussion on the properties of electricity, see the WTO Secretariat paper, 'Energy Services' (S/C/W/52), 9 September 1998.

- Second, one could look at the effects in the economy brought about by the measure: Is the *economic impact* of the measure predominantly in the field of goods or in the field of services?
- And, third, one could look at the measure itself: Does the measure, explicitly or by necessary implication, regulate trade in goods or trade in services?

The first method would concentrate on what preceded the adoption of the measure (the legislature's intent); the second on what followed the adoption of the measure (the economic impact of the legislative action); the third on the measure itself (the regulatory scope of the measure).

In my view, a reliance on the policy objective for the purpose of determining the legal status of a measure under the basic provisions of the GATT and the GATS would be incompatible with the legal structure of these agreements. The basic provisions of these agreements prohibit measures with defined characteristics (e.g., customs duties exceeding the bound rate, restrictions, limitations on the number of service suppliers, etc.). They do not make distinctions between measures serving different policy purposes. For instance: a high charge on importation falls under the provisions of Article II of the GATT governing import charges but not under Article XI of the GATT governing import prohibitions, even if the charge was imposed with the objective of eliminating all imports and had the effect of discouraging all imports. Or: a production subsidy accorded to domestic breweries is, in principle, permitted under the GATT, while an exemption from sales tax for beer produced by domestic breweries violates the national-treatment requirement of Article III:4 of the GATT, even though the two measures are likely to have the same policy objective.

While the basic provisions of the GATT and the GATS do not distinguish between measures serving different policy purposes, many of the exceptions set out in these agreements permit measures that serve a defined policy purpose (e.g., 'to protect human health', 'to safeguard the external financial position'). The judicial organs of the WTO will normally examine the measure at issue in the light of such an exception only if the defendant has invoked it and, in doing so, declared which policy purpose its measure serves. The judicial organ's task is then limited to determining whether the measure has the characteristics, and was taken in the circumstances, described in the exception invoked. To take an example: if an import restriction inconsistent with Article XI:1 of the GATT protects both the imposing Member's domestic industries *and* its balance-of-payments, the complainant need not demonstrate which of these two purposes the measure served. Rather, it is the defendant that would have to invoke an exception justifying the restriction (for instance, the provisions permitting balance-of-payments measures) and to demonstrate that the measure complies with the conditions of that exception.

Under the basic legal scheme of the GATT and the GATS, therefore, the thorny question of the policy purpose of the measure at issue normally does not arise. This has the advantage that the complainant's claims and the rulings of the judicial organs can generally be limited to tangible facts: the characteristics of the measure at issue and the circumstances in which it was applied. That advantage would be lost if one were to define measures 'affecting' products or services as measures intended to affect goods or services. Every dispute under these agreements could then be resolved only after the intent behind the measure at issue had been ascertained. As a result, the complainants' and the judicial organs' tasks would be greatly complicated, and the normative force of the GATT and the GATS would be weakened.

If the intent behind a measure should not be used to determine the categorization of a measure under the GATT or the GATS, should one focus instead on the economic impact of the measure?

Most of the measures that fall under the GATT have an impact on the supply of services. Thus, a restriction on the importation of a product is bound to have an impact on the supply of distribution services. And most services cannot be supplied without goods – transportation services require vehicles, communication services electronic equipment. Consequently, if 'affecting' were interpreted to mean 'having an economic impact', the GATT and the GATS would simultaneously apply in almost *all* instances. The carefully negotiated differences between the legal regime governing trade in goods and that governing trade in services would be lost.

The economic impact of a law, regulation, or requirement generally depends on the market's reaction to it, which, in turn, depends on the decisions of private actors. The WTO can hold its Members responsible only for the laws, regulations, and requirements they adopt, not for the reactions of private actors to those measures. Consequently, the categorization of a measure under these agreements cannot appropriately depend on something that WTO Members do not control. Moreover, it is always extremely difficult and frequently impossible to segregate the market impact of a governmental measure from the market impact of other factors. Usually, this can be done only by observing the market over a period of time. If the economic impact of a measure were to determine its categorization under the GATT and GATS, therefore, a complaint against the measure could not be brought immediately upon its adoption, but only after the impact of the measure on the market could be determined. For this reason also, the 'having an economic impact' definition would be unworkable.

What then should 'affecting' mean?

I believe that the definition of this term must be in harmony with the basic function of the GATT and the GATS. These agreements do not oblige Members to pursue specific policy objectives; nor do they oblige Members to attain specific results in the marketplace. GATT and WTO panels and the Appellate Body have therefore consistently interpreted the basic provisions of the GATT and the GATS as norms setting out the conditions of competition that Members must create for actual and potential trade, and not as norms prescribing goals or results.[4] A definition of 'affecting' that would be in harmony with the basic function of the GATT and the GATS would therefore be 'modifying conditions of competition in respect of'. With that definition, the interpreter facing the question of whether a measure falls under the GATT or the GATS would examine the distinctions made in the law, regulation, or requirement at issue and the necessary consequences of those distinctions.

In *China–Publications and Audiovisual Products*, the Appellate Body followed this approach. It examined whether the Chinese law at issue regulates the importation of a product or the supply of a service. The Appellate Body thus focused on the distinction made in the Chinese law, rather than on the policy objective of the Chinese government or the impact that the Chinese government sought to achieve through the law. For the reasons outlined above, I believe that there is no alternative to the approach adopted by the Appellate Body.

The authors ask whether 'the law' should 'follow economic reality' or 'stick to physics'. This implies that the judicial organs of the WTO should determine the scope of the market-access obligations under the GATT and the GATS in the light of prevailing economic realities. As the drafters of these agreements decided – for very good reasons – to 'stick to physics' in delineating the scope of obligations under these agreements, the judicial organs have no option but to do the same. If economic realities are such that a tariff concession for a product (e.g., hard-copy cinematographic films) is only meaningful when there is also a specific commitment on the cross-border supply of a service (for instance, entertainment services supplied by electronic means), the negotiators can add to the GATT concessions on products corresponding GATS commitments. If the negotiators failed to do so, the judicial organs of the WTO cannot step in and correct the omission without going beyond their mandate.

2. Could a measure inconsistent with one WTO agreement be justified by an exception contained in another?

Under the GATT, WTO Members may establish import and export monopolies and reserve the right to trade to state-owned enterprises. This follows from Article II:4, the note to Article XI, Article XVII, and Article XX(d) of the GATT. These provisions attempt to ensure that the GATT provisions applicable to private trading are not circumvented through state trading operations, but they do not curtail the right to establish import and export monopolies and other state trading enterprises. Moreover, under Article XX(d) of the GATT, Members may take all measures necessary to secure compliance with their laws and

4 For a recent confirmation of this jurisprudence see: Appellate Body Report, *Brazil – Measures Affecting Imports of Retreaded Tyres*, WT/DS332/AB/R, adopted 17 December 2007, para. 229 and footnote 437.

regulations relating to the enforcement of monopolies operated under Articles II and XVII.

In paragraph 5.1 of its Protocol of Accession, China assumed the obligation to accord all enterprises in China the right to trade, with respect to all goods except those listed in an Annex to the Protocol. Paragraph 5.1 defines the right to trade as the right to import and export goods. Unlike the other Members of the WTO, therefore, China may not establish monopolies on the importation of a product and enterprises with 'exclusive or special privileges' of the kind referred to in Articles II:4 and XVII:1 of the GATT with respect to the goods not listed in the Annex to the Protocol.

Paragraph 5.1 contains an introductory phrase, which states that China's trading-rights obligation is 'without prejudice to China's right to regulate trade in a manner consistent with the WTO Agreement'. The Appellate Body interpreted this phrase in its examination of a regulatory regime adopted by China under which films and other audiovisual products could be imported only by specified state enterprises charged with the review of their content. This regime restricted both *what* may be imported (audiovisual products with a certain content) and *who* may import (the specified state enterprises). The regime could thus be viewed to consist of:

- a *measure that regulates trade* within the meaning of the introductory phrase of paragraph 5.1 of the Protocol, namely the restriction on the importation of audiovisual products with a proscribed content, and
- a *measure that denies trading rights* guaranteed under the main clause of the first sentence of paragraph 5.1 of the Accession Protocol, namely the requirement that certain audiovisual products be imported exclusively by specified state enterprises.

The United States did not pursue any claim under the GATT in respect of the restriction on the importation of products subject to content review. The United States did, however, claim that China's failure to accord all enterprises in China the right to import audiovisual products was inconsistent with its obligation to provide the right to trade under the first sentence of paragraph 5.1 of the Protocol. China responded that its right to regulate trade consistently with the WTO Agreement, which it explicitly reserved under the introductory phrase, included the right to deny trading rights to protect public morals under Article XX(a) of the GATT.

The Panel and the Appellate Body thus faced a most curious situation: China invoked as a justification for a restriction on trading rights an exception to an agreement that it was not found to have violated. Was that legally possible? The Panel had avoided the issue by assuming *arguendo* that China could invoke Article XX(a) of the GATT and then finding that the denial of trading rights was not 'necessary' to protect morals and therefore did not meet the conditions of this exception. The Appellate Body, however, considered it appropriate to rule on the issue even though it, too, ultimately concluded that the denial of trading rights was not 'necessary to protect public morals' within the meaning of Article XX(a).

China's argument implies that the phrase 'without prejudice to China's right to regulate trade in a manner consistent with the WTO Agreement' entitles China to invoke in respect of its trading-rights commitment a GATT exception that applies to trade regulations. This is, however, not what this phrase states. Put simply: it does not say that China may deny trading rights consistently with the GATT; it says that the trading-rights commitment does not extend to WTO-consistent trade regulations.

The phrase was added to China's trading-rights commitment to take into account that, in fact, virtually every import or export regulation limits the number or types of enterprises that can exercise their right to trade. For instance, if a WTO Member accords shares in a tariff-rate quota to traders in accordance with their historical trade shares, it will limit the range of enterprises that are in a position to trade. A regulation that permits the importation of a dangerous chemical only by enterprises that meet certain safety standards would have the same effect. If a Member imposes a ban on the importation and production of meat with hormones, all enterprises are denied the possibility to import and export that product. In all these cases, the affected enterprises still have the right to trade, but cannot exercise that right because they do not meet the conditions set out in a trade regulation. In other words, in all these cases the regulations do not restrict the right to trade of particular enterprises (as envisaged in the main clause of the first sentence of paragraph 5.1), but impose conditions that all enterprises must observe in exercising their right to trade (as envisaged in the introductory phrase).

The paragraph 5.1 thus invites the interpreter to distinguish measures regulating trade from measures restricting the right to trade. By making that distinction, the interpreter ensures that China's right to regulate trade is not undermined by its additional commitment to provide the right to trade. Thus, if China takes a measure regulating trade that has the effect of narrowing the range of enterprises that can import or export, that effect should not, by itself, be considered to constitute a denial of the right to trade. Instead, it should be treated as an incidental consequence of the exercise of the right to regulate trade. Only direct limitations on the right to import or export are covered by China's trading-rights commitment, such as the grant of the exclusive right to import or export to a designated monopoly, state-owned enterprises, or enterprises owned by nationals. In my view, the threshold question before the Appellate Body was therefore whether the US claim concerned a measure *regulating trade* within the meaning of the introductory phrase (in respect of which the United States would have to make a claim under the GATT, and China could subsequently invoke Article XX of the GATT) or a *measure restricting trading rights* (in which case China could invoke only the exceptions from its trading-rights commitment set out in the Protocol).

Would that approach deprive China of the policy space accorded to other WTO Members under Article XX? I do not think so. Article XX lists nine policy areas in which WTO Members may, under specified conditions, take measures inconsistent with their obligations under other provisions of the GATT. These are public morals; human, animal, or plant life or health; importation or exportation of gold and silver; products of prison labour; national treasures of artistic, historic, or archaeological value; exhaustible natural resources; commodity agreements; stabilization of the price of domestic materials; and products in short supply. WTO Members do not pursue any of the policy goals listed in Article XX through denials of trading rights but through trade regulations. If a Member wishes to prevent the importation of plants carrying diseases, it must prohibit the importation of all such plants by *all* enterprises. It is not sufficient to exclude some enterprises. If a Member wishes to ensure that dangerous chemicals are imported only by enterprises capable of meeting certain safety standards, it will normally adopt a trade regulation imposing those safety standards on *all* importers. It is neither necessary nor efficient to deny to a category of enterprises the opportunity to meet those standards and thereby restrict their right to trade.

In practice, governments often deny the right to import and export to all but state-controlled enterprises in order to regulate the domestic prices of basic agricultural products and to improve their bargaining position in international markets for such products. State trading also occurs when governments take control of enterprises importing or exporting products of strategic importance. These and the other common reasons for denying trading rights are not mentioned in Article XX. It must be kept in mind that this provision is *not* a list of the most important societal values of the Members of the WTO. It lists those areas in which policy goals unrelated to trade cannot be achieved without imposing import or export restrictions, measures discriminating against imported products or products destined for export, or other measures inconsistent with the basic provisions of the GATT. The denial of trading rights as such is not inconsistent with the basic provisions of the GATT. There was therefore no reason for the drafters of the GATT to extend the scope of Article XX to the policy goals that governments pursue through the denial of trading rights.

The interpretative approach outlined above would thus not deprive China of the policy space accorded to all Members of the WTO under Article XX, because the policy goals listed in Article XX cannot be achieved through the denial of trading rights, and the policy goals that governments commonly seek to realize by reserving the right to trade to state trading enterprises and trade monopolies are not mentioned in Article XX.

At one stage in its analysis, the Appellate Body appears to lean towards the approach advocated here. It notes that the China Accession Working Party Report specifies that 'foreign enterprises and individuals with trading rights ha[ve] to comply with all WTO-consistent requirements related to importing and exporting, such as those concerning import licensing, TBT and SPS'.[5] The Appellate Body

5 Appellate Body Report, *China–Publications and Audiovisual Products*, para. 224.

read this as a confirmation that 'China's obligation to grant the right to trade cannot impair China's power to impose WTO-consistent import licensing, TBT, and SPS measures'.[6] In its subsequent reasoning, however, the Appellate Body took a different approach. It found that '*the regulation of who may import and export specific goods will normally be objectively related to, and will often form part of, the regulation of trade in those goods*'. '*When such a link exists*', the Appellate Body concluded, '*then China may seek to show that, because its measure complies with the conditions of a GATT 1994 exception, the measure represents an exercise of China's power to regulate trade in a manner consistent with the WTO Agreement* ...'[7] On the basis of this reasoning, it permitted China to invoke Article XX(a) of the GATT to justify a measure inconsistent with its trading-rights commitment.

According to the Appellate Body, China can thus invoke Article XX of the GATT in respect of the denial of trading rights if three conditions are met:

- the measure must regulate 'those who may engage in the import and export of goods',
- it must be 'objectively related to ... the regulation of trade in those goods', and
- it must 'form part of, the regulation of trade in those goods'.[8]

The criteria established by the Appellate Body cannot be found in the text of paragraph 5.1, in prior GATT or WTO jurisprudence, or in any principle of law. The wording of the introductory phrase clearly safeguards China's right to regulate trade in goods consistently with WTO law notwithstanding its trading-rights commitment. However, it does not make China's trading-rights commitment subject to its rights under the GATT. Since the provisions of the GATT permit China to channel trade through state-owned enterprises and trade monopolies, China's additional commitment to provide trading rights serves no purpose if its rights under the GATT delineate the scope of that commitment. The Appellate Body's ruling therefore gives a meaning to the introductory sentence that renders China's trading-rights commitment redundant.

WTO law makes numerous legal distinctions between measures that are in practice 'objectively' linked, for instance between measures affecting goods and those affecting services, between exchange restrictions and trade restrictions, and between foreign-investment regulations and foreign-trade regulations. However, there is no previous Panel or Appellate Body ruling that applied the rules governing one type of measure to another type of measure governed by other rules solely on the ground that the two types of measures were 'objectively' linked.

The Appellate Body suggests the contrary by referring to previous GATT and WTO cases 'where measures that did not directly regulate goods, or the importation

6 Ibid.
7 Ibid., para. 230.
8 Ibid.

of goods, have nonetheless been found to contravene GATT obligations. Thus, for example, restrictions imposed on investors, wholesalers, and manufacturers, as well as on points of sale and ports of entry, have been found to be inconsistent with Article III:4 or Article XI:1 of the GATT 1947 or 1994.'[9] However, in none of these cases did the Panel or the Appellate Body rule that, by virtue of the close 'objective' link between the disputed measure and another policy area, the rules applicable in that other policy area could be invoked by the respondent. For instance, the GATT Panel that examined measures discriminating against imported products adopted by Canada under its foreign-investment law clearly distinguished between the trade measures and the investment measures adopted by Canada in the context of this law. It did not rule that Canada could impose a trade measure inconsistent with the GATT by virtue of the right to regulate investments that it had retained under the GATT. The cases cited by the Appellate Body do not support but undermine its conclusion because they demonstrate that the national-treatment obligation of the GATT, and its general prohibition of quantitative restriction, apply in all areas of policy making and that WTO Members cannot escape their GATT obligations by taking trade measures in the context of regulations extending to non-trade matters.

There is also no previous Panel or Appellate Body ruling in which the fact that the measure at issue forms part of a domestic regulation extending to other measures was considered to be legally relevant. In all previous cases, Panels and the Appellate Body avoided attributing legal relevance to an aspect of the measure at issue that is open to manipulation by Members. Thus, the Appellate Body ruled in *China–Auto Parts* that, in determining whether a charge is a 'border charge' falling under Article II of the GATT or an internal charge falling under the national-treatment provisions of Article III of the GATT, 'a degree of caution must be exercised in attributing decisive weight to characteristics that fall exclusively within the control of WTO Members, "because otherwise Members could determine by themselves which of the provisions would apply to their charges"'.[10] Whether two measures are taken under a single or under two separate regulations falls exclusively within the control of WTO Members. The sound principle of GATT and WTO jurisprudence reflected in the ruling in *China–Auto Parts* was not applied in the present case.

In support of its 'objective link' criterion, the Appellate Body points out that the types of WTO-consistent requirements that China may impose according to the Working Party Report on China's Accession 'are not limited to requirements that apply directly to goods themselves, nor to requirements that apply to the activity of importing or exporting'.[11] The Appellate Body states that '[i]mport licensing

9 Ibid., para. 227.

10 Appellate Body Report, *China – Measures Affecting Imports of Automobile Parts* (WT/DS339/AB/R, WT/DS340/AB/R, WT/DS342/AB/R), adopted 12 January 2009, para. 178, quoting in part the Panel.

11 Appellate Body Report, *China–Publications and Audiovisual Products*, para. 225.

requirements, for example, are requirements relating to the activity of importing goods. Typically, licensing requirements and their attendant procedures apply to and are satisfied by those who wish to import the goods, rather than by the goods themselves.'[12] It is difficult to see how these considerations support the conclusion that China's obligations regarding the right to import are qualified by its rights under the GATT. All laws are addressed to persons and all requirements must be fulfilled by persons, not objects or actions and hence not goods or services. A law regulating trade and a law restricting the right to trade, therefore, necessarily have the same addressee, namely persons engaged in the activity of trading. What distinguishes these laws is that the former regulates *what* may be imported (and may therefore fall under the GATT or one of the agreements supplementing the GATT) and the latter regulates *who* may import (and may therefore fall under paragraph 5.1). Only the content of the measures, not their addressees, can be relevant to their legal status under WTO law.

The Appellate Body argues that the 'introductory clause of paragraph 5.1 cannot be interpreted in a way that would allow a complainant to deny China access to a defence merely by asserting a claim under paragraph 5.1 and by refraining from asserting a claim under other provisions of the covered agreements relating to trade in goods that apply to the same or closely linked measures, and which set out obligations that are closely linked to China's trading rights commitments'.[13]

The statement implies that the measure at issue in this dispute – the measure on which the Appellate Body had to rule – was China's regulatory regime for the importation of audiovisual products *as a whole*. However, in a WTO dispute-settlement proceeding the measure at issue is defined by the complainant. Only the facts on which it bases its legal claim and the provisions it invokes in support can therefore be the basis of a ruling against the defendant. In this case, the United States did not base its claim on that part of China's regulatory regime that restricts *what* may be traded and that might therefore be inconsistent with the GATT, and there was consequently no need for China to invoke the defence of Article XX of the GATT. The United States, by basing its claim on that part of China's regulatory regime that restricts *who* may trade and on its rights under the Protocol of Accession rather than those under the GATT, therefore did not deny China access to a defence under the GATT. The Appellate Body's argument is essentially a *petitio principii*: It is intended to demonstrate that China has the right to invoke Article XX of the GATT as defence against a claim not based on the GATT, but in fact presupposes that this is so. The objective-link criterion possibly reflects a concern that in taking measures to regulate trade, Members may need to restrict simultaneously the right to trade and that it would be inappropriate to deny China the right to invoke Article XX of the GATT in such situations. However, as discussed above, while trade regulations, such as import-licensing, TBT, and SPS

12 Ibid., footnote 428.
13 Ibid., para. 229.

regulations, may narrow the range of enterprises that can in fact exercise their right to trade, they do not restrict the right to trade as such. The introductory phrase to paragraph 5.1 makes clear that such regulations must not be treated as denials of trading rights even if in practice not all enterprises are able to meet the requirements imposed by such regulations. If trade restrictions are clearly distinguished from restrictions on trading rights and China's trading-rights commitment is properly interpreted not to extend to the incidental impact of trade restrictions, there is no need to qualify China's trading-rights obligation by its rights under Article XX of the GATT and to develop a novel theory justifying that qualification.[14] Put differently: the need to develop a tool to extract trade regulations covered by Article XX from the box 'trading rights' only arises if one has incorrectly put such trade regulations into that box in the first place.

Just as the authors and others,[15] I have for these reasons difficulties fathoming the legal basis, the practical need, and the policy rationale of the objective-link principle. The Appellate Body takes pains to emphasize that its ruling is based on the introductory phrase in paragraph 5.1 of China's Protocol of Accession and that it applies only 'in this case'. However, while its ruling is of course case-specific, the reasoning underlying that ruling is not. The Appellate Body reasoned that links made by Members in their laws between 'objectively' linked measures can determine the scope of their obligations. That new principle puts the legal relationships between the various WTO agreements on an entirely new footing.

The agreements annexed to the WTO Agreement were negotiated separately as self-contained regimes.[16] Where the drafters intended the obligations under one of these agreements to be qualified by rights under another legal instrument, they made that explicit. Under the new principle of WTO law posited by the Appellate Body, the relationships between these WTO agreements are no longer determined solely by the expressed intentions of the drafters; 'objective' and regulatory linkages between the measure at issue and another measure subject to other rules under another agreement become relevant. This raises legal issues such as the following: Could the provisions on regional trade agreements of Article XXIV of the GATT now be invoked to justify measures inconsistent with WTO agreements that

14 This is not to say that the distinction between trade regulations and trading-rights limitations can easily be made in all cases. However, the difficulty of making that distinction does not exceed the difficulty of distinguishing for example between internal regulations and restrictions on importation (Articles III:4 and XI:1 of the GATT), between standards for services and market-access limitations on the supply of services (Articles VI:5 and XVI:2 of the GATS), or between measures prohibiting the sale of a product and those prescribing product characteristics (Article III:4 of the GATT and Annex 1, paragraph 1, of the TBT Agreement).

15 Fernando Piérola (2010), 'The Availability of a GATT Article XX Defence with Respect to a Non-GATT Claim: Changing the Rules of the Game?', *Global Trade and Customs Journal*, 5: 172–175.

16 Some of these agreements were taken over from the GATT era, during which they operated as independent agreements concluded among different GATT contracting parties with separate dispute-settlement procedures. The decision to incorporate these agreements into the WTO Agreement was taken only in the final stages of the Uruguay Round. Only then were the acceptance procedures set out in the drafts of each of these agreements replaced by a single acceptance procedure in the WTO Agreement.

do not permit discrimination in favour of regional trading partners, such as the SPS, TBT, and TRIPS agreements? Could Article XX of the GATT now be invoked to justify export subsidies inconsistent with the Subsidies Agreement even though that Agreement contains an exhaustive list of exceptions to the prohibition of export subsidies? Can the rights that the Members of the WTO have retained under the GATS be invoked to justify trade measures inconsistent with the GATT? Can Members, by creating 'objective' and regulatory links between policy measures covered by different WTO agreements, now manipulate the scope of their obligations under these agreements? In the past, the answer to all these questions was clearly negative; now we no longer know.

The dispute could easily have been settled without a ruling on the relationship between Article XX and China's trading-rights commitment. The Panel did so; the Appellate Body could have followed its example. The new theory developed by the Appellate Body does not provide China with additional policy space because the denial of trading rights is not a policy instrument with which any of the policy goals mentioned in Article XX can effectively be implemented. Perhaps future jurisprudence will reveal why the Appellate Body justified an unnecessary ruling with no impact on the respondent's policy options on the basis of a new principle that casts a shadow of uncertainty over the whole of WTO law.

'Optimal' Retaliation in the WTO – a commentary on the *Upland Cotton* Arbitration

GENE M. GROSSMAN
Princeton University
ALAN O. SYKES
Stanford University

Abstract: The *Upland Cotton* case raises a range of interesting issues regarding the rationale for retaliation in the WTO system and the proper approach to its calibration. These include: Should the approach to retaliation differ in cases involving prohibited or actionable subsidies? When should cross-retaliation be allowed? Should retaliation be based only on the harm to the complaining nation, or to other nations as well? And, most importantly, what economic content can be given to the standard of countermeasures 'equivalent to the level of nullification or impairment'? We address these and other issues from both a legal and economic perspective, with particular attention to the question of what level of retaliation will restore the lost welfare of the complaining nation.

The United States is a leading producer and exporter of cotton. Its market share in world cotton trade has averaged 37% since the year 2000, and some 70% of US production on average has been exported.[1] The US cotton industry has also long been the beneficiary of various forms of government support, averaging some $3.55 billion per year since 2000, as compared with average annual cotton output in the United States of $4.26 billion.[2] These statistics alone suggest that US government programs for cotton production have had a sizeable impact on the competitive position of US cotton growers.

In 2002, Brazil requested consultations with the United States regarding various US government programs benefiting producers of upland cotton. A Panel was constituted in 2003 to adjudicate claims that US programs constituted actionable subsidies under Part III of the Subsidies and Countervailng Measures (SCM) Agreement, prohibited subsidies under Part II of the SCM Agreement, illegal export subsidies under the Agreement on Agriculture, and actionable subsidies

1 Schnepf (2010: 6).

2 Ibid.: 7. Schnepf uses data from the USDA Farm Service Agency, Budget Division, available at http://www.fsa.usda.gov/FSA/webapp?area=about&subject=landing&topic=bap-bu-uc.

under Article XVI of GATT. The Panel ruled that a variety of US programs were inconsistent with the Agreement on Agriculture, and thus not exempt from actions under pertinent provisions of the SCM Agreement and GATT Article XVI.[3] On appeal, the Appellate Body confirmed that certain US programs were actionable subsidies that had caused serious prejudice to Brazil, and that other programs were either prohibited export subsidies or prohibited subsidies contingent on the use of domestic over imported goods.[4]

The United States subsequently introduced various modifications to its programs affecting the production of upland cotton, but some of the problematic provisions remained little changed. Brazil thus initiated a compliance proceeding pursuant to Dispute Settlement Understanding (DSU) Article 21.5. The compliance Panel ruled in 2007 that certain marketing loan and countercyclical payments by the United States were being provided under the same conditions and criteria as those found to cause serious prejudice by the original Panel, and that the United States had failed to bring these measures into compliance. Likewise, the Panel ruled that the United States continued to provide certain export credit guarantees that amounted to a circumvention of the US commitments under the Agreement on Agriculture and thus to prohibited export subsidies under the SCM Agreement.[5] The United States again appealed, and although the Appellate Body modified several findings of the Panel, it nevertheless upheld the Panel's key results.[6]

In the interim, Brazil requested authorization to retaliate against the United States following the expiration in 2005 of the 'reasonable periods of time' for the United States to bring its policies into compliance.[7] The United States objected to the proposed retaliation and the matter was referred to arbitration under DSU Article 22.6. The arbitration was suspended during the compliance litigation, but in 2008 Brazil requested that it be resumed.

Our focus in this paper is on the two arbitration decisions regarding the proposed level of retaliation by Brazil, one pertaining to the prohibited subsidies,[8] and the other pertaining to the actionable subsidies.[9] Both decisions calculated an allowable level of retaliation in goods sectors based on the magnitude of US subsidies during prior years, and offer a formula for retaliation based on future subsidy levels. They further provide authority for Brazil to suspend concessions under

3 Panel Report, *United States – Subsidies on Upland Cotton*, WT/DS267/R, 8 September 2004.

4 Appellate Body Report, *United States – Subsidies on Upland Cotton*, WT/DS267/AB/R, 3 March 2005.

5 Panel Report, *United States – Subsidies on Upland Cotton*, Recourse to Article 21.5 of the DSU by Brazil, WT/DS267/RW, 20 December 2007.

6 Appellate Body Report, *United States – Subsidies on Upland Cotton*, Recourse to Article 21.5 of the DSU by Brazil, WT/DS267/AB/RW, 2 June 2008.

7 The 'reasonable period' expired earlier for the prohibited subsidies than for the actionable subsidies.

8 WT/DS267/ARB/1, 31 August 2009 (hereafter Prohibited Subs. Arb.).

9 WT/DS267/ARB/2, 31 August 2009 (hereafter Actionable Subs. Arb.).

TRIPs or GATS in the event that the total allowable retaliation in goods sectors exceeds a certain threshold.

The analysis of the Arbitrator in each decision is complex and raises a wide range of issues. We cannot hope to address all of them in this brief commentary, and will focus on the issues that seem to us to be the most central for the remedial system, and to have the broadest implications for other possible disputes.

Sections 1 (prohibited subsidies), 2 (actionable subsidies), and 3 (cross-retaliation) set out the core legal issues that we wish to address, and the decision of the Arbitrator with respect to each set of issues. They also contain our own legal commentary on the issues, a commentary that is brief due to the lack of much useful guidance in the treaty text or from any well-established WTO practice. Section 4 contains our economic analysis.

1. Key issues and legal analysis – prohibited subsidies

A number of US programs were found to constitute prohibited subsidies in the original *Upland Cotton* litigation. These included payments under a program known as 'Step 2', found to constitute import substitution subsidies, along with export credit guarantees under programs known as GSM 102, GSM 103, and SGCP, which were found to constitute export subsidies. The 'reasonable time' for the United States to bring these programs into compliance with its obligations expired on 1 July 2005. The United States stopped accepting applications for export guarantees under GSM 103 on 30 June 2005, and announced a new fee structure for GSM 102 and SGCP at the same time. In October 2005, it announced an end to the SGCP program altogether. The Step 2 program continued until it was repealed, effective 1 August 2006. After that time, only GSM 102 remained in effect, as modified in June 2005. Brazil argued before the compliance Panel that the new fee structure for GSM 102 did not solve the problem of subsidization, and the Panel and Appellate Body agreed.

This chronology raised two core issues regarding retaliation. First, could Brazil retaliate for the now repealed programs that had continued after 1 July 2005? Second, what was the proper measure of retaliation with respect to the ongoing GSM 102 program?

Expired programs

In its request to the Dispute Settlement Body, Brazil sought authorization for 'one-time' countermeasures in the amount of US$350 million, which was based on the Step 2 payments made between 1 July 2005 and 30 June 2006 before the program was repealed. Brazil bolstered its argument for countermeasures against this expired program by arguing that the 2008 US Farm Bill enacted new programs benefiting upland-cotton producers that Brazil believed to constitute illegal subsidies. Those new programs had not been the subject of a WTO complaint by Brazil, however, and had not been addressed by the compliance Panel. Likewise,

Brazil did not ask the Arbitrator to adjudicate the issue of their WTO consistency, but simply urged the Arbitrator to 'take into account' the existence of these new programs.[10]

The Arbitrator noted the repeal of Step 2 and the fact that the compliance Panel made no findings regarding the program because of its repeal. It then noted various textual provisions of the DSU to the effect that countermeasures were an extraordinary remedy to be used on a temporary basis following the 'reasonable period' for compliance. Most prominent in this respect is DSU Article 22.8, which provides:

> The suspension of concessions or other obligations shall be temporary and shall only be applied until such time as the measure found to be inconsistent with a covered agreement has been removed, or the Member that must implement recommendations or rulings provides a solution to the nullification or impairment of benefits, or a mutually satisfactory solution is reached.

Brazil argued that this provision relates only to the duration of countermeasures and not to their initial authorization, but the Arbitrator had little difficulty dismissing this distinction, holding that countermeasures are impermissible after a WTO-inconsistent measure has been repealed, absent a finding that the measure has been replaced by a new measure that amounts to substantive noncompliance.[11]

As a legal matter, we have no quarrel with the analysis of the Arbitrator. The treaty text is clear that countermeasures are limited to a window of time following the reasonable period for compliance, and delimited by the date of compliance or one of the other enumerated events in DSU Article 22.8. WTO practice has been consistent in this regard. We also see no legal basis for departing from these principles simply because a complaining nation alleges that some new violation exists that has not yet been adjudicated by an original Panel or examined as part of a compliance Panel proceeding.

Of course, the effect of these principles is to insulate a violator from retaliation for violations that it cures within a 'reasonable period of time', perhaps supplemented by a further period of compliance litigation. At first blush, such a system might appear to create an 'engraved invitation' for temporary cheating in the system, and indeed has come to be known colloquially as the 'three-year free pass'.[12] It is thus open to question from an economic standpoint, an issue that we address in Section 4.

10 See Prohibited Subs. Arb., para. 3.93.

11 See ibid., para. 3.95.

12 One potential abuse has been addressed by the Appellate Body. If a nation repeals a program that violates WTO rules, and replaces it with another that has much the same effect, it cannot then argue that retaliation is impermissible because the new program has not been the subject of an adjudication. Rather, a compliance Panel may examine the new program for 'substantive compliance' with the original ruling, and retaliation may be authorized if the new program fails this test. The difference in *Upland Cotton* is that the new US Farm Bill programs were enacted two years after the repeal of Step 2, and had not been examined by the compliance Panel.

Continuing programs – the retaliation metric

Of the programs originally found to constitute prohibited subsidies, only GSM 102, an export credit guarantee program, remained in effect at the time of the Article 22.6 arbitration. The compliance Panel had ruled earlier that the modifications introduced in 2005 were inadequate to put the program into compliance, and that it continued to confer prohibited export subsidies. The amount of retaliation requested by Brazil was based on the value of the interest-rate subsidy under the program, plus Brazil's estimate of the marginal additional exports by creditworthy borrowers ('marginal additionality'), plus the value of all exports by noncreditworthy borrowers on a number of unscheduled products, plus rice, poultry, and pork ('full additionality'). Brazil calculated these amounts as $237.4 million, $62.3 million, and $855 million, respectively.[13]

The United States argued in response that Brazil's proposed method of calculation was flawed. It noted that the export credit guarantee program was found to constitute a subsidy with reference to illustrative item (j) in Annex I of the SCM Agreement, which provides that export credit programs constitute a subsidy when the fees for participation do not cover the costs of the program.[14] Accordingly, the United States argued, the appropriate measure of the subsidy was the net cost of the program to the US government, an amount that it urged should cap the amount of retaliation. The United States did not specify this amount but offered to calculate it. The United States further argued that 'a reduction should be made' because 'Brazil may only take such countermeasures with respect to the impact of the alleged subsidy on itself. If Brazil were permitted to take countermeasures for the entire amount of the subsidy, it would create a conflict for other Members who may have an interest in the GSM 102 program.'[15]

One core issue here, therefore, concerns the proper metric for calibrating retaliation. Is it the value of the subsidy, as had been the case in some prior prohibited-subsidies cases? Is it the impact of the subsidy on the volume of trade? Or is it something else? A second core issue concerns the retaliation rights of an individual country in relation to a subsidy program that affects the trade of many countries – can the complaining nation retaliate based on the global effect of the subsidy, or only the effects on itself? Finally, once these questions are answered, it remains to calculate the amount of retaliation under the chosen standard, a potentially complex calculation that itself raises a variety of issues.

13 Prohibited Subs. Arb., para. 4.110.

14 Item (j) states: 'The provision by governments (or special institutions controlled by governments) of export credit guarantee or insurance programmes, of insurance or guarantee programmes against increases in the cost of exported products or of exchange risk programmes, at premium rates which are inadequate to cover the long-term operating costs and losses of the programmes.'

15 Prohibited Subs. Arb., para. 4.114.

The decision of the Arbitrator

The usual standard for WTO countermeasures is found in DSU Article 22.4: 'The level of the suspension of concessions or other obligations authorized by the DSB shall be equivalent to the level of the nullification or impairment.' This standard is understood to refer to the harm done to nations adversely affected by a violation – the 'nullification or impairment' of the benefits to which they are entitled under the WTO bargain. Accordingly, in the typical case governed by DSU Article 22.4, the focus is on the trade impact of the violation, and the allowed retaliation is to be 'equivalent'. Thus, an Arbitrator will commonly calculate the value of lost trade due to the violation, and then authorize retaliation in an equal amount – complaining nations, for example, may impose prohibitive tariffs on imports from the violator nation to a degree sufficient to choke off exports from the violator in an amount equal to the value lost because of the violation.

In prohibited-subsidies cases, however, the SCM Agreement introduces another wrinkle. Article 4.10 states: 'In the event the recommendation of the DSB is not followed within the time-period specified by the panel, which shall commence from the date of adoption of the panel's report or the Appellate Body's report, the DSB shall grant authorization to the complaining Member to take appropriate countermeasures…' A footnote to the word 'appropriate' further states: 'This expression is not meant to allow countermeasures that are disproportionate in light of the fact that the subsidies dealt with under these provisions are prohibited.' The 'appropriate countermeasures' standard was interpreted in prior prohibited-subsidies cases – *Brazil–Aircraft*,[16] *Canada–Aircraft*,[17] and *United States–Foreign Sales Corporations* (*FSC*)[18] – to authorize countermeasures in an amount equal to the value of this subsidy. And, in the *FSC* decision, the complainant (Europe) was permitted to retaliate at a level equal to the full value of the subsidy. No reduction was made for the fact that other nations had also suffered adverse effects due to the subsidy.

The US position on retaliation, which focused on the value of the subsidy, followed directly from these earlier cases. Of course, the United States was also seeking to avoid the *FSC* outcome, by insisting that Brazil's retaliatory rights should be reduced in some fashion to reflect the fact that other nations were also affected by the subsidy and might in principle seek their own retaliation rights in the future.

16 *Brazil – Export Financing Programme for Aircraft*, Recourse to Arbitration by Brazil under Article 22.6 of the DSU and Article 4.11 of the SCM Agreement, WT/DS46/ARB, 28 August 2000.

17 *Canada – Export Credits and Loan Guarantees for Regional Aircraft*, Recourse to Arbitration by Canada under Article 22.6 of the DSU and Article 4.11 of the SCM Agreement, WT/DS222/ARB, 17 February 2003.

18 *United States – Tax Treatment for 'Foreign Sales Corporations'*, Recourse to Arbitration by the United States under Article 22.6 of the DSU and Article 4.11 of the SCM Agreement, WT/DS108/ARB, 30 August 2002.

Brazil's position, by contrast, sought an entirely new measure as the standard – it wished to sum the value of the subsidy with the value of worldwide exports stimulated by the subsidy. It also wished to avoid any reduction in retaliation rights based on the fact that the subsidy had adverse effects on other countries besides Brazil.

The Arbitrator rejected both proposals. It agreed with Brazil and with prior case law that the 'appropriate countermeasures' standard was looser than the 'equivalence' standard of DSU Article 22.4. Yet, emphasizing the footnote that cautions against 'disproportionate' countermeasures, the Arbitrator concluded:

> [C]ountermeasures, in order to be 'appropriate', should bear some relationship to the extent to which the complaining Member has suffered from the trade-distorting impact of the illegal subsidy. Countermeasures are in essence trade-restrictive measures to be taken in response to a Member's application of a trade-distorting measure that has been determined to nullify or impair the benefits accruing to another Member. Countermeasures that would ensure a relationship of proportionality between the extent to which the trade opportunities of the Member applying the countermeasures has been affected and the extent to which the trade opportunities of the violating Member will in turn be adversely affected would notionally restore the balance of rights and obligations arising from the covered agreements that has been upset between the parties. This would ensure a proper relationship between the level of the countermeasures and the circumstances out of which the dispute arises.[19]

The Arbitrator further noted the standard for countermeasures in 'actionable subsidies' cases under SCMs Article 7.9, which contemplates countermeasures 'commensurate' with the adverse effects of the subsidy. It viewed the 'appropriate' standard of SCMs Article 4.10 as a 'more flexible' standard, and concluded that the adverse effects of the subsidy on the complaining member in effect provide a floor for the level of retaliation.[20] Finally, while acknowledging that an objective of all WTO countermeasures is to 'induce compliance', the Arbitrator rejected the notion that this objective delinked the level of countermeasures from the adverse effects of the violation.[21]

For these reasons, the Arbitrator rejected the notion put forward by the United States that the value of the subsidy was necessarily the proper standard in prohibited-subsidies cases. It also rejected the US claim that the proper way to value the subsidy should focus on the net cost to the government, observing that the benefit to the recipient of subsidies was the typical standard for valuing subsidies under WTO law. The proper valuation must thus ask what borrowers would have had to pay for credit in the private market.

19 Prohibited Subs. Arb., para. 4.190.
20 Ibid., para. 4.205.
21 Ibid., paras. 4.213–4.215.

The Arbitrator also rejected the Brazilian proposal to base retaliation on the total value of the subsidy plus the increase in worldwide US exports due to the subsidy. This amount was not properly linked to the adverse effects suffered by Brazil.

But the Arbitrator did accept Brazil's notion that the harm from the subsidy included a lost-volume-of-trade component, and a price-suppression component. It found that the additional export sales stimulated by the subsidy were an approximation of the lost quantity of sales by all other producers, recognizing that it might overstate that amount. It also argued that the value of the subsidy (measured against market interest rates) was an approximation to the price-suppression effect suffered by all non-US producers. These amounts could thus be summed to approximate the adverse effects on non-US producers. What remained was to adjust the calculation to capture the harm to Brazil in particular. To estimate the adverse effects on Brazil in its export markets, the Arbitrator suggested that these total price and volume effects in those markets should be multiplied by Brazil's market share of the products in question. The total price and volume effects in Brazil's home market would then be added to obtain the total amount of permissible retaliation.[22]

In the end, therefore, the Arbitrator adopted a variant of Brazil's original proposal. It suggested that Brazil's calculation of the value of the subsidy approximated the lost revenue abroad, while the exports stimulated by the subsidy approximated the lost volume of sales abroad. The Arbitrator recognized that these estimates were crude and might overstate the harm, but argued that they were nevertheless acceptable under the 'appropriateness' standard of SCMs Article 4.10. The key departure from Brazil's original proposal was the requirement that the harm be apportioned to the harm suffered by Brazil, which was done by adjusting it downward using Brazil's market share in its export markets.

Much of the remainder of the decision focuses on the details of the calculations pursuant to this standard. The Arbitrator undertook to value the subsidy based on the spread between the subsidized export credit price and the market price of credit, taking account of the creditworthiness of borrowers. It also sought to value the additional quantity of exports to noncreditworthy and creditworthy borrowers. Ultimately, the amounts calculated for fiscal year 2006 for these three components were US$25.3 million, $80.8 million, and $41.3 million, respectively, for a total figure of $147.4 million, in contrast to Brazil's original proposal in the amount of $1.12 billion.[23] The Arbitrator's calculation also provides a formula for retaliation in future years when US subsidy expenditures may increase or decrease.

Legal analysis

The textual standard for countermeasures under WTO law is at best vague. The 'equivalence' standard under DSU Article 22.4 does seem to require that

22 Ibid., paras. 4.285–4.305.
23 Ibid., para. 4.381.

countermeasures bear relation to the harm suffered by aggrieved parties, but offers little guidance as to how this arm should be measured. The looser 'appropriateness' standard of SCMs Article 4.10 provides even less clarity.

Neither can one rely much on established practice. Formal sanctions under GATT were nonexistent save for one case in the 1950s (in which they were authorized but not used). The brief period of WTO practice since 1995, involving a rather small number of cases, divides into a focus on lost trade volume in cases under DSU Article 22.4, and a focus on the value of the subsidy in prior cases under SCMs Article 4.10. The Arbitrator in *Upland Cotton* obviously departed from the value of the subsidy as the measure of retaliation, but we cannot condemn this departure as a legal matter simply because of its inconsistency with three prior unappealed (and unappealable) arbitrations involving prohibited subsidies. The 'appropriateness' standard confers significant discretion on a process that has no appellate oversight, and we have no basis for suggesting that the Arbitrator here abused its discretion.

Likewise, the Arbitrator's determination that retaliation should be apportioned based on the amount of harm suffered by Brazil was a departure from the outcome in the *FSC* case. But the *FSC* arbitration has been criticized on the grounds that if complaining nations could each retaliate based on the effect of the subsidy on all nations, cumulative retaliation might ultimately prove 'disproportionate' (see, e.g., Howse and Neven, 2005). This critique is not without logic, and the decision of the Arbitrator in *Upland Cotton* to apportion retaliation rights based on market share seems a reasonable response to this concern.

In short, although *Upland Cotton* departs from prior 'precedent'[24] in significant ways, we cannot say that it is at odds with any element of the treaty text or any well-established practice. The issues here are much more issues of policy and economics, which we reserve for Section 4.

2. Key issues and legal analysis – actionable subsidies

The programs at issue as actionable subsidies were nonrecourse marketing loans (ML) and counter-cyclical payments (CCP) that resulted in payments to farmers when prices fell below a target level. Both the original Panel and the compliance Panel determined that these programs were subsidies because they provide net payments from the government, and that they had caused 'serious prejudice' to Brazil in the form of price suppression in violation of SCMs Article 6.

The United States argued that these programs, part of the 2002 Farm Bill, had expired at the time of the arbitration. The Arbitrator responded that the compliance Panel had ruled against the United States when these programs were examined, and that essentially the same programs had been reenacted in the

24 Of course, we recognize that *stare decisis* and formal precedent are not part of the WTO system.

2008 Farm Bill. Accordingly, it rejected the suggestion that retaliation was impermissible because of the expiry of the 2002 Farm Bill.[25]

The standard in the SCM Agreement for countermeasures against actionable subsidies is found in Article 7.9: '[T]he DSB shall grant authorization to the complaining Member to take countermeasures, commensurate with the degree and nature of the adverse effects determined to exist...' This language is similar to that in DSU Article 22.4, which refers to countermeasures 'equivalent to the level of nullification or impairment'. The Arbitrator suggested that the two standards are not identical, and that the requisite linkage to the harm suffered by the complaining nation is less strict under SCMs Article 7, but that nevertheless Article 7 links countermeasures to the harm suffered: '[T]he term "commensurate" connotes a less precise degree of equivalence than exact numerical correspondence. Nonetheless, the term "commensurate" does indicate, in our view, a relationship of *correspondence* and proportionality between the two elements.'[26]

To Brazil's suggestion that stiffer countermeasures ought be allowed for the purpose of 'inducing compliance', the Arbitrator responded: '[T]he terms of Article 7.9 of the *SCM Agreement*, which refer exclusively to the "degree and nature of the adverse effects determined to exist", do not suggest that there would be any basis for increasing their level, in a subjective sense, to specifically take into account a superadded objective of inducing compliance. We are not empowered to "adjust" the level of countermeasures beyond what these terms allow'.[27] Likewise, as it had ruled with respect to the prohibited subsidies, the Arbitrator held that the 'adverse effects' relevant to the calibration of countermeasures are the adverse effects *on Brazil*, not the entirety of the adverse effects on non-US producers.[28]

Finally, recall that the basis for the finding of 'serious prejudice' under SCMs Article 6 was 'significant price suppression'. The United States argued from this language that only the amount of price suppression above the 'significance' threshold should be considered for retaliation. The Arbitrator rejected this suggestion, concluding that:

> [t]he threshold of 'significance' is set in order to ascertain whether the price suppression at issue is sufficiently 'important, notable or consequential', as the original panel put it, to fall within the scope of Article 6.3(c) and form the basis of a finding of 'serious prejudice' under Article 6 of the *SCM Agreement*. Once it is determined that the price suppression *is* significant, and therefore that it is within the scope of the provision, then it is the entirety of that existing 'significant price suppression' that is the basis for the determination of 'serious prejudice'. To adjust the level of price suppression downwards, for the purposes of estimating the level of countermeasures that Brazil is entitled to, would mean that we would not in fact take into account the entirety of the situation that has given rise

25 Actionable Subs. Arb., paras. 3.64–3.68.

26 Ibid., para. 4.39.

27 Ibid., para. 4.62.

28 Ibid., para. 4.92.

to the findings, namely the fact that a certain degree of price suppression exists on the world cotton market, that has been found to be 'significant'.[29]

After disposing of a few other minor issues that we omit here, the Arbitrator turned to the task of calculating the appropriate countermeasures. The calculation relied on a simulation model of the world cotton market that sought to estimate the effect on world market prices and non-US production of the subsidy programs at issue. The conceptual approach was summarized by the Arbitrator as follows:

> Brazil's calculation of adverse effects from US marketing loans and counter-cyclical payments can be graphically represented by Figure 1. It represents the supply curve of a cotton producing country in the rest of the world. With US subsidies in place, the world price is at OP and quantity produced in the country at OQ. Without the US subsidies, the world price would be at the higher level OP' and cotton producers in the country would have responded by producing more cotton, represented here by OQ′.
>
> Figure 1. Adverse Effects on Producers in the Rest of the World
>
> 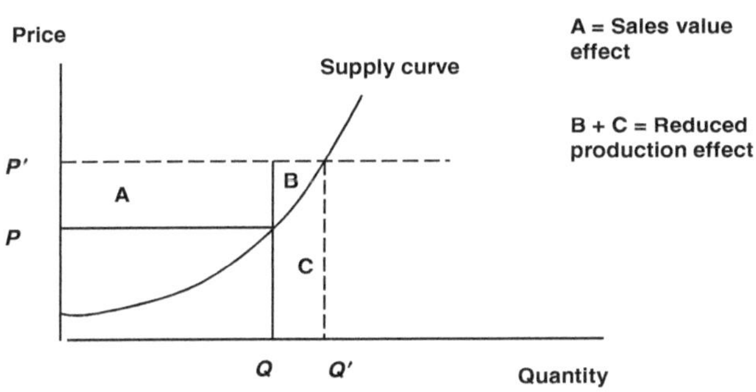
>
>
> The area **A** in Figure 1 is what Brazil terms the 'sales value effect' while the sum of the areas **B** and **C** is what it terms the 'reduced production effects'. The Arbitrator notes that the United States has not disputed Brazil's decomposition of the adverse effects from the actionable subsidies into this sales value and reduced production effects. An alternative way of characterizing these effects can be provided using standard economic concepts. The sales value effect is the increase in producer surplus that farmers in the rest of the world would have received based on their current output of cotton had world prices been at the counter-factual (no subsidies) level. The reduced production effects are made up of two parts: the producer surplus from the additional production *QQ′* (area **B**) and the opportunity cost of the resources needed to produce the additional cotton (area **C**). The Arbitrator notes that if one were only interested in measuring how US cotton subsidies have reduced producer welfare in the rest of the world, then this would be represented by the loss in producer surplus (sum of areas **A** and **B**). This is because those resources used to produce *QQ′* of cotton would have

29 Ibid., para. 4.104–4.105.

> found employment elsewhere and consequently, there would have been no loss associated with those resources to the rest of the world. However, the Arbitrator understands that adverse effects may have a wider meaning than producer surplus and that Brazil's economic analysis of adverse effects is consistent with the language of Article 6.3(c) of the *SCM Agreement*, particularly in its reference to 'lost sales'.[30]

Having endorsed the conceptual approach of Brazil (with the proviso that retaliation should be limited to the harm suffered by Brazil), the Arbitrator proceeded to examine a number of detailed issues that bear on the resulting numerical calculation. We will omit discussion of most of these issues, but note one of fairly broad significance. To calibrate the simulation model, elasticity estimates are required, and the question arises whether these should be based on long-run or short-run elasticity estimates. Long-run elasticities, of course, are higher as they assume free entry and exit of capital in response to price changes. The use of long-run supply elasticities for rest-of-world cotton producers results in a calculation more favorable to the United States, because the larger production response by these supplies mitigates the effect of any change in US output on the world price.

Accordingly, the United States argued for long-run elasticities for rest-of-world suppliers, while Brazil argued for short-run elasticities. The Arbitrator noted that the United States had the burden of proving that Brazil's approach was inappropriate, and then ruled for Brazil:

> Brazil has established a plausible case that it will take time for consumers and producers to fully adjust to the removal of marketing loans and countercyclical payments. As we have noted in our analysis, this means that producers in the rest of the world would continue to experience the adverse effects of the subsidies even after they have been removed. Since the calculated countermeasures must be 'commensurate with the degree and nature of the adverse effects determined to exist', the Arbitrator believes that the economic modelling must account for these rigidities. This makes a short-run analysis, and the use of short-run elasticities, not inappropriate for the economic modelling.[31]

After sorting through these and a variety of other issues pertaining to the calculation, the Arbitrator recalculated the price and output effects of the US subsidies using data from the reference period. It concluded that the total adverse effect on non-US producers was approximately US$3 billion. Applying Brazil's market share of roughly 5 %, Brazil's retaliation rights were estimated at roughly $150 million.[32] Combined with its rights relating to prohibited subsidies as discussed earlier, Brazil's total retaliation rights were then set at roughly $300 million.

30 Ibid., paras. 4.128–4.129.
31 Ibid., para. 4.147.
32 Ibid., paras. 4.194–4.195.

Legal analysis

We endorse the Arbitrator's unwillingness to allow the United States to avoid retaliation based on the formalist argument that the 2002 Farm Bill had expired, given that the essential programs had been renewed in the 2008 Farm Bill. A contrary position would allow violators to escape all sanction by 'repealing' offending policies and then reenacting them under another name, a result that would render countermeasures inutile.

Regarding the magnitude of countermeasures, the standards in the WTO are loose and provide only limited guidance. The standard in SCMs Article 7.9 is no different – 'commensurate with the adverse effects' simply requires some degree of correspondence between the countermeasures and the adverse effects, but the precise correspondence is unclear and the concept of 'adverse effects' is nowhere defined. The Arbitrator's interpretation of the standard seems broadly reasonable, and we see no basis in the treaty text or in settled practice for any serious quarrel. The decision to limit countermeasures based on the harm done to Brazil, rather than to allow Brazil to retaliate based on the global effects of the violation, is inconsistent with the approach in the *FSC* arbitration as we noted earlier, but seems sensible in light of the critique of the *FSC* decision and the resulting potential for retaliation out of proportion to the harm done to trading partners. Likewise, the decision to allow retaliation based on the totality of price suppression, and not just the amount by which it exceeds a 'significance' threshold, seems reasonable and consistent with the principle of countermeasures 'commensurate with the adverse effects'.

We might quibble somewhat with the Arbitrator's willingness to allow retaliation based on the entire lost production effect in Figure 1 above. As the Arbitrator acknowledges, areas A and B capture the lost surplus to firms and workers due to the violation, whereas area C reflects a savings of resources that are diverted to other productive uses. It is difficult to understand conceptually how a shift of resources into other productive uses is properly deemed an 'adverse effect' of the subsidy, although we recognize that the concept of 'adverse effects' is not necessarily limited to lost producer surplus. We will have more to say about this issue in Section 4, but simply remark at this point that the Arbitrator offers no theoretical basis for treating area C as an 'adverse effect'.

Finally, the debate over short-run versus long-run elasticities seems to us to come down to the question of which parameters do the best job of capturing the 'adverse effects' of a subsidy program. Without a clear theory as to the proper conceptual measure of 'adverse effects', it is difficult to say what parameters should be used to estimate them. Again, we will have more to say about these issues in Section 4.

3. Key issues and legal analysis – cross-retaliation

Aside from questions about the permissible magnitude of retaliation, *Upland Cotton* raises important questions about the appropriate subject of retaliation.

In particular, as in *EC Bananas–III*[33] and *United States–Gambling*,[34] Brazil sought authority to use its retaliation rights to suspend concession under the TRIPs. The United States objected, arguing that the conditions for cross-retaliation set forth in the DSU were not met.

The decision of the Arbitrator

An initial question was whether countermeasures governed by SCMs Article 4.10 (or 7.9 in the case of the actionable subsidies) are also required to conform to pertinent provisions of the DSU, in particular, Article 22.3, which provides:

> In considering what concessions or other obligations to suspend, the complaining party shall apply the following principles and procedures:
>
> (a) the general principle is that the complaining party should first seek to suspend concessions or other obligations with respect to the same sector(s) as that in which the panel or Appellate Body has found a violation or other nullification or impairment;
> (b) if that party considers that it is not practicable or effective to suspend concessions or other obligations with respect to the same sector(s), it may seek to suspend concessions or other obligations in other sectors under the same agreement;
> (c) if that party considers that it is not practicable or effective to suspend concessions or other obligations with respect to other sectors under the same agreement, and that the circumstances are serious enough, it may seek to suspend concessions or other obligations under another covered agreement;
> (d) in applying the above principles, that party shall take into account:
>
> (i) the trade in the sector or under the agreement under which the panel or Appellate Body has found a violation or other nullification or impairment, and the importance of such trade to that party;
> (ii) the broader economic elements related to the nullification or impairment and the broader economic consequences of the suspension of concessions or other obligations.

Brazil argued that this provision was inapplicable because the SCM Agreement contained its own provisions for retaliation. The Arbitrator ruled, however, in accordance with the Appellate Body's remarks in *Guatemala–Cement*,[35] that special or additional rules such as those in the SCM Agreement do not displace more general rules unless there is a conflict between them. Here, it was possible to

33 *European Communities – Regime for the Importation, Sale and Distribution of Bananas*, Recourse to Arbitration by the European Communities under Article 22.6 of the DSU, WT/DS27/ARB, 9 April 1999.

34 *United States – Measures Affecting the Cross-Border Supply of Gambling and Betting Services*, Recourse to Arbitration by the United States under Article 22.6 of the DSU, WT/DS285/ARB, 21 December 2007.

35 Appellate Body Report, *Guatemala – Anti-Dumping Investigation Regarding Portland Cement from Mexico*, WT/DS60/AB/R, 2 November 1998.

adhere to both sets of rules, and hence they should be applied together as complementary.

The Arbitrator also ruled that the text requires a fair amount of deference to the complaining nation – the phrase 'if that party considers that it is not practicable or effective' places considerable discretion in the hands of the complaining party, and the Arbitrator must simply ensure that it 'takes into account' the factors in paragraph (d). The United States had the burden of proving that Brazil had not met its obligations, and the Arbitrator could only 'broadly judge' whether Brazil had behaved inappropriately.[36]

Turning to the standards for cross-retaliation under Article 22.3(a)–(c), the question is whether retaliation in the same sector (a) or in other goods sectors (b) is 'practical and effective'. The Arbitrator read 'practical' to refer to the 'actual availability or feasibility' of the retaliation[37] – for example, is there enough trade in the pertinent sector(s) to exhaust retaliation rights? The term 'effective' relates to the ability of retaliation to induce compliance, although the Arbitrator ruled that a complaining member cannot elect cross-retaliation just because that would be more effective at inducing compliance – the issue is whether retaliation in the same sector or under the same Agreement would be effective.[38] Such retaliation might tend to be ineffective, however, if it imposed more harm on the complaining nation than on the violator.[39] Ineffective means something like the retaliation would impose more harm on the sender than the target. Finally, Article 22.3(c) provides that retaliation under another Agreement is acceptable when the circumstances are 'serious enough'. In this regard, the Arbitrator concluded that 'an assessment of whether same-sector or same-agreement suspension is "not practicable or effective" and of whether "the circumstances are serious enough" may legitimately, and indeed *should*, take into consideration not only the trade to which the suspension would apply, but also the economic consequences arising from the suspension.'[40]

Applying these standards, the Arbitrator noted that Brazilian imports of goods from the United States totaled US$18.7 billion,[41] yet its total retaliation rights relating to both prohibited and actionable subsidies for fiscal year 2006 were only on the order of $300 million. The question thus arose whether Brazil could identify $300 million worth of US goods with respect to which retaliation was 'practical and effective'. The Arbitrator accepted the argument that retaliation on 'capital goods, intermediate goods and other essential inputs' would harm Brazil unduly because many such goods are tailored for particular buyers, and substitute sources

36 Prohibited Subs. Arb., para. 5.430.
37 Ibid., para. 5.455.
38 Ibid., para. 5.460.
39 Ibid., para. 5.461.
40 Ibid., para. 5.472.
41 Ibid., para. 5.517.

of supply are not readily available.[42] It also allowed Brazil to carve out 'important' consumer goods like autos and books, and certain other important categories like medicine and food if the US market share of Brazil's imports exceeded 20 %, raising a presumption that substitution from other sources of supply would be difficult. After making these adjustments, the Arbitrator concluded that retaliation in goods sectors could be practical and effective up to an amount of $410 million.[43] Only if Brazil's total retaliation rights exceeded that amount in some future year might it justify retaliation under another Agreement.

In the event that future retaliation rights exceeded this threshold, however, the Arbitrator was prepared to accept that the circumstances were 'serious enough' to permit cross-retaliation. It based this conclusion largely on a finding that the subsidies in question have a large trade distortive impact that gave the United States a 'persisting competitive advantage'.[44]

Legal analysis

We have little quarrel with the legal analysis of the Arbitrator. The decision to treat the retaliation provisions of the SCM Agreement as complementary to the provisions of the DSU was reasonable and supported by Appellate Body precedent. The interpretation of the terms 'practical' and 'effective' likewise seems reasonable. Finally, we concur that the text of Article 22.3 vests discretion in the complaining member, and that the standard of review by the Arbitrator is appropriately deferential.

The application of these standards to the facts of the case is somewhat more questionable. The great bulk of Brazilian goods imports from the United States fell into Brazil's category of 'capital goods, intermediate goods, and other essential inputs'. The notion that retaliation against any of these goods would impose undue harm on Brazil seems speculative. No doubt in some cases alternative sources of supply would be difficult to obtain, but it is difficult to imagine that to be the case across the board. Likewise, the presumption that alternative sources of supply for consumer goods would be difficult to obtain anytime the US market share of imports exceeded 20 % seems quite arbitrary.

More fundamentally, the implicit premise that retaliation on consumer goods is generally more 'practical' or 'effective' than retaliation on input products seems questionable. There is no apparent reason to suppose that 'effectiveness' would always be greater with consumer goods. As for what is 'practical', perhaps the Arbitrator is implicitly sensitive to the interest-group politics of retaliation, and in effect views politically difficult retaliation (which hurts producer groups) as impractical, while viewing retaliation that mainly harms consumers as more practical as long as the harm is not too great. It is hardly obvious that the concept of 'practical' under the DSU should be interpreted in this fashion.

42 Ibid., para. 5.535.
43 Ibid., para. 5.565.
44 Ibid., para. 5.601.

The Arbitrator's application of the 'serious enough' standard is also somewhat conclusory. While it is assuredly true that subsidies can distort trading patterns, it is unclear why the violations at issue here are any more 'serious' than a myriad of other violations of WTO law. Unless one is prepared to say that 'serious' circumstances arise anytime 'prohibited' subsidies are in play – a move that the Arbitrator did not make – it would be helpful to have somewhat more guidance on the principles that distinguish 'serious' circumstances from less serious circumstances. We acknowledge, however, that the inherent vagueness of the 'seriousness' standard makes it difficult to lay down tight rules. And, given the appropriately deferential standard of review in assessing Brazil's determination, we cannot say that the Arbitrator's decision was incorrect.

4. Economic analysis

One cannot assess the soundness of the Arbitrator's decision in *Upland Cotton* from an economic perspective without a theory of the objectives that countermeasures are intended to achieve. Unfortunately, no generally accepted theory of their purpose exists, and indeed a lively academic debate exists over the issue.[45]

Roughly speaking, the various theories of countermeasures divide into two camps. The first, which we term the 'compliance' theory, holds that the function of countermeasures is to punish breach of obligations and induce WTO members to bring their behavior back into compliance. The second, which we term the 'efficient-breach' theory, holds that countermeasures seek only to achieve the 'efficient' level of compliance, and thus allow WTO members to deviate from their obligations when the benefits of deviation exceed the costs of deviation to other WTO members ('efficient breach'). Variations on the efficient-breach theme suggest that the goal of countermeasures is to 'compensate' for breach,[46] to 'rebalance' concessions following breach,[47] or to provide a 'safety valve' for political pressure that makes trade negotiators more willing to make trade concessions in the first instance.[48]

The debate among these competing theories invokes various considerations. Aspects of the treaty text can be cited on both sides.[49] Both sides can also point to elements of the dispute-settlement system that are consistent with their position,

45 The most thorough surveys are perhaps those of Lawrence (2003) and Schropp (2009).

46 If countermeasures compensate aggrieved parties for their losses, then they restore those parties' welfare to its level prior to breach – if a violator is willing to pay such 'compensation' and can still remain better off, breach is efficient.

47 Rebalancing is a somewhat vague concept, but it can be understood either as a version of the compensation idea, or as the economic equivalent of 'rescission' in a contractual setting, so that the welfare of the aggrieved party is restored to its level prior to the exchange of concessions in question.

48 The safety-valve story is also a variant of the efficient-breach claim – a safety valve is valuable if the costs of deviation *ex post* under the safety valve are exceeded by the mutual gains due to the facilitation of a greater number of concessions *ex ante*.

49 See Jackson (1997); Sykes (2000).

and inconsistent with the position of their detractors. Proponents of the efficient-breach perspective, for example, emphasize that the general standard for countermeasures under DSU Article 22 requires measures 'equivalent to the level of nullification or impairment', which is interpreted (as in *Upland Cotton*) to capture the harm done to complaining nations by the violation, and will not ensure retaliation at a level sufficient to produce compliance. Critics of the efficient-breach camp emphasize the fact that countermeasures do not really 'compensate' aggrieved nations very effectively, for example, and question whether the approach to calculating them in practice has any realistic hope of optimizing the breach decision. We make no attempt to settle the debate here, and simply offer a few basic observations from each perspective.

Implications of the 'compliance theory'

If the goal of countermeasures is to ensure compliance (or, equivalently, to force any deviation from commitments into a renegotiation process), then it is impossible to specify any unique 'optimal value' for countermeasures. Rather, any system of countermeasures that punishes the violator to a degree that wipes out the gains from the violation will suffice – the gains from the violation thus offer a lower bound on retaliation, but there is no necessary upper bound.

This statement requires several caveats. First, countermeasures are not necessarily the only sanction for violations. Violators may suffer damage to reputation that imposes future costs on their ability to negotiate valuable agreements, for example, or they may suffer various informal sanctions relating to trade issues or other aspects of international relations. If so, the countermeasures required to induce compliance are lessened. Second, as the level of countermeasures increases, expenditures on litigation costs in the WTO system will tend to increase, as will the deadweight costs of whatever countermeasures it employs. These costs offer further reasons why it may make sense to limit countermeasures even if the goal of the system were compliance. Third, if legal error is possible, error costs must be factored into the analysis. The possibility of error in favor of the complainant will weigh in favor of weaker countermeasures, while the possibility of error benefiting respondents will weigh in the other direction. Finally, countermeasures are of little utility unless the threat of them is credible. There is no value in setting countermeasures at a level so high that they will not be employed.

Nevertheless, the 'equivalence' standard of Article 22, which focuses on the harm to aggrieved nations caused by the violation rather than the gains to the violator, is a peculiar standard from the compliance perspective. Likewise, none of the standards for countermeasures in prior arbitrations, whether focused on the lost trade volume suffered by aggrieved nations or on the value of the subsidy bestowed by the violator in a prohibited-subsidies case, has any obvious connection to the level of countermeasures that will ensure compliance. The Arbitrator in *Upland Cotton* acknowledged this problem as we noted earlier, but insisted that authority for stiffer measures was lacking in the treaty text. If the *goal* of the system is to ensure compliance, therefore, its *design*, at least as interpreted in the decisions to date, is hard to square with that objective.

Accordingly, we will focus most of the remainder of our remarks on the possible implications of the efficient-breach approach to retaliation. Prior to that discussion, however, we briefly consider the issue of retroactive retaliation.

Retroactive retaliation

As the Arbitrator held in *Upland Cotton*, and has been the consistent practice in the WTO, countermeasures are allowed only after the 'reasonable period' for compliance has expired and only then until such time as the violation has been cured. Retaliation for violations in the past is impermissible.

From both the compliance and efficient-breach perspectives, this aspect of the system is puzzling. It seemingly allows members to cheat on their obligations with impunity for extended periods of time, weakening compliance with obligations generally, and doing so in a manner that does nothing to limit violations to cases of 'efficient breach'.

Commentators have offered some speculations about the rationale for limiting retaliation in this fashion. For example, perhaps informal sanctions discourage flagrant cheating to a great extent, and many actual disputes may then involve good-faith disagreements about the content of obligations. Because sanctions in the system are costly and because litigation can provide useful clarification of the bargain for all members (a positive externality), it may make sense to allow parties to litigate these good-faith disputes to conclusion without fear of sanctions if they lose, as long as they are willing to bring their behavior into compliance thereafter.[50] Related, some nations may have limited compliance capacity due to a lack of technical expertise, especially developing countries, and it may not make sense to impose costly sanctions on them for their 'accidental' violations.

The *Upland Cotton* case itself casts doubt on this rosy account, however, inasmuch as the US programs at issue – particularly the prohibited subsidies – were rather straightforward violations of WTO rules. It is not difficult to think of other cases as well that do not look much like 'good faith disputes'. Thus, although we are not prepared to say definitively that the system should be modified to allow retaliation for violations in the past, especially given the fact that sanctions are costly and create their own deadweight losses, we do worry that the existing dispute-resolution system may unduly encourage temporary cheating.

Implications of the efficient-breach theory in a model of competing exporters

We now turn to the heart of our economic analysis, which presupposes that the objective of countermeasures is to induce violators to internalize the costs that their violations impose on others. This objective, as noted, comports with the idea

50 Schwartz and Sykes (2002).

that retaliation is not intended to ensure compliance in all cases, but merely to ensure that any violations are approximately 'efficient'. Our approach is based on that of Bagwell and Staiger (2002), who view trade agreements as a mechanism for helping nations to internalize terms-of-trade externalities and to achieve 'reciprocity' in their commercial relations. Howse and Staiger (2006) apply this theory in a two-country, two-good framework with tariffs to suggest how retaliation at a level equal to the lost volume of trade valued at original (pre-violation) prices can enable a complaining nation to restore its welfare (approximately) to what it was before the tariff violation.[51]

The idea underlying the Howse and Staiger proposal is that of 'expectation damages', a so-called 'liability rule' familiar from contract law. In the case of domestic contracts, a liability rule that compensates the injured parties for any damages that are suffered as a result of a breach of contract ensures that breach occurs if and only if joint welfare is enhanced by deviation from the contract provisions. Howse and Staiger apply this idea in the trade context by searching for a set of retaliatory measures ('withdrawal of concessions') that leave the injured countries as well off as they would have been, absent the violation of the trade agreement. As they show in the two-country, two-good setting, sometimes this can be accomplished by an increase in tariffs in the injured country that reduces trade volume by an amount equal to the trade opportunities lost as a result of the violation (valued at pre-violation prices).

However, as Beshkar (2010) has pointed out recently, this expectation-damages rule does not have the same efficiency properties in the trade context as it does in the context of domestic contract law. Its efficiency there relies on the availability of cash transfers as a means of compensation. The cash transfers from one private party to another in the case of a contract violation can make the injured party whole without generating excess burden for the party that undertakes the breach. Accordingly, a party will breach if and only if the joint welfare of all parties to the contract is enhanced by that action.

In contrast, cash transfers typically are not available as countermeasures in WTO disputes.[52] Instead, the injured parties are offered the opportunity to withdraw concessions; that is, to erect barriers or otherwise impede trade by the party that has violated the agreement. This method of compensation is not the same as a cash transfer, because the retaliation mechanism itself generates efficiency loss. Thus, when a party retaliates with a trade barrier, such as that described by Howse and Staiger, that restores the welfare of the complainant to its level absent the violation, the cost to the violator is larger than the benefit to the injured party. A system that utilizes trade barriers to make the injured party whole is thus overly

51 See also Bown and Ruta (2010).

52 A violator is of course free to offer cash as compensation, as has been done by the United States in the *Copyright* (United States – Section 110(5) of the US Copyright Act, WT/DS160) and *Upland Cotton* cases.

conservative relative to a 'first-best' standard of 'efficient' breach, because the excess burden of the distortive retaliatory measure discourages breach in circumstances where joint welfare would be enhanced by a violation of the agreement. Perhaps such conservatism is appropriate if we take the view that violations should be tolerated only when they generate a *Pareto* welfare improvement for the parties to the agreement and not just an increase in their joint welfare.[53] In any case, we shall assume the principle – that the 'suspension of concessions or other obligations authorized by the DSB shall be equivalent to the level of the nullification or impairment' – should be interpreted to authorize retaliatory measures that restore the welfare of the injured party to the level that it would have achieved absent the violation.

In what follows, we extend the approach of Howse and Staiger (2006) to a setting that incorporates domestic and export subsidies and competing exporters. We ask whether it justifies any differences in the retaliatory response to violations involving domestic (actionable) subsidies on the one hand, and export (prohibited) subsidies on the other. We also ask whether it supports using lost trade volume as a metric for retaliation, or supports an approach that ties retaliation to the amount of the subsidy. More generally, we develop the implications of the model for the level of countermeasures that will restore the welfare of the injured party, assuming that retaliation is intended to allow efficient breach, using *Pareto* improvement as the (high) standard for efficiency.

Consider two countries, Brazil and the United States. Both are net exporters of cotton. The cotton market is competitive and all cotton is perfectly substitutable. Let the world price of cotton be $p^*(x_u, s_u, s)$ where x_u is the US export subsidy and s_u (s) is the US (Brazilian) domestic subsidy.

The Brazilian government has a welfare function that includes consumer surplus (CS), producer surplus (PS), and government revenue (R) as components

$$W = \alpha PS + CS + \gamma R,$$

where

$$\alpha \geq 1 \text{ and } \gamma \geq 1.$$

We thus assume that producer surplus receives at least as much weight as consumer surplus, a conventional political economy assumption (see, for example, Baldwin, 1987). The weight given to government revenue perhaps reflects the excess burden of taxation.

Let the United States create a dispute by increasing x_u or s_u. For simplicity, assume a 'small' change in US policy. The political welfare cost to Brazil is given by

$$dW = (\alpha y - c - \gamma s y')\, dp^*, \quad (1)$$

53 Such a principle is questionable, of course, because the opportunity for efficient breach *ex post* can yield expected *Pareto* gains to all parties *ex ante*, or else other terms of the bargain can potentially be adjusted to make all parties better off.

where y is Brazilian output, y' is the slope of the Brazilian supply curve, c is Brazilian consumption, and dp^* is the induced change in the world price of cotton (which is negative). The effect on Brazil can thus be decomposed into a loss of producer surplus, a gain in consumer surplus, and a savings in government revenue because the induced reduction in domestic output of cotton lowers the associated domestic subsidy payment. We can think of the welfare effect as a terms-of-trade effect in that the harm to Brazil is transmitted entirely through the reduction in the world price of a good for which Brazil is a net exporter.

This expression suggests several observations. First, the welfare effect on Brazil does not depend on whether the US policy involves a change in the domestic subsidy or in the export subsidy. What matters to Brazil is simply the magnitude of the induced effect on the world price. Second, the overall effect on Brazil depends on the welfare weights given to the different terms in the welfare function. Finally, the welfare effect depends on Brazil's own domestic-support policies (s).

This last point raises some subtle issues. Suppose, for example, that the Brazilian domestic subsidy has been chosen in the context of an 'optimal' international-subsidies agreement, which induces members to choose their subsidies to maximize their domestic welfare without regard to international terms-of-trade externalities (they behave 'as if' these externalities are internalized). This assumption is in the spirit of Bagwell and Staiger (2002), who note that a politically optimal trade agreement is one that sets trade policies at levels that neglect their implications for the terms of trade. When thinking about tariffs, it may be reasonable to use the politically optimal tariffs as the starting point for assessing violations. But this approach seems much less realistic where subsidies are concerned. For example, if importing nations were parties to such an agreement, the agreement might encourage exporters to *increase* their level of subsidies due to the positive terms-of-trade externalities that they impose on importers. Nothing in the WTO system, of course, does anything of the sort, and, indeed, the treatment of subsidies in the WTO system raises some puzzles for the terms-of-trade theory of trade agreements (see Bagwell and Staiger, 2006). Nevertheless, we will begin our analysis with the implications of this assumption.

If the subsidy s has been chosen by Brazil to maximize W ignoring the terms that involve a change in p^*, then the level of subsidy would be such that

$$dW/ds|_{p^*} = \alpha y - \gamma s y' - \gamma y = 0;$$

i.e., it would expand Brazilian production to the point where the political gain from higher domestic producer prices (αy) matches the marginal revenue cost ($\gamma s y' + \gamma y$). Substituting this condition into the expression for dW, we have

$$dW = (\gamma y - c)dp^*.$$

Since the Brazilian domestic subsidy ensures that the gain in Brazilian revenue when output falls offsets part of the loss in producer surplus, what remains from a worsening of terms of trade in cotton is the benefit to consumers and a portion of the loss in producer surplus. Notice that if $\gamma=1$, this expression is simply the terms-of-trade loss to Brazil due to the induced change in the world price (i.e., it is the excess of Brazilian production over Brazilian consumption, multiplied by the (negative) change in the world price caused by the increased US subsidy).

As another possibility, suppose that the Brazilian subsidy is set noncooperatively to maximize Brazil's welfare, taking into account the adverse effects of such a subsidy on Brazil's terms of trade. The first-order condition for an optimal Brazilian subsidy (including terms-of-trade effects) implies

$$dW/ds=\alpha y-\gamma sy'-\gamma y+(\alpha y-c-\gamma sy')(\partial p^*/\partial s)=0.$$

Substituting this condition into the expression (1) for the change in Brazilian welfare induced by the US violation, we find

$$dW=[(\gamma y-\alpha y+\gamma sy')/(\partial p^*/\partial s)]dp^*.$$

In this case, Brazil suffers harm from the US policy only to the extent that producer surplus carries greater weight in the government's objective than tax revenues and that Brazilian output is not too responsive to the local price. The optimal Brazilian policy sets the domestic subsidy at a level where the harm from a worsening of terms of trade is balanced by a gain in producer surplus that exceeds the revenue cost of the subsidy. The only reason that Brazil can be harmed by the US policy at all in this case is that the Brazilian subsidy does not affect the incentives facing local consumers and therefore does not fully optimize the initial export level before the US violation.[54]

As a final possibility, suppose the Brazilian government does not subsidize its local cotton growers whatsoever; i.e., $s=0$. The formula for the harm to Brazil from the US policy in expression (1) implies in this case that

$$dW=(\alpha y-c)\ dp^*.$$

If it happens that $\alpha=1$, the welfare loss is again simply the terms-of-trade loss. With $\alpha>1$, the more typical political-economy assumption, the welfare loss exceeds the terms-of-trade loss as conventionally measured when the subsidy is zero. Producers lose and consumers gain from the US subsidy, but the former weighs heavier in the political calculation than it does in a straight welfare calculation that is the basis for measuring terms-of-trade loss.

In general, the harm imposed on Brazil by a US violation of its WTO obligations depends on a number of factors, including the relative weights that the Brazilian government attaches to producer surplus, consumer surplus, and tax revenue, and the extent of Brazilian support for its own cotton industry, be it zero, 'optimal', or

54 If Brazil were to employ an optimal *export* subsidy instead of an optimal output subsidy, there would be no marginal harm to Brazil from a small change in US policy.

otherwise. Of course, the harm to Brazil will be less the closer the initial level of cotton production is to what the Brazilian government would deem to be the optimal scale.

Having characterized the welfare loss to Brazil as a result of the change in US subsidy policy, the next question is: What sort of retaliation can restore Brazilian welfare? Suppose that Brazil retaliates by raising its per-unit tariff t on some good that it imports from the United States – say, automobiles. If Brazil raises the border tax it imposes on each imported car by dt, the change in its political welfare is given by

$$dW = \{[\alpha y_a - c_a + \gamma t(c_a' - y_a')](1 + \partial p_a^*/\partial t) + \gamma(c_a - y_a)\}dt. \tag{2}$$

The tariff change that compensates Brazil for the loss from the violation in cotton is one that equates the welfare gain from the tariff on automobiles in (2) to the welfare cost of the illegal US subsidy in (1).

The degree of retaliation that restores Brazil's welfare will depend on how the subsidy on cotton and the tariff on automobiles are set initially. Suppose first that both have been set in the context of a Bagwell–Staiger 'optimal' trade agreement that has induced Brazil to internalize the externalities from its policy choices. Then, as we showed earlier, the welfare loss to Brazil from the US subsidy is simply the political-economy-weighted terms-of-trade loss, $dW = (\gamma y - c)\ (\partial p^*/\partial x_u)\ dx_u$. If the tariff on automobiles was also set to maximize Brazilian political welfare, but ignoring terms-of-trade effects, it satisfies the first-order condition

$$\alpha y_a - c_a + \gamma t(c_a' - y_a') + \gamma(c_a - y_a) = 0,$$

where the subscript a denotes a variable in the automobile industry. Now substituting this condition into the above expression (2) for the welfare change, we find the gain to Brazil from a change in its automobile tariff beginning at the Bagwell–Staiger political optimum, which is

$$\begin{aligned} dW &= \{[\alpha y_a - c_a + \gamma t(c_a' - y_a')](\partial p_a^*/\partial t)\}dt \\ &= -\gamma(c_a - y_a)(\partial p_a^*/\partial t)dt. \end{aligned}$$

The term on the right-hand side corresponds to the weighted gain in tariff revenue on the initial volume of imports. This is the marginal gain to Brazil from increasing its tariff, considering that the initial tariff was set to optimize the political outcome, but neglected the implications for the terms of trade.

Finally, if we equate the gain from the retaliatory tariff increase on automobiles to the loss suffered by Brazil as a result of the US violation, we have

$$(\gamma y - c)\ (\partial p^*/\partial x_u)\ dx_u = \gamma(c_a - y_a)\ (\partial p_a^*/\partial t)dt. \tag{3}$$

A sufficient condition for the tariff change to be positive ($dt > 0$) in this expression is that $\gamma \geqslant 1$. Then, Brazil's welfare will be restored by an increase in the tariff on autos that offsets the terms-of-trade loss on cotton. To calculate the appropriate value of dt, however, one must know the relative welfare weight attached to government revenue relative to consumer surplus.

If the welfare weight that Brazil attaches to government revenue is the same as that on consumer surplus ($\gamma=1$), then (3) mandates a retaliatory tariff that generates a terms-of-trade improvement on automobile imports that exactly matches the terms-of-trade loss suffered by Brazil on its cotton exports, both measured in the conventional way; i.e., as the initial volume of trade multiplied by the change in the border price. As Lawrence (2003) and Bagwell (2008) have aptly noted, however, this result rests on the assumption that the US violation is a small one. A larger violation will cause Brazilian cotton exports to fall significantly short of the level dictated by the political optimum, and the retaliatory tariff will similarly generate a sub-optimally low level of automobile trade. Thus, in general, the tariff that induces a terms-of-trade gain for Brazil in automobiles just equal to its terms-of-trade loss in cotton will not suffice to restore Brazil's welfare to its initial, pre-violation level.

Things become considerably more complicated if the cotton subsidy and auto tariff are not initially set at their 'politically optimal' values. Then we must use the general expression for the welfare effects of a tariff change (given above in (2)), which requires information not only on the relative weight on revenues compared to consumer surplus, but also on the political-economy weight for producer surplus. The former may be approximated by the excess burden of taxation – for which estimates are available for many countries – but the latter is much more difficult for the Arbitrator to assess.

In sum, although there exists a change in the auto tariff that restores Brazil's welfare, the task of calculating it is a difficult one. It requires assumptions about the relevant political-economy weights on different components of Brazilian welfare, as well as assumptions about how the initial values of Brazil's policy instruments have been determined.

But we can identify a simple benchmark case that arises when political-economy weights in Brazil are the same for producer surplus, consumer surplus, and government revenue, and the Brazilian cotton subsidy is zero. On the assumption that all components of welfare receive equal weight, the politically optimal level of subsidy is zero (because the politically optimal subsidy ignores terms-of-trade considerations, and with a national income maximizing government, there is no reason to subsidize for purposes of domestic redistribution). Then, with an initial subsidy of zero, we can use our earlier result for the case where the subsidy level is politically optimal to conclude that Brazil's welfare will be restored by retaliation in the import industry that exactly offsets the terms-of-trade loss – the resulting change in the world price of the import good, multiplied by the initial volume of Brazilian imports, should match the change in world price of cotton induced by the violation multiplied by the initial volume of Brazilian cotton exports. Once again, this proposition is subject to the caveat that for a 'large' breach, this level of retaliation will fall somewhat short of restoring lost welfare.

Furthermore, although the point may seem obvious from the mathematics, we think it worth underscoring that the approach here suggests a level of retaliation that restores the level of welfare for *Brazil*, not for the world as a whole. It is thus broadly consistent with the approach of the Arbitrator in *Upland Cotton* (and contrary to the approach in the *FSC* case), in that proper countermeasures depend on the harm suffered by the complaining Member.[55]

We conclude with a comment and extension on some prior work, which has suggested that appropriate retaliation can be approximated by equating the 'trade volume' effects of the retaliatory measure with those of the initial violation. This observation is particularly significant inasmuch as it comports with the way that some Arbitrators have calculated permissible retaliation.

Howse and Staiger (2006) and Bown and Ruta (2010) consider the consequences of a violation that reduces a country's exports of some good, call it good 1. They suggest that a retaliatory tariff on, say, good 2, which reduces the *value* of good 2 imports by an amount equal to the *value* of lost exports of good 1 valued at the original (pre-violation) prices, will restore the welfare of the aggrieved exporter. In other words, they suggest that the appropriate terms-of-trade changes needed to compensate an injured party can be achieved in some circumstances by focusing on trade-volume (value) effects, rather than on terms-of-trade (price) effects *per se*. They develop this claim in a model with only two goods and two countries, and we now ask whether it is valid in a more general setting.

Let us continue to suppose that the United States and Brazil export cotton to the rest of the world and that Brazil imports automobiles from the United States. Brazil retaliates for a US violation in cotton by raising its import tariff on automobiles. Besides these two goods, there are others that are traded, so that changes in Brazil's exports of cotton need not be balanced by changes in its imports of automobiles. We examine a tariff increase for Brazil that restores its welfare to the level before the US violation and ask under what conditions this policy change also implies a decline in the value of automobile imports that matches the decline in the value of Brazilian exports of cotton.

To keep the analysis simple, let us now assume that the Brazilian government is a national-welfare maximizer in the traditional sense – all components of welfare receive equal weight ($\alpha = \gamma = 1$). Let the retaliatory tariff be set so that the gain to Brazil from the fall in the (world) price of autos just offsets the loss of welfare due to the fall in the world price of cotton. Condition (4) captures this requirement

$$(y - c)dp^* = (c_a - y_a)dp_a^*. \tag{4}$$

55 We must acknowledge, however, that if the goal is to facilitate efficient breach and discourage inefficient breach, it is important that the welfare effects of a violation on all WTO Members be internalized by the potential violator. To the degree that some injured nations lack the resources to bring complaints or lack retaliatory capacity (notwithstanding the possibility of cross-retaliation), the price for breach can become too small.

We ask now what are the trade effects induced by the US subsidy and the retaliatory tariff that satisfy (4).

Standard supply-and-demand analysis can be used to link the change in the world price of cotton to the change in the US subsidy. The price change induced by a given subsidy will depend on the export-supply elasticities in Brazil and the United States and the import-demand elasticity in the rest of the world. Similar analysis can be used to link the change in the price of US automobiles to the change in the Brazilian tariff; this will reflect the export-supply elasticity in the United States and the import-demand elasticity in Brazil. Finally, we require that the terms-of-trade effects are compensatory; i.e., the Brazilian tariff is set in response to the US subsidy to ensure that condition (4) is satisfied. In this way, we can calculate the effect of the US subsidy on Brazilian exports of cotton and the effects of the retaliatory tariff on its imports of automobiles, and we can check when these trade effects will match.

We find that the trade effects of the compensatory tariff match those of the US cotton subsidy if and only if the US elasticity of export supply for automobiles is equal to the elasticity of Brazilian export supply for cotton. Put differently, a retaliatory tariff that equates the trade-volume effects valued at the original prices will restore Brazil's welfare if and only if the supply of US automobile exports responds to a percentage change in the US price of autos by the same percentage amount as Brazilian cotton exports respond to a percentage change in the Brazilian price of cotton. Of course, there is no reason that this should be the case, especially if the sector for retaliation (in this example, 'automobiles') is chosen somewhat arbitrarily. We conclude that the approach to retaliation that balances trade effects is not likely to achieve its ostensible purpose in a world with more than two countries, more than two goods, and an arbitrary sector in which the retaliatory measure is applied.

It should also be noted that the trade-effects remedies applied by previous Arbitrators differ in an important way even from those proposed by Howse and Staiger (2006) or Bown and Ruta (2010). These commentators have provided limited justification (subject to the strong caveat discussed above) for retaliatory tariffs that reduce the volume of trade by an amount equal to the trade lost by the complainant as a result of the violation, but that nonetheless leave imports at a positive level. The idea behind retaliation in their framework is that the complainant should be able to import more cheaply so that its terms of trade improve. But an improvement in terms of trade requires that there be positive trade after the tariff hike. In contrast, Arbitrators in the past have simply calculated a total amount of trade that may be the subject of retaliation. The subsequent retaliation has then often taken the form of *prohibitive tariffs* on a volume of trade equal to the trade lost by the complainant in the industry where the violation occurred. A prohibitive tariff cannot induce an improvement in the terms of trade, and therefore it cannot be used to restore the complainant's welfare to what it would have been absent the violation.[56]

Perhaps the reason that prohibitive tariffs have been popular in the past is that they are relatively easy to apply. Once the Arbitrator calculates how much trade has been lost due to the violation, there is no further information about the supply-and-demand conditions in the industry of retaliation that is needed to ensure an equal trade-volume effect when prohibitive tariffs are used. But prohibitive tariffs will generally *reduce* welfare in the complainant country, and so are an odd instrument of retaliation given that alternative, nonprohibitive tariffs could impose the same harm on the violator while generating a gain for the complainant.[57]

Our analysis suggests that a more rational approach to retaliation would employ nonprohibitive tariffs that enhance the terms of trade. But the application of the equal-trade-effects principle with nonprohibitive tariffs requires information about supply-and-demand elasticities in the retaliation industry in order to calculate the requisite tariff hike. But then, as we have also argued, there will be no guarantee that the implied tariffs will restore welfare to something close to what it would have been absent the violation.

Note, however, that once the Arbitrator has information about supply-and-demand elasticities in the industry where retaliation will take place, there is no need to use the equal-trade-effects approach to approximate proper retaliation. The Arbitrator could instead directly calculate the tariff that would generate a terms-of-trade gain in the retaliation industry equal to the loss in the violation industry, using the same information necessary to calculate the tariff that would generate equal trade effects in the two sectors. The tariff that induces a terms-of-trade gain equal to the loss suffered due to the violation is likely to be closer to the one that ensures efficient levels of breach than the one that induces an equal trade effect for the reasons given above. We conclude that Arbitrators ought to devote more attention to the terms-of-trade implications of retaliation, and less to the effects of retaliation on the volume of trade than has been true in the recent past.

Other issues: cross-retaliation, elasticities

Cross-retaliation

We will not attempt to model the implications of cross-retaliation under GATS or TRIPS, which raises a range of issues that range beyond our simple modeling

56 Put more precisely, a prohibitive tariff on some good can only generate a terms-of-trade improvement for the importing country if it results in a reduced price of imports of some other good, or an increased price of exports of some other good. But this would require a particular pattern of substitution between the good with the prohibitive tariff and other imports and exports, and there is no reason to believe that the prohibitive tariff with equal trade effects would improve terms of trade in other sectors by just the right amount to compensate both the loss of welfare due to the violation plus the loss of welfare associated with the cessation of imports in the industry subject to retaliation.

57 Of course, prohibitive tariffs can, in principle, cause the violator to suffer harm equal to the harm suffered by other WTO Members. In this sense, they can confront the violator with a penalty that leads to efficient breach in the Kaldor–Hicks sense.

framework. Instead, we offer a few informal thoughts on the wisdom of allowing complaining nations to choose either the industry or sector in which to retaliate.

Consider first a case involving a violation of the rules with respect to trade in goods (like *Upland Cotton*). Under WTO practice, the complaining nation will have considerable flexibility to choose the *goods* industry or industries in which to exercise retaliation rights. Is this desirable? Intuitively, the modeling framework here suggests that retaliation should come in the industry where the (politically weighted) terms-of-trade gain to the retaliator (which is what compensates the injured party) comes at the least deadweight loss. If the initial tariff rates before retaliation are all politically optimal in the sense of Bagwell and Staiger, then there is no deadweight loss from a small change in any tariff, and it does not matter which tariff (or tariffs) is chosen for retaliation. It matters only that the total magnitude of retaliation (and the attendant terms-of-trade gain) is appropriately calibrated.

If the initial tariffs are not politically optimal, then the details of the retaliation that restores the complaining nation's welfare will affect the amount of collateral deadweight loss. If the rule for retaliation does NOT take this fact into account (which is the case in practice), then the retaliator will, given the choice, tend to choose the industry where the retaliation does the least harm to itself. This observation affords one reason in favor of letting the retaliator choose the industry in which to retaliate. But of course the retaliatory option that is optimal for the retaliator may not be optimal from a global perspective, and an argument might be made for channeling retaliation into the instruments that cause the smallest global loss. As a practical matter, however, it is difficult to imagine how Arbitrators could accomplish this task.

What about retaliation under other WTO Agreements ('cross-retaliation' in WTO parlance)? In past arbitrations, the goal of complaining nations seeking cross-retaliation rights, of course, has been an authorization to retaliate under TRIPs. Such retaliation involves a host of issues that go beyond conventional trade models. On the one hand, for example, TRIPs retaliation might adversely affect incentives for innovation and be relatively unattractive for that reason. On the other hand, perhaps TRIPs retaliation might have little effect on incentives and primarily amount to a transfer of rents from interest groups in the violator country to the complaining nation. If so, it may have the nice property that it is much closer to a 'transfer' than traditional trade sanctions, which may make it relatively attractive. Indeed, if TRIPs retaliation could be orchestrated in such a way as to avoid damaging innovation incentives (or other valuable interests served by intellectual property rights), and could be made to resemble pure transfers as a first approximation, then it might dominate trade sanctions quite broadly.

Finally, and as others have recognized, cross-retaliation empowers nations with little capacity to retaliate under GATT or GATS with some prospect of meaningful and credible sanctions. To this extent as well, it has potential merit.

Long-run versus short-run elasticities

Consider a violation of WTO rules that will remain in place for an extended period of time – perhaps, for example, it is an 'efficient breach'. The harm from the violation over time will be the present discounted value of a sequence of annual harms. Initially, the harm will tend to be greater because resources in the industries harmed by the violation have not been able to redeploy themselves to opportunities that may earn higher returns. In time, the harm will decline as resources are reallocated and sunk capital depreciates.

The first-year's harm is best calculated with short-run elasticities, the second year with somewhat longer-run elasticities, and so on. Thus, if an Arbitrator is calculating the allowable retaliation for the near term only, short-run elasticities may be appropriate (although one must ask how long the violation has been in place, and whether a lot of adjustment may already be underway). If the Arbitrator wishes to establish a formula for retaliation that will apply for many years to come, by contrast, it is inappropriate to rely solely on short-run elasticities.

The more general point is that the harm caused by a violation is time variable, and will typically decrease over time as affected industries adjust and reallocate resources elsewhere. The Arbitrator's formula in *Upland Cotton* was apparently intended to govern retaliation for a period of years, and indeed has been applied on an ongoing basis. One might argue that if the goal is to afford compensatory retaliation to Brazil over time, the formula should have included some mechanism for adjusting downward the estimate of harm to Brazil over time, holding constant the value of the underlying subsidies. To be sure, the precise adjustment required would be difficult to specify.

Summary

Economic analysis can say little about 'optimal' retaliation in the WTO system, absent a theory of what retaliation is supposed to accomplish. If the goal is 'ensuring compliance', then the focus ought be on guaranteeing that violators cannot profit from their violations, a focus that is at odds with the treaty text as presently interpreted. If the goal is 'efficient compliance' (and its corollary 'efficient breach'), then the emphasis should be on 'compensating' WTO members harmed by a violation through countermeasures that restore their lost welfare.

The fact that WTO members can 'cheat' for an extended period of time without suffering any formal sanction raises a puzzle under either perspective. Perhaps the system can be explained by a desire to minimize the use of costly sanctions, by the role of informal sanctions that discourage flagrant cheating, and by the positive externalities associated with formal litigation to clarify the bargain (which might be discouraged by stiffer sanctions), but these explanations are at best speculative.

Putting this puzzle to the side, the 'equivalence' standard for countermeasures under DSU Article 22.4, and the determination by the Arbitrator in *Upland Cotton* that sanctions should be linked to harm suffered by Brazil, all point to a system that is focused more on rebalancing the bargain and at least crudely on restoring the welfare losses caused by the violation than on ensuring 'compliance'. Accordingly, we have focused our economic analysis on the task of identifying the level of retaliation that will restore lost welfare.

This is not an easy task. Although we can derive expressions for the proper level of retaliation, they depend on the welfare weights that each nation gives to various components of welfare, which are unobservable. The welfare implications of retaliation through changes in trade-policy instruments also depend importantly on how those policies have been chosen in the first instance. It is thus unrealistic to expect that WTO arbitrators can do a good job at identifying the retaliatory measures that will restore lost welfare with much accuracy.

Under certain quite restrictive assumptions, however, the analysis provides some support for an approach to retaliation that allows the retaliator to reduce the value of its imports by an amount equal to the value of its lost exports due to the violation. We extend the result in Howse and Staiger (2006), in particular, to show that this approach can approximately restore lost welfare *if* one is willing to assume that all components of welfare receive equal weight, and that trade in other goods is not affected significantly following the violation and the subsequent countermeasure. Although these assumptions are probably unrealistic in general, our analysis provides at least weak support for the trade-volume-effects calculation in past arbitrations.

The use of prohibitive tariffs for purposes of retaliation is more puzzling, as they cannot in general restore lost welfare for the complainant – nonprohibitive tariffs that enhance the terms of trade seem to make more sense. To this end, our analysis suggests that the same information required to compute the nonprohibitive tariffs that will produce an equal trade-volume effect could instead be used to compute the tariffs that would offset the terms-of-trade loss due to the violation. Such an approach seemingly holds more promise as a way to approximate the level of retaliation that would restore the welfare of the complainant.

Finally, nothing in our analysis provides any support for the measure of retaliation used in prohibited-subsidies cases prior to *Upland Cotton* which has been the amount of the subsidy. Likewise, our analysis suggests no reason why the approach to retaliation should differ in subsidies cases generally, or in prohibited-subsidies cases in particular. Perhaps there is some basis for treating the 'prohibited subsidies' as a more pernicious practice subject to greater condemnation, but if the concern is for their effect on the welfare of other nations, it is the magnitude of the terms-of-trade effect that matters and not the formal structure of the subsidy program.

References

Bagwell, Kyle (2008), 'Remedies in the WTO: An Economic Perspective', in Merit E. Janow, Victoria J. Donaldson, and Alan Yanovich (eds.), *The WTO: Governance, Dispute Settlement and Developing Countries*, Huntington, NY: Juris Publishing, pp. 733–770.

Bagwell, Kyle and Robert W. Staiger (2002), *The Economics of the World Trading System*, Cambridge, MA: MIT Press.

—— (2006), 'Will International Rules on Subsidies Disrupt the World Trading System?', *The American Economic Review*, **96**(3): 877–895.

Baldwin, Richard E. (1987), 'Politically Realistic Objective Functions and Trade Policy: PROFS and Tariffs', *Economics Letters*, **24**(3): 287–290.

Beshkar, Mostafa (2010), 'Optimal Remedies in International Trade Agreements', *European Economic Review*, **54**(3): 455–466.

Bown, Chad P. and Michele Ruta (2010), 'The Economics of Permissible WTO Retaliation', in Chad P. Bown and Joost Pauwelyn (eds.), *The Law, Economics and Politics of Retaliation in WTO Dispute Settlement*, Cambridge: Cambridge University Press, pp. 149–193.

Howse, Robert and Damien J. Neven (2005), '*United States – Tax Treatment for "Foreign Sales Corporations"*, Recourse to Arbitration by the United States under Article 22.6 of the DSU and Article 4.11 of the SCM Agreement (WT/DS108/ARB), A Comment', in Henrik Horn and Petros C. Mavroidis (eds.), *The WTO Case Law of 2002: The American Law Institute Reporters' Studies*, Cambridge: Cambridge University Press, pp. 36–63.

Howse, Robert and Robert W. Staiger (2006), '*United States – Anti-Dumping Act of 1916* (Original Complaint by the European Communities) – Recourse to Arbitration by the United States under 22.6 of the DSU, WT/DS136/ARB, 24 February 2004: A Legal and Economic Analysis', in Henrik Horn and Petros C. Mavroidis (eds.), *The WTO Case Law of 2003: The American Law Institute Reporters' Studies*, Cambridge: Cambridge University Press, pp. 254–279.

Jackson, John H. (1997), 'The WTO Dispute Settlement Understanding – Misunderstanding on the Nature of Legal Obligation', *American Journal of International Law*, **91**(1): 60–64.

Lawrence, Robert Z. (2003), *Crimes and Punishments? Retaliation Under the WTO*, Washington, DC: Peterson Institute for International Economics.

Schnepf, Randy (2010), *Brazil's WTO Case Against the US Cotton Program*, Washington, DC: Congressional Research Service.

Schropp, Simon A. B. (2009), *Trade Policy Flexibility and Enforcement in the WTO: A Law and Economics Analysis*, Cambridge: Cambridge University Press.

Schwartz, Warren F. and Alan O. Sykes (2002), 'The Economic Structure of Renegotiation and Dispute Resolution in the World Trade Organization', *The Journal of Legal Studies*, **31**(1): S179–S204.

Sykes, Alan O. (2000), 'The Remedy for Breach of Obligations under the WTO Dispute Settlement Understanding: Damages or Specific Performance?', in Marco Bronckers and Reinhard Quick (eds.), *New Directions in International Economic Law: Essays in Honour of John H. Jackson*, The Hague: Kluwer, pp. 347–357.